NEWS-LETTER DESIGN

W9-DAI-608

Broughton

An imaginative illustration on a philosophical theme was art directed by Beth Singer for the IBM publication FSD Manager. *(See page 144.)*

Edward A. Hamilton

NEWS-LETTER DESIGN

A Step-by-Step Guide to

Creative Publications

VAN NOSTRAND REINHOLD
I(T)P™ A Division of International Thomson Publishing Inc.

New York • Albany • Bonn • Boston • Detroit • London • Madrid • Melbourne
Mexico City • Paris • San Francisco • Singapore • Tokyo • Toronto

Thanks to the many designers, editors, and publishers who generously consented to be interviewed and have their newsletters featured on these pages. Materials published by International Typeface Corporation were helpful to me in explaining the techniques of type and typography design. I am especially indebted to Time-Life where years of contact with editorial and publishing professionals gave me inspiration, a sense of standards, and taught me how to design with words and pictures.

Copyright © 1996 by Van Nostrand Reinhold

I(T)P™   A division of International Thomson Publishing Inc.
         The ITP logo is a trademark under license

Printed in the United States of America
For more information, contact:

Van Nostrand Reinhold
115 Fifth Avenue
New York, NY 10003

Chapman & Hall GmbH
Pappelallee 3
69469 Weinheim
Germany

Chapman & Hall
2-6 Boundary Row
London
SE1 8HN
United Kingdom

International Thomson Publishing Asia
221 Henderson Road #05-10
Henderson Building
Singapore 0315

Thomas Nelson Australia
102 Dodds Street
South Melbourne, 3205
Victoria, Australia

International Thomson Publishing Japan
Hirakawacho Kyowa Building, 3F
2-2-1 Hirakawacho
Chiyoda-ku, 102 Tokyo
Japan

Nelson Canada
1120 Birchmount Road
Scarborough, Ontario
Canada M1K 5G4

International Thomson Editores
Campos Eliseos 385, Piso 7
Col. Polanco
11560 Mexico D.F. Mexico

All rights reserved. No part of this work covered by the copyright hereon may be reproduced or used in any form or by any means—graphic, electronic, or mechanical, including photocopying, recording, taping, or information storage and retrieval systems—without the written permission of the publisher.

1 2 3 4 5 6 7 8 9 10 HAM 01 00 99 98 97 96 95

Library of Congress Cataloging–in–Publication Data
Hamilton, Edward A.
    Newsletter Design / Edward A. Hamilton.
        p.   cm.
    Includes bibliographical references
    ISBN 0–442–01668–9
    1. Printing, Practical—Layout.   2. Newsletters—Design.
3. Graphic arts.   I. Title.
Z246.H36   1995   94–42373
686.2′252—dc20   CIP

To G.D.H.
for encouraging words

CONTENTS

HOW TO USE THIS BOOK

Some people set their eyes on their future profession at an early age—sometimes as young as ten or 12 years. I did my first newsletter in pale purple ink on a Ditto machine when I was in eighth grade. Hand-delivered, it lasted for three issues. Since then I've never been far from the medium, even though I ventured early into the field of national magazines.

I've had this book in mind for a long time. The idea grew as I became aware of the proliferation of newsletters in every guise imaginable. Now and then some stood out visually—lively with clever words and ideas, clearly the work of practiced professionals. A sad number were blandly neutral and downright ineffectual.

Recently, I heard a successful editor comment: "For some reason many newsletters are edited by people who really don't want to edit a newsletter." It is true that a great many are edited by noneditors and designed by nondesigners. The list of people in diverse fields who are

called upon to "do a newsletter" can go on and on.

There is great satisfaction in producing effective and appealing editorial pages. I want you to share that pleasure so that the urge to create something of value will be so strong that nothing between heaven and hell can stop you. Of course, realize your own limitations. But also realize that this is a competitive society where you are expected to be better or best.

Every creative field has its masters whose work can be imitated as a point of departure. In the exacting craft of editorial design, you develop by steady practice, not just on alternate Saturdays. Serious practice invariably means that your project becomes your steady companion. I once had a boss who told me that "If you want to lock the door on your work each afternoon, go work in a shoe store."

This book displays many model newsletters to follow and you will never go wrong by studying the best. In the last chapter there are 80 pages of successful newsletters from all corners of the country. I have sketched brief background information to give you some insight into how the best and brightest operate. There are also detailed marginal annotations. This section can be a valuable learning experience. Occasional "Scenario" pages provide interludes of newsletter activity drawn from real-life situations.

Step-by-step, the chapters describe specific editorial-design techniques based on my professional experience in producing national magazines, newsletters, and visual books. Much of the content deals with work phases that take place before you sit down with the keyboard, mouse, monitor, scanner, and printer.

Time and again you will notice the word "simplicity" related to page layout—not childishly simple but mercifully uncomplicated. In short, this is a book of concepts—editorial, design, verbal, and pictorial—and how the parts and pieces come together to create an outstanding newsletter that is *unboring*.

1. PLANNING A NEWSLETTER

Make it dramatic, make it enjoyable reading, make it believable, use striking graphics, avoid the junk-mail look—*be outstanding!*

The criteria for creating an outstanding newsletter could be expanded on at length. The objective of this book is to enable you to produce a top-notch visual-and-verbal editorial product.

Every newsletter requires a master plan as well as day-to-day and week-to-week planning. This chapter is addressed in particular to the editor or team assigned to the task of originating or revitalizing a publication. This information should also be shared or discussed with the publication's art director or designer.

Design Is a Broad Term

Editing, writing, the very act of choosing and using pictures are all part of the design process. Likewise, the choice of stories, page organization, and copy/picture ratio are design functions as much as page layout, graphics, and typographic planning. Let no one say that editors do not "design."

This book prepares you for the task of designing an appealing publication—whether you work with the most sophisticated software programs or with a typewriter, drawing board, and hand tools. You may be an editorial novice, a skilled art director, a journalism graduate, or a versatile administrative assistant. Whatever the subject or theme of your publication, the need for creative thinking and planning is universal.

Know Your Audience

One characteristic is common to most newsletters' readership: Americans are busy people. Not only are they preoccu-

"Never underestimate your readers' intelligence but never overestimate their interest."

pied with daily activities but they are besieged with media—visual and verbal. Television, radio, fax, computers, and tons of junk mail constantly vie for their attention. Your challenge is to craft such an appealing and unboring newsletter that it will grab and hold their hard-won attention.

Most newsletters target people with specialized needs and interests—a "captive" audience with more than a casual interest in the publication's contents.

This gives the editor and designer an obvious advantage. It's critical to conceptualize your readers. Are they a high-style audience? Then give them a high-style newsletter. Are they more conventional in their tastes and habits? Then give them a clean, simple, dramatic layout that packs plenty of punch!

But whether your readers are tool-and-dye makers, bankers, bakers, truck drivers, or tax accountants, no reader is attracted to dull-looking literature.

Henry Luce, founder of Time-Life and one of the world's great communicators, often impressed upon his editors, "Never underestimate your readers' intelligence but never *overestimate* their interest."

Planning for Visual Vitality

Consider the overall appearance of your publication. Does it all work together? Do word content and graphic content merge and mingle throughout the pages? Do the verbal and visual succeed together as a well-constructed complex?

Near the top of your priority list are the cover and logotype designs. In fact, this is the most conspicuous feature in any newsletter. Determine your cover objectives early. Assuming that you have already chosen a scintillating name for your publication, the logo design is a most important step. Hopefully, it will be distinctive, versatile, and "timeless." Remember: You'll live with your design issue after issue.

Ten Major Tasks

1. Outline objectives

2. Decide tone and style

3. Determine printing specifications

4. Develop writing style

5. List content sources

6. Develop overall design style

7. Plan visual content

8. Develop staffing needs

9. Determine production plan

10. Draft budget

The cover design is a challenge to even the most experienced designer. Once it's been prepared and okayed by everyone concerned, your task is to use this standard cover scheme with visual material that gives each issue a fresh, new look. More about covers in the next chapter.

A Handy Page Size

Choose your page dimensions carefully. There are many alternatives. The vast majority of newsletters are letter size—8½ × 11—and there is nothing wrong with this conventional size—*it's what you put into it that makes the difference!*

Occasionally, you see bona-fide newsletters that are tabloid size and very pictorial. I've run across some that are 18 inches high. You may feel that a large format will give your publication a look of importance, but I believe that it can be a deterrent because readers will resist juggling a clumsy page. In the other direction, there are nifty little 6x10 newsletters, accordian folded, with a single type col-

Well-planned on desktop with a three-column grid, this subscription newsletter is one of a group produced by Wentworth Publishing Company in Lancaster, PA.

A full-time staff at Time Inc. edits and produces this newsletter read by the savvy, in-house business and editorial staffers. More about this on page 108.

Planned with high professional standards, the Osprey is designed, edited, and produced by Communications Director Carl Herrman at the University of North Florida.

A nationwide audience subscribes to this vigorous health newsletter. A light, informal editorial and design plan makes the serious theme of nutrition very readable.

Planning a Newsletter

umn. Consider your size options early in the game when you determine your method of distribution.

The Visual Plan, Overall

For obvious reasons, publications that appear too frequently could dilute your content by causing you to spread the material too thin. Likewise, too few or too many pages in an issue can affect the visual quality, making the publication appear too jam-packed or too empty.

While your particular field and subject matter may offer limited sources for story material, there needn't be a similar problem with the visual content: There are many prospects for photos, drawings, and other visuals. This is where creative *effort* comes into play—no simple task! Scan the selection of newsletters on page 107 and you'll see the results of creative thinking and planning in a broad range of subject areas. Without exception, these outstanding publications resulted from the efforts of trained professionals—editors, writers, and designers.

Typographical Matters

Also very conspicuous is the design of your typographic page. (This is covered in detail starting on page 53.) Above all, your major design consideration must be CLARITY—and this requires the right choice and combination of type styles and sizes. For the best results, design should be handled by an experienced designer who is familiar with the complex world of typefaces.

Concentrating on Content

What kinds of articles and features will you run in each issue? You may decide on one fairly long (perhaps a page or more) interpretive piece as a regular feature. You'll always need several short updates

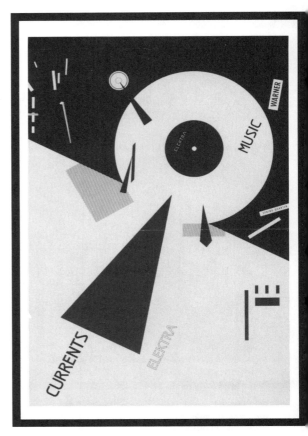

Warner Currents, *designed by Pentagram's Peter Harrison and Harold Burch, has a spatial cover with flowing geometric shapes.* Campaign '60, *a KIDSNET tabloid, art directed by Beth Singer for A&E Cable Network, shown below, dramatizes a political history series.*

15 Final Steps to Production

1. Plan Content
List ideas for articles and features. Explore all sources and think creatively about opportunities for visual content.

2. Draft Work Schedule
Forecast as realistically as possible all key editorial and production dates with work flow that will meet deadline.

3. Information and Research
Assemble story material and data by phone, letter, or in person. Plan writing assignments, if any.

4. Assemble, Assign Photos/Art
Interpret your visual possibilities. Plan, gather, or assign drawings, charts, and photos early.

5. Rough Thumbnail Sketch
Achieve a bird's-eye view of your proposed issue with all major stories indicated as first-stage layout of pages.

6. Full-Size Rough Layout
Block out your issue on the computer screen using a basic text-column grid in your page-layout program. Indicate spaces for copy and illustrations.

7. Rough Draft of Text Copy
Keyboard copy in the typeface you choose and, with a designer's help, place into position on the grid. Outline areas for visuals.

8. Rewrite, Edit, and Fit Copy
Output hard copy on your printer. Make necessary copy changes and appraise your layout plan.

9. Write Headlines and Captions
Weigh relative importance of headlines and compose to fit spaces indicated. Draft picture captions.

10. Complete Page Makeup
Impose all visual material and keyboard headlines and captions into position.

11. Final Checking
Output hard copy for final checking and approvals. Everything is now in position.

12. Printing Stages
Send disk to printer by messenger or modem. Printer makes high-resolution negative film in preparation for plates.

13. Specifications
Furnish printer with detailed instructions regarding paper stock, quantity, and discuss layout details.

14. Bluelines
Printer returns blueline proofs—your last chance to catch mistakes or make minor changes before printing.

15. Printing
The moment of truth. Your printing quality shouldn't be a routine matter: Be present at the press and check the first sheets off the press for overall quality.

The San Francisco Museum of Modern Art publishes newsletters tied in with specific shows. The typography in Linda Hinrichs' cover design is in complete harmony with the illustration.

as well as longer newsy, focus articles. Also consider a close-up column about a person within the organization and a useful calendar of events. For each feature, think about visual ideas that will breathe life into your pages.

Who Does the Work?

In terms of sheer labor, most of the writing, editing, copy editing, designing, and the many other skills that will bring pieces all together to fit smoothly into a well-designed issue is frequently handled by one person, the *editor*.

Occasionally that same person will also sit in front of a Mac or drawing board and wear other hats—as layout designer and production manager.

This amount of responsibility can be overwhelming. Consider some alternatives. If a newsletter is worth publishing, it is worth the enlistment of qualified talent. Organizations often overlook this most important aspect of the planning phase, which is one reason for the blizzard of mediocre publications that shower the country.

One constructive step toward a well-designed newsletter is the use of a freelance designer or art director who will style your publication at the start-up stage. If you're fortunate enough to have a MAC or PC and publication software such as Page-Maker or Quark XPress, the designer can program your layout design and typographic style with sufficient variations for all future issues.

If your newsletter is by definition a humble enterprise and you have appropriate desktop equipment, print it in house. However, if you're working with a variety of graphics, photos, and typefaces, you'd be wise to use the services of a quality print shop.

A realistic and well-planned work schedule is the businesslike way to assure that your newsletter will come out on time. In the publishing world, meeting deadlines is a traditional mark of professionalism. So is a realistic budget plan.

Budget for High Standards

Whether you work for a commercial organization or nonprofit group, someone will expect you to tally the budget as you move ahead with editorial and design planning. Shoot for high standards. Just as a house planned by a talented architect may cost no more than a house designed by an inept architect, the same is true in publishing, where high standards of planning and production may cost no more than mediocre concept and execution. Think quality. It is possible and attainable at all stages.

Cathy, an administrative assistant and onetime English major, works for an aluminum fabricating company. Her boss, J.B., a self-made man, is CEO and proud of his company, his 1200 employees, their line of specialized products, and the number of customers they have from coast to coast.

One morning, J.B. called Cathy into his office. "For several months I've thought about starting up a newsletter for our employees. We could send it to many of our distributors, too." He continued, "You've been pretty close to the action. I know you write good, clear English. I'm convinced you can take on the project."

Cathy, ambitious and alert but untrained, listened uneasily and was somewhat shocked.

"I've never worked on any publication. I'm not sure I'd know how to go about it," she said with the thought that she shouldn't sound unwilling but not overconfident, either.

"You'll learn." J.B. replied. "Learn by *doing*. Let's talk about what we're trying to do."

J.B. continued, "It'll fit in ideally with your everyday activities. And I'll be able to watch over your shoulder."

"You'll want me to carry stories about plant activity, the salespeople, the managers, marriages, births, and so forth?"

"Yes, all kinds of interesting material. We can commission the managers to do some of the writing under your guidance. I'm sure we'll have lots of stories. We can print it on nice gray paper. I like blue ink. You know, my nephew Harry is a commercial artist. He's got some desktop equipment. He can help you make it look pretty and prepare it for printing.

"Think about it. Tomorrow we'll talk some more. I want to get started right away. We'll print it every three months—and I'll want a spot for myself on the front page, upper left-hand corner, with a small picture and a couple hundred words' viewpoint, which you'll write."

Cathy went back to her desk in the outer office, took a deep breath, sat down in front of her word processor, and wondered what to do.

Thinking Out Loud

Here's a newsletter off to a poor start—a victim of casual and arbitrary planning.

- **Choice of an editor.** This is a gamble. Instead of Cathy, J.B. might have looked for *a bright, freelance professional* who could report to her. (Would he choose an untrained person to do his accounting or legal work? Hardly.)
- **Choice of a designer.** The second key person selected could be an unfortunate mistake. J.B.'s nephew may be a talented, bright artist, but they learned that he specializes in the design of cosmetic displays and labels for a local canning company. He has no publication design in his background. J.B. needs *a smart designer with publication experience.*
- **Visual sources.** The ill-considered mention of "interesting material" is some cause for alarm. Photos, cartoons, and other visual items are rarely found in administrative offices. There is a need to *identify who will produce this material.*
- **Story plan.** Early in the game Cathy will have to prepare story lists. It's unlikely that story copy written by corporate managers will be lively reading, though it may be factual. Here again, *freelance talent should be used* to interview managers and write stories.
- **Layout experiments.** Cathy will have to develop a cover and page format. She might learn to utilize PageMaker, Quark XPress, or some other desktop facility, but this requires many decisions about type and typography—and the computer can't give the right answers! With *the help of a design consultant* she can make critical decisions.

Milepo

A Publication for Metro-North Customers   Nover

2.
IMAGE
AND
IDENTITY

Air Directors Club of New York

Society of Publication Designers

The American Institute of Graphic Arts

Three distinctive logotypes used by the newsletters of three professional design organizations. The top one, aimed at a savvy membership, uses a whimsical sign language. Grids symbolizes a key word of publication designers. The third, an elegant italic hand-drawn for a prestigious club.

What's in a name? *Plenty.*

In 1936, the founders of a new picture magazine were searching for an appropriate name. Ultimately, they purchased the name LIFE from a humor magazine that had used it since 1882. They paid the phenomenal price of $92,000! It's a well-known fact that LIFE went on to become the most valuable publishing property in the world.

While a different order of magnitude, your newsletter's name is an essential key to its visual appeal. Be strong. Resist the temptation to use an overworked name. There are scads of them: To name a few— "Insight," "Outlook," "———News," "Connections," or simply "Newsletter." It's difficult to be outstanding with a trite name. If an original word or term poses a problem, try the obvious—which in itself may be distinctive. For example, if you work for The Amalgamated Decalcomania Corporation, there's nothing wrong with calling your publication ADC. If your organization is The Kennel Club, simply call your publication that. Your readers are insiders who'll react to the name.

Logotype Verities and Varieties

The famous industrial designer Raymond Loewy once wrote a book titled, *Never Leave Well Enough Alone.* You might apply that wisdom to your logotype (or nameplate) design. Unfortunately, too many newsletters display a logo that is bland and undistinguished. Someone decided, "That's good enough"—and so mediocrity prevails for untold issues ahead. Many people do not have the background and training to judge a good logo from a bad one.

Your logo design does much to define your publication and your organization. If

International Typeface Corporation

Cape Cod Museum of Natural History

Standard & Poor's

Council for the Arts in Westchester

SEPTA Railworks

T. Rowe Price Inc.

it's well designed, it can stand out brightly, attract readers, and virtually pull them into your pages. In most cases, the outstanding logos are designed by professionals as part of a publication design package or specific assignment. Review the collection of logos on these pages. This random sampling of design quality runs the gamut from bold and conventional to inspired and clever. For inspiration, note the logo for the typographic newsletter "U&lc." Designed by the late Herb Lubalin, one of the most noted designers of our era, it has originality, power, and classic distinction.

Don't be put off by the fact that NBC once paid an astounding six figure sum for a less-than-original logo design. Quality can be within your reach at a reasonable price and will be well worth the cost.

If You "Go It Alone"

Logotypes are as different and varied as the thousands of newsletters that display them. It's difficult to prescribe a specific direction for your individual needs. Here's one logical approach: Compose your design in all capital letters, blown up to a size that is impressive and commanding. Select a typeface that is strong and distinctive. (Don't necessarily settle on one from the limited choices in your software program.) Look for a type style that seems to express your newsletter's subject matter. For obvious reasons, if your subject is cosmetics, your typeface shouldn't be the heavy Helvetica Extra Bold Condensed. Likewise if your subject is concrete products, the typeface shouldn't be the delicate, classic Caslon Light.

Each of the logotypes at the left is in harmony with its subject and theme. Most are based on interpretations of known typefaces. The spectacular cover at the right, designed by noted West Coast designer Kit Hinrichs, has an elegant, formal logo that combines effectively with the dynamics of bold and light sans-serif typematter beneath— an ideal cover for the Museum of Contemporary Art, San Diego.

VIEW

C M A

JULY · AUGUST · SEPTEMBER · QUARTERLY NEWSLETTER 1992

EXHIBITIONS Noboru Tsubaki · Julie Bozzi: *American Food* · Selections from the William I. Koch Collection, including Modigliani, Corot, Picasso, Cezanne, Arp, Renoir, Remington, Buttersworth, Wood **PROGRAMS** Orquestra de Baja California · Henry Jaglom's film *Eating* · Paper Conservation: What Every Collector Should Know **SPECIAL EVENTS** *C'est Magnifique!* Gala · M.A.C. Day at the Races · Art After Five · Best of the Festival of Animation **MUSEUM NEWS**

THE LOTUS POSITION

March, 1992

Working Together:
A Spreadsheet
Perspective

THE ADVERTISING DIRECTOR of a major consumer electronics company is putting together a six-month advertising plan to present to the senior management team. She sends an e-mail to the seven account managers who report to her, asking each of them to submit a six-month plan for their product line that includes costs. ¶ Using a common spreadsheet to which they all have access from their desktop PCs, each manager sends the director a worksheet that includes their plans and related

costs — some include alternative plans at different budget levels. Each proposal is dated and includes the name of the person who created it. Most of the ideas submitted are workable within the annual advertising budget, but the high-end numbers for the CD player division are unrealistic. The director sends that manager an e-mail, asking him to submit a less expensive alternative. When the manager changes the numbers on his worksheet by adding a new alternative, the entire spreadsheet is updated automatically to reflect the change. Moreover, the manager attaches a note to his worksheet, explaining why he made the changes he did. This annotation, too, can be read by everyone on the network who has access to the model.

Using the information submitted by all her direct reports, the director completes her six-month plan. During the presentation to senior management, she is able to support her plan with a fully documented history of her group's decision-making process that includes all of the alternatives submitted by each member.

The scenario above, though not yet exemplary of the way most businesses operate today, is exemplary of the way businesses *could* operate — and a portent of things to come, driven by one of the many software developments underway at Lotus.

A decade ago, when Lotus introduced its flagship 1-2-3 spreadsheet, it caught on like wildfire,

Lotus.

A distinguished work of typography was crafted by well-known Boston publication designer Ronn Campisi. Starting with a giant capital initial, he designed the type in subtly declining sizes. A single word punctuates the page.

A happy logo design that changes with the seasons is the work of an accomplished illustrator. Decorative effects such as this "F" can be executed with a drawing program. Content is aimed at visitors to Hudson River historic sights.

Comment

Published for the customers of COM/Electric

January/February 1992

August 19, 1991: Hurricane Bob adds a twist to COM/Electric's daily operations.

A message from the President

Dear Customer:

The January Comment will share with you Commonwealth Electric's efforts to enhance community involvement and reduce its costs to provide safe and reliable service.

I have listened closely to the needs of our customers, local officials, businesspeople and the media, and I believe we have developed a positive working relationship with our community members. Looking back, many of your suggestions have assisted us in improving Commonwealth Electric's operation and communication efforts. I am confident that the time we have spent has proven beneficial to all parties involved, and that the fruits of those efforts will become more apparent as plans unfold during the coming years.

During the first three months of 1992, Commonwealth Electric residential rates will be well over 2¢ per kWh lower than they were in early 1990. Industrial rates will see similar reductions.

1992 promises to offer customers additional changes. On January 1, 1992, William G. Poist became the president and chief executive officer of Commonwealth Energy System, whose principle retail utility companies include: Commonwealth Electric, Cambridge Electric Light and Commonwealth Gas Company. Mr. Poist joined Commonwealth Gas Company in 1971, and has served as president and chief operating officer during the last seven years.

On behalf of the staff at COM/Electric, we wish you and your families a healthy and happy

---

The logo for a utility customers' newsletter is a traditional Roman typeface, made distinctive with white lines as shading. The news photo with a concise caption gets attention and leads readers to a straightforward president's letter.

The logo is classic Roman type with outline and shadow and it brings to mind words chiseled in stone on ancient Roman buildings. This handsome publication is distributed to the alumni of Printing Management and Sciences at R.I.T.

DISCOVER HISTORIC HUDSON VALLEY   FALL/WINTER 1992

INSIDE:
- A special pull-out of Calendar of Events
- Down at the farm— New arrivals at Philipsburg Manor
- Legend has it... a spooky Halloween Weekend
- Romantic Candlelight Tours for the holidays
- An Autumn Crafts and Tasks festival

An Orchard With A View:
Apple Picking Along The Hudson

If there's a better place to be than nestled in the back of a hay wagon, breathing in the crisp autumn air as you're led to the apple orchards at Montgomery Place, please write and tell us!

October 10-11, the Montgomery Place Harvest Fair returns to this spectacular 400 acre property, overlooking the Hudson River and Catskill Mountains.

Visitors to the Harvest Fair can pick their own apples, press cider, make a scarecrow, or enjoy a woodland walk amidst the blaze of fall foliage.

Saturday's events include tractor-pulled hay rides and a rag-time jazz band from 1-3. On Sunday, a team of draft horses will pull the hay wagon!

It's harvest time at Montgomery Place! This year's Harvest Fair takes place on October 10-11. Call (914) 758-5461 for details.

QUARTO

An Alumni Newsletter from the School of Printing Management & Sciences   Fall 1992

From the Director

The school has gone through an amazing change over the past 12 months. Students and faculty have met the challenge of reorganizing the laboratories to make room for our new Integrated Electronic Prepress Laboratory. The faculty have completed a self-study and are actively implementing their direction-setting objectives, which incorporate adaptability to change and an integrated definition of graphic arts systems into the core curriculum.

The College of Imaging Arts and Sciences was officially established in June under Dean Margaret Lucas. The new college combines the colleges of Fine and Applied Arts and Graphic Arts and Photography. The School of Printing Management and Sciences is leading the combination by providing opportunities to our colleagues in our new lab.

Some other good news: Our entering class for Fall 1992 is slightly higher than Fall 1991. Our graduating class from May has had significant success in entering the work force.

Much of this change and our enrollment success were brought about by alumni and friends who, over the years, have demonstrated significant support for the school. We thank you for your help.

George H. Ryan

George H. Ryan, Interim Director
School of Printing Management and Sciences

Integrated Electronic Prepress Laboratory: The Complete Publishing Center

Students studying photography, printing, and art and design now have the ability to integrate all the disciplines into one marketable resource.

The new 1,000-square-foot Integrated Electronic Prepress Laboratory, developed in conjunction with the Technical & Education Center and the school, is a Macintosh-based prepress facility that allows students in every area of graphic arts to explore the possibilities of desktop publishing. The laboratory will integrate the 15 Macintosh Quadra systems with scanners, electronic still photography, and design workstations to allow students to output to a wide variety of proofing and printing systems.

The laboratory will be used for class demonstrations and T&E Center seminars and will also be available for student and faculty use outside of class. The goal of this

Integrated Electronic Prepress Laboratory is to encourage designers, photographers, printers, and publishers to put their heads together and learn how to harness new technology in a systematic, controlled, and cost-effective manner, said George Ryan, interim director of the School of Printing Management & Sciences.

RIT received donations of money and equipment to establish the laboratory from major corporations, including Du Pont Company, F. Process Company, Rockwell International, Eastman Kodak Company, 3M Company, Apple Computer, and the Gravure Education Foundation.

"The creation of the Integrated Electronic Prepress Laboratory is one step further toward the integration of the College of Graphic Arts and Photography and the College of Fine and Applied Arts into the new College of Imaging Arts and Sciences," Ryan said.

Using optical or computer techniques, you may slant the type, stretch it, bend it, outline it, run it in circles, or choose from a variety of other typographic tricks. Remember, however, that the best logos are simple, strong, and clear. If you're tempted to use typographic trickery, use it with caution. Best of all, don't use it.

A logo that you've admired on an existing magazine or other publication may inspire you to move in a certain direction. A degree of imitation can be constructive—nothing is altogether new. Everything in the creative world is influenced to a degree by existing models.

Cover Design Concepts

During the start-up period of a new publication, the cover concept is a primary problem. A well-conceived master plan at the outset will make all future covers smooth sailing. Your cover must blend the design scheme and the editorial theme so as to please, attract, and *win* readers. Try to achieve a *memorable image*.

The most successful covers from a publishing standpoint may never win an art director's award for graphic design. Neither is an "aesthetic" cover necessarily the answer. The advertising business learned long ago that a "pretty" ad may not elicit a response; nor does the slickest, most costly printing job.

What, then, *are* the secret qualities that win readership? Let's assume that you are an editor with a firm hold on the pulse of your readership. You want a cover scheme that will rivet their attention. You may go the route of the single, large picture. Many newsletters are quite magazinelike. You may feature a photo of a known and admired personality, or it might be an action shot with several figures. Or, you might want to forget about the familiar representational photo and try a drawing instead. Preferably the drawing would not be clip art, but would

Here is the world's most understated logo—spoken by a youth in knickers and cap. Washington designer Phil Jordan drew it on the WASP 1928 using Adobe Hacienda. It is aimed at an "in group" of readers, the Washington Chapter of the AIGA.

Newsletter or magazine? A slim, lively public television program publication for WGBH has generous feature material and a single-photo cover. Douglass Scott and Cathleen Damplo designed it with QuarkXPress, using conventional mechanicals.

A popular science theme is vividly represented on the cover of this museum newsletter. A logo in basic sans serif, upper and lowercase becomes a theme type with swirling white lines. The museum name stands out in casually drawn script.

be custom drawn to evoke your special editorial qualities. If you have appropriate software on the shelf—and someone on your staff is creatively inclined—consider a computer graphics composition. It might result in an image to remember. However, be aware that an unconventional or "arty" image may repel as much as it attracts. It might also distract from the serious purposes of your publication. If your newsletter is directed toward an "in" group such as an art directors' club or rock music society, then your approach would be to artfully devise a cover style that will make this special group happy. You must decide what is most likely to work best for your readership.

Newsletters Should Appear "Newsy"

Logically, a newsletter's cover should convey that it contains news, predictions, interpretations, and other helpful or entertaining content. There is a strong case for a journalistic, editorial style of picture, as described in Chapter 7. The cover should have compelling editorial qualities or a controversial rather than a humdrum theme.

You may be totally unable to obtain suitable photographs or illustrations (you may be faced with dull "headshots" or bland "handshake shots"), or you may feel the subject matter is altogether nonpictorial (is anything nonpictorial?). Perhaps the pressure of time or the burden of work makes the effort impractical. If any of these situations exist, then establish an all-type cover. This cover style can be both elegant and forceful, as you'll see when you review the typographic covers throughout this book. Rather than settle on poor photographs, by all means take the all-type route!

If your newsletter deals with finance, demographics, or something statistical, a well-designed graph or chart will enliven your page and can be high in message value. A pictograph dressed up with a clever cartoon spot could help soften

Stewart had never suggested to anyone that he was an editor. In fact, his job as Human Resources Director at Davenport, a large retail chain, was his principle interest. That's why he was perturbed and upset when his CEO, Mr. H, wrote a terse comment across the front page of a recent issue of Stewart's newsletter, "The Davenporter." The penciled inscription read: "What's this all about??"

Increasingly, Stewart noticed copies of his publication on the floor and crumpled up in wastebaskets. To learn what reader reaction was to his publication, he circulated a questionnaire to the 4500 employees. About 100 people responded, but no one had much to say. One anonymous staffer suggested that the newsletter "should be killed to save money." Another simply wrote, *"This paper is boring!"* Clearly, his newsletter wasn't paying off and he decided to meet with Mr. H to discuss the matter. But first, to prepare himself, he would review in his own mind what he believed to be the strong points in his publication.

He felt sure the name, "The Davenporter," couldn't be more appropriate. The logotype, a scrawling brush script had a dashing, progressive look. The cover, designed by an unknown someone in the company's computer department, had a network of lines and boxes and a few small photos. He thought it was clever, a bit complex but certainly interesting looking. Printing and paper quality were excellent—paper stock was richly glossy and printing was in a soft gray ink, very easy on the eyes, he thought.

Every issue included a picture of the boss or other officers greeting someone, making a speech, or posing with staff members.

As a regular feature, he tried to run at least three portraits of staff people who had done something noteworthy. For this, he would ask them to bring in a photo from home. Usually, to personal-ize the feature, he would have the featured subjects write their own copy.

So much for what he considered the good qualities. However, he also wanted to be truthful with himself: The publication *didn't* have much personality, he thought, and there's a need for some help.

Thinking Out Loud

Stewart had stumbled onto the perfect prescription for boredom. He was not reaching or pleasing his readers, including his own boss!

• The retailing field and the people who work in it can be interesting enough, so his subject was no problem and his readers were intelligent, though busy. However, Stewart was an active personnel administrator, deeply concentrating on his objectives—he was not a creative part-time editor.

• The name "The Davenporter" in dashing script was okay, but there was a major problem with the cover: Stewart wasn't aware of the principle of design simplicity. Rarely are good covers complex.

• High-gloss paper stock may look "classy" but the shine is a meaningless cosmetic device that can also look "chintzy." The use of gray ink makes copy more difficult to read.

• Articles about the boss and his associates are not necessarily exciting, are possibly boring, and to the rank and file, may appear obviously planted.

• Portraits of staff members (mug shots) printed in soft gray, can be a real turnoff.

• Stewart needed a selection of stronger visual material. He was also lacking one other visual resource—the help of a *knowledgeable art director*.

• In our age of frequent surveys, Stewart's open admission of concern by questionnaire is not the way to obtain editorial ideas. He needed a bright, creative, part-time editor.

THE NEWSLETTER OF THE ART DIRECTORS CLUB, INC. FOR ADVERTISING, GRAPHIC AND PUBLICATION DESIGNERS • SPRING 1992

McDESIGN: *Is design better after the computer revolution? What we've lost and what we've gained.*

The revolution is over. The computer has won. Today, just about every advertising agency and design studio uses computers. Art directors and designers who swore they would never go near a Mac just a few years ago are now scrambling to learn how to operate one. The reality is, one simply can't get business without owning computers.

"Ten or fifteen years ago, a designer could go into business with a phone, a drawing board and a T-square. Today you need a twenty thousand dollar system just to compete," observes John Waters, an early convert who bought his first computer in 1983.

"Designers used to argue with me about it," he says. "Many felt this technology was anti-design. I think they felt that way because artists come from a craft tradition."

Lost craft

"Creating a piece of graphic used to be a labor of love," says Peter Hirsch, principal and creative director of Calet Hirsch & Spector Advertising. "There was more of a hands-on feeling to it. We were trained to draw a Caslon letter and relish every curve. We talked about negative space and positive space, and spent a whole weekend drawing a "C". Now you can punch the computer and get 400 versions of a "C". Everything is automatic. We don't handcraft the work anymore. It's like the artists have left the Village and moved uptown with a computer."

If a designer is no longer a craftsman, is he any different from an accountant or an engineer using a computer? "Yes, our guys wear ponytails," laughs Hirsch. "The

JOY — NOT

CLEMENT MOK

problem is I'm losing my hair and by the time I learn the computer I'll be totally bald!"

Lost jobs

Every technological change in history is fraught with controversy and emotional upheavals. Each threatens to annihilate a cherished craft tradition and put a generation of craftsmen out of business. Ten years ago, designers feared they would lose their jobs to secretaries who would learn to operate a computer, and today, we see that it is the designers who are taking jobs away from typesetters, layout artists and color separators.

Martin Solomon, creative director of the Royal Composing Room, fears that the computer may be turning too many designers into technicians. "A designer's job is to art direct. They should spend their time on coming up with the ideas, not producing the art," he argues. "Besides, we're living in an era of specialization. We don't have one doctor taking care of all parts of the body. We have specialists. Design should be the same way."

Interestingly, it is precisely because the computer offers a designer a greater degree of independence that Clement Mok was smitten by it. Mok, a former creative director at Apple Computers, now heads his own design studio, Clement Mok Designs in San Francisco.

"There are illustrations that on a craft level I can't achieve, but I have visions of these images and with the help of a computer, I can create them. I don't have to rely on other people to interpret my vision," Mok explains. "If you think of the computer as a way to help with the developmental process, then I think the technology is very valuable. Before computers, you might have four rounds of misinterpretation and still not be happy with the final product two weeks later."

Though a big fan of the computer, Mok concedes there is a downside. "On the mainstream level, it will

CONTINUED ON PAGE 5

your most stern reader. If you can afford a second color, a dash of red or blue can go far to enhance the overall effect. Any of these graphic features should be designed with strength and style.

An intriguing, brief table of contents on the cover is a familiar device that can attract readers who will—hopefully—be unable to resist turning the page. The same is true of a cover blurb or "sell" line.

Simplicity Is a Necessity

Think simplicity. Beware of clutter and confusion! Novelty for the sake of novelty can defeat your purpose.

The collection of covers on these pages represents a variety of objectives within active publishing programs. Each succeeds in one way or another and has stood the tests of time. Try to interpret the thinking and planning that went into these designs, as well as others featured throughout this book.

Design Your Page to Invite Readers

Scan the pages of any successful newsletter and you'll see an array of design characteristics that meld into an individual "look." If the pages appear gray overall—and this is a common problem—you are looking at an unsuccessful editorial product. The same is true of clutter.

In the field of national newspapers, *The New York Times, The Times of London, USA Today,* and *The Village Voice* all have widely different characteristics. The same is true of major magazines and outstanding newsletters. The upshot is that you should try to give your pages a one-of-a-kind, distinctive style that is uniquely your own.

What visual qualities will make your

On your left is the Art Directors Club logo gracing the cover of the club's iconoclastic newsletter. It's produced by noted New York designers Seymour Chwast and Sara Giovanitti, with graphic support from other members. (Read the text. It is relevant to the theme of this book.)

Mileposts

A Publication for Metro-North Customers   November/December 1991

Disaster Drill

On a Sunday in late October, hundreds of Metro-North employees came to work to put out a fire that never happened, to rescue 517 customers and "victims" from a derailed train that was sitting on the tracks all the time, to keep other trains running around this accident-that-didn't-occur, and to work with other city agencies on the same simulated mission.

It was a disaster drill, held to practice all aspects of managing a serious emergency in Grand Central and its acres of underground track. This "emergency" was a simulated collision under Park Avenue and 50th Street. After a phone call from a signal tower in the Park Avenue Tunnel to a dispatcher in the Metro-North Control Center at 347 Madison Avenue, the New York City Police Department, the Fire Department, the Transit Police, the Department of Transportation, the Emergency Medical Service, the Long Island Rail Road Police Command Center Unit, the American Red Cross, and the Salvation Army all came within minutes to help carry out the "rescue" operation. The work of all agencies was then coordinated through the New York City Office of Emergency Management.

A command center was established at Vanderbilt and 43rd Street, necessitating the closing of the taxi stand, and all com-

munication and command units operated from there.

"Victims"—those injured in the "accident"—were moved to the end of the nearest platform, where a medical triage area was set up for the evaluation and disposition of those injured. All "victims" were Metro-North employees. Other employees directed fire and rescue crews from the accident site to the platform and through the Terminal while still other crews worked to "rerail" the equipment so that it could be moved out of the way.

Twenty-eight minutes after the drill began, a serious smoke condition was reported. That meant "evacuation" of the whole Terminal—customers, employees, tenants, tourists. It was the first time that a complete evacuation had been ordered for a practice drill and it was "accomplished" in just over 20 minutes.

Fifty-two minutes into the drill, the fire was reported out, and two minutes later word came that the train had been evacuated. Twelve minutes after that it was reported that there had been "517 customers and four crew members on the train, two fatalities, ten injured customers, and two injured employees." Also at that time, damage reports to the train cars and the tracks were available, a list of train changes was compiled, and the

Mileposts is so appealing and readable that it rated a three-column review in The New York Times. *Its quaint charm captivates 60,000 commuters on New York's Metro-North Railroad. Staff produced, it features line art, often historical, in a $5\frac{1}{2} \times 11$, six-page folder on gray stock.*

publication stand out as welcome reading? Your best answer is to study and analyze existing publications that you admire. Six examples displayed on pages 28–31 illustrate six widely different styles.

Illus. 1) A nonprofit public-interest research organization uses an all-type, four-column approach. The typeface is familiar Times Roman with a few accents of sans-serif type and initials. This is an elegant typographic page that has subtle layout features. Note the handsome box on the left and the blown-up quotations set in caps and small caps.

Illus. 2) Playful original graphics and typographic devices strategically placed add interest to a three-column layout of an IBM management newsletter. Air space at the top of the spread gives it an open, inviting look.

Illus. 3) This journalistic look is appropriate for a major international funding organization. This newsletter uses words and pictures to report on economic mat-

ters. A strong visual dynamic results from contrasting the large photo adjacent to three smaller ones.

Illus. 4) Aimed at garden enthusiasts, this publication is clearly in harmony with its subject: It uses a generous selection of decorative illustrations. Published by a Cape Cod nursery, its three-column pages are set in friendly Goudy Old Style Bold.

Illus. 5) An alumni publication representing the Art Institutes International, a prestigious group of art schools, this spread (designed by the author) has the look of traditional, forceful picture journalism. A technique to remember: an eye-catching picture with storytelling content can justify its presence with a minimum-sized copy block.

Illus. 6) A page from *Warner Currents*, aimed at a corporate audience, has a look of stylish elegance. The typographic style varies from spread to spread. Its sophisticated approach is appropriate for the readership, which is involved in the media world.

1. Pure Typography

In the hands of publications designer Walter Bernard, type alone has subtle elegance: well-placed initials, pull quotes in caps and small caps, a simple system of hairline rules, and a reverse panel at the top.

2. Playful Graphics

A clever illustration and typographic elements adorn a spread in a management newsletter designed by Pentagram. The subject lends itself to odd bits of copy and the symbolic illustration, at top, left.

3. Journalistic Integrity

In a news-magazine style, a spread from THE IDB (see page 117) has a 50-50 blend of words and pictures that enlivens factual reporting about Latin America. Narrow columns give the copy a fast pace.

4. A Garden of Images

Frankly a promotional newsletter for a Cape Cod landscape nursery, its pages set in Goudy Old Style are readable and appealing to its audience. Produced in PageMaker, its illustrations are mostly clip art.

5. "Picture-Friendly"

Every picture is a story. Every story is a picture. A national group of art schools published this alumni newsletter, which was unusual for its lively photography—resulting from the Photography Major in the curriculum.

6. Sophistication

E LEKTRA

Few record companies have experienced the dramatic rise that Elektra Records has achieved in recent years. Throughout its history Elektra has been unique in the discovery and development of a wide range of artists, among them — Jackson Browne, The Cars, The Eagles and Linda Ronstadt. However, Elektra's fortune has soared recently under the astute direction of Bob Krasnow. He assumed leadership of Elektra in 1983. Elektra's biggest year, 1988, was highlighted by several popular new releases — Anita Baker, Linda Ronstadt, Tracy Chapman and Metallica among others. In 1988, Elektra's revenues increased by more than a third over the previous year. In addition, Elektra's artists won some of the industry's top honors, including eight Grammy awards. Krasnow, in a recent interview says his company's success is no surprise:

▲ It's something that we've been building towards. It's actually been the last three years that this kind of momentum has been building, and I just characterize this as the re-establishing of Elektra as one of the great companies that services the needs of the great American music public and the world's music public.

🐦 Elektra was in the doldrums before you took over the company, and some believed the label wouldn't survive. What was the turning point for the company?
▲ This is a business of talent. To say that Elektra wasn't in as good a shape as it is now is the understatement of the year. I think *The Los Angeles Times* characterized it best when it said Elektra Records went from being "an outhouse to a penthouse". I think *Time* magazine also characterized us as being the "Intrepid" record label. But I think that Elektra is so tied

in to what it does musically, it's hard to separate.

This company puts out very few records, and each record has a very clear raison d'etre — that's the difference.

We make very specific types of recordings, whether its to work with Linda Ronstadt on her Mexican album that she did or to sign on someone with the character of Reuben Blades or choose to take the path with a Tracy Chapman, someone who is flying in the face of the Gordon Gekko, Wall Street, 'Greed is Good,' the '80s Reagan philosophy, or to choose to work with someone like Anita Baker who is not a manufactured product. Metallica is another example. We choose our

product very carefully.
🐦 What were the building blocks which led to today's success?
▲ The artists are your building blocks. We're not chemists here. We don't manufacture anything here. We choose people to work with, that's the blocks. The quality of our artists, the fact that we were awarded 21 Grammy nominations by our own peers, I certainly think distinguishes us from anyone else. Such publications as *Time, Newsweek, The New York Times, The Los Angeles Times,* and *The London Times* — the most important and most serious newspapers and weekly newsmagazines — cover what we do on a consistent basis. They don't do that with other people. We don't put out purely pop or fluff. Again I'm not criticizing anyone else. What distinguishes us is that we have a philosophy and that philosophy is to try to be our best and to try to do the best with the best
🐦 What about Nonesuch's recent critical and sales success involving such classical and contemporary artists as John Adams, Steve Reich and the Kronos Quartet?
▲ When we rebuilt Nonesuch, I brought in Bob Hurwitz. And Bob and I decided together that we would not try to compete with Deutsche-Grammophon and do some Beethoven Symphonies done by some of the greatest conductors in the world, or try to do string quartet music or chamber music by traditional people. We decided we would go into the American culture and market, and choose people like John Adams, Steve Reich, Phillip Glass and the

Kronos Quartet. We would choose artists working in a contemporary field, and do contemporary music and carve our niche. We can't compete with Deutsche-Grammophon or Columbia Masterworks, the Columbia classical label. They've been doing it 50 years and they've been doing it incredibly well.
If we wanted to succeed in it, we had to find a place where first of all, we had competence, and where we had a relationship with what the musical genre was all about. Also, that we appreciated it, that we sympathized with it, and we were able to support it emotionally and in every other way. And from that philosophy, of saying yes, there are great American composers out there, they're out there, now, it's just up to us to find them. To separate the wheat from the chaff, and say, 'Hey, let's find these people. Let's record Steve Reich. Let's record John Adams. Let's support these big operas. Let's support the Kronos Quartet. Let them do unrecorded classical pieces, classic pieces. Just because somebody didn't write them two hundred years ago does not in any way make them less valuable. Let's pursue that area.' I think our success speaks for itself. Let's bring the Bulgarian Singers to America. Let's record the Gypsy Kings. Let's do something everyone in the world isn't doing. That's what I demand from myself and of everybody that's on this team. And it is a team. I am not certainly sitting in this chair doing all of this myself. We have a great staff of people here.
🐦 What do you look for in

Incisive type columns are emboldened by a structure of heavy rules that bring to mind paintings by Mondrian. A distinguished work by Pentagram Design, it reports on Elektra Records. Well-leaded text type is Futura Book.

Logotype

e panel

Shoulder head

Main head

Three-line drop
initial

Advantages of Size

When Bigger

5-STAR
Inve

Morningstar's Gu

A

lthough large
lions of do
often m
sluggish than sm
generally been
the past deca
largest fun
period fr
large fi
coun
enr

ation

3.
THE ACT OF EDITING

It all begins with the editor. The act of editing might also be called the art or craft of editing, but whatever you call it, an effective editor sits in a pivotal position of creative control. Sometimes, with a staff that includes a designer, the editor orchestrates a visual-verbal production.

The Editor's Selective Judgment

Editorial thinking is almost completely a process of selective judgment. On the subject of the mind-set of an editor in the act of planning, Wilson Hicks, onetime Executive Editor of the Associated Press, once wrote: "The only reader he can be sure of is himself. So, instead of editing by 'reader appeal,' he edits by 'editor appeal.' The editor's curiosities and concerns are the curiosities and concerns of many other people whose interests he shares. The editor does not permit the exercising of his peculiar gifts to interfere with his human sympathies with those interests. He is adept at sensing shifts in thought trends and public tempers, in noting changes in customs and mores. He recognizes significances more quickly than noneditors. Therefore, as often as he reports and interprets events and ideas in which he believes his readers *will* be interested, he reports and interprets events and ideas in which he believes they *should* be interested. In this latter respect he is unabashedly presumptive."*

The Editor's Role as Visualizer

The subject of this book is design in a broad sense and all subject matter is af-

*Wilson Hicks, Words and Pictures *(New York: Harper, 1952).*

fected by phases of the editor's work. Therefore, let's define the editor's role as it relates to the visual newsletter. Each of a thousand newsletters may have a thousand different circumstances so it's difficult to generalize, but many of the editor's priorities are universal whether they produce a subscriber financial letter, a nonprofit fund-raiser, an in-house corporate newsletter, a P.R. medium, or scores of other subjects with different aims and audiences. The following are concepts and work routines that fill an editor's day. They are as true for a one-person staff as they are for a larger editorial operation. An untold number of companies and organizations have their newsletter produced by one versatile person. Many blue-chip companies and publishers may have several full-time staff members.

Design for Popular Appeal

Basically, you, as the editor, may be a word person, but if your publication requires visual content, you must develop selective judgment in the use and control of the visual. This doesn't necessarily mean that you must try to invade the "secret realm of the artist," but it does mean that you should be able to express your editorial aims and convictions in a way that will guide your designer effectively.

Consider design as an editorial tool. The editor's primary goal is to transmit ideas from the printed page to the eyes and minds of the readers. You want your publication to communicate by every possible means. You also want it to look good—but good looks is, and should be, the natural result of successful communication. In the newsletter field, the best design is functional design. *Your designer's role is to communicate, not decorate: He/she should be content oriented.*

Your designer manipulates the raw material—words and type, pictures, informational graphics—within a framework of space so as to communicate ideas as defined by you. If you are a word person you can't use the dodge that you know nothing about art. Editorial design *isn't art.*

Good editorial design is not cosmetic and not a form of artistic expression—it is inherently a part of the story itself. It makes the story's message visible on the printed page. There is no one better qualified than the editor to judge the editorial effectiveness of a layout. Your challenge is to locate a designer who will read your stories, who cares about the message, and who will assist you in making design work for your publication. If you cannot hire a designer, you will reconcile matters of design with your own alter ego!

The Anatomy of a Newsletter

Starting from point zero, know your terms. The principle parts of a newsletter are derived from the tradition of newspapers and magazines. This is also true of most of the editorial work routines.

Copy preparation—fitting in particular—greatly affects the visual quality of your layout. You should know the average number of type characters per line in your text column and rough out your copy accordingly.

If your layout plan looks great, your copy will be cut or extended as required. *This effort is vital to assure a quality visual product.* There's a danger that, as text copy rolls onto the columns on the computer screen, quick, arbitrary decisions will be made. Filler clip art may be added at the expense of your well-conceived layout plan. Or, if the text is running long, a major visual element may be cropped unsatisfactorily or sacrificed altogether. You should resist making a compromise.

With its quintessential cover, 5-Star Investor, *published by Morningstar, displays many functional newsletter features in a layout design that is simple, handsome, and readable.*

Labels (clockwise): Logotype · Head margin · Expanded type · Rule · Dateline · Reverse panel · Shoulder head · Main head · Three-line drop initial · Line illustration · Text runaround · Flush left · Foot margin · Body copy, justified lines · Continued slug

5-STAR Investor

October 1992

Morningstar's Guide to Building a Winning Fund Portfolio

Advantages of Size

When Bigger Funds Are Better Bets

Although large funds, with billions of dollars in assets, are often more unwieldy and sluggish than smaller funds, they have generally been a good investment over the past decade. An analysis of the 10 largest funds for each year during the period from 1976 to 1991 shows that large funds outperformed their smaller counterparts in four out of the six different investment categories (see table on page 10, column 1).

One of the biggest reasons for the megafunds' stellar performance has been superior management, a magnet that has frequently played a major role in attracting so many assets to these funds. This is particularly true of the largest equity funds, whose managers include such renowned investors as John Templeton, Peter Lynch and John Neff.

Equally, if not more important to performance, however, has been fund costs. Over the past 15 years, expense ratios for the 10 largest funds in our study have been about 30% lower, on average, than those of their smaller counterparts in the six categories examined (see table on page 8, column 3). This is in spite of the fact that expenses for the average mutual fund have increased dramatically in the same period.

The reason larger funds can keep their costs lower is that their size provides economies of scale. Because large funds trade such huge blocks of stock, they can pressure the brokerages through which they deal to keep the funds' trading costs very low. Moreover, large funds have the ability to spread costs associated with research, management and fund administration over a large asset base.

see Big Funds on page 8

D. Hoffman

INSIDE

News & Views 2
International currency turmoil, Japan's market rally, managers' increased cash positions, new fund offerings, load reductions and more.

Portfolio Makeover 4
A young widow needs to plan for her children's college education and for her own future.

Fund Profile 6
Third Avenue Value is every bargain hunter's dream.

The Morningstar 500 11
Comprehensive coverage of 500 elite stock, closed-end, hybrid and bond funds.

The Last Word 32
Now more than ever, it pays to watch costs when picking funds.

Not So Fast, Fidelity

Who's the True King of Sector Funds?

When investors think of sector funds, one name generally comes to mind: Fidelity. This isn't surprising, since the Fidelity select group's comprehensive list of three dozen specialty vehicles runs the gamut from automotive to utilities, and nearly everything in between. In comparison, Fidelity's next biggest rival, INVESCO (which runs the Financial Strategic funds), only sports eight sector funds, and second runner-up, Vanguard, has only five funds in its Specialized sector series. In all, Fidelity has roughly four times the assets of its two biggest sector-fund rivals. And whereas its rivals will have one, or at best two, funds for a given sector, Fidelity can offer as many as four (as in the case of specialty technology).

Yet, when it comes to performance, Fidelity is definitely not the top banana. We compared the performance of six Fidelity Select funds with their direct counterparts at Vanguard and INVESCO and found that, far from carrying the day, Fidelity tended to lag behind its rivals. For example, when we compared Fidelity's mainstream health-care fund with Financial Strategic Health Sciences and Vanguard Special Health Care, we found that the Fidelity fund couldn't boast a single winning year. (Financial Strategic's fund was actually the most consistent winner.)

see Sector Funds on page 9

The Act of Editing

An Issue Is Born!

The work stages in the editing of a newsletter are not stages at all, but processes that blend together during creation and move ahead concurrently.

A. INVESTIGATION. As editor, you know your audience, what's going on in your field, and your sources. To begin, sort out the current events and data that are the raw material for your issue. This editorial investigation is cumulative during the planning stages. If you have full- or part-time staff members, this is when you sit together and brainstorm the issue.

B. PREPARATION. Your story list will invariably include some subjects that are routine and worth reporting. Broader issues and subjects of widespread concern will be on the list—people to interview or who may have an article or speech for possible use. At this point, make photo, art, and writing assignments.

C. MANIPULATION. All your idea material is in mind and on your desk. It may be in notes on slips of paper, perhaps a few photos have arrived. You begin to look for some kind of pattern. You may shuffle the material, look at it sideways, make a few phone calls.

D. INCUBATION. As you wrestle with the raw material, answers don't appear immediately. You may turn to other things—but surprisingly, the unconscious mind continues to wrestle with the original problem.

A statistic may catch your attention—a timely item that you know is foremost in your readers' minds. As you probe the underlying information, it triggers a human story with visual possibilities. An idea is about to be born. It may well up in the consciousness like light before the dawn.

E. ILLUMINATION. Eureka! You're on to something. You explore your opportunities and limitations. It's time for visual thinking. If this appears to be your leading story, you'll review your best prospects for visual media. Explore this with your art director or design consultant. Should you use photos, drawings, diagrams? What are your sources?

As the text is drafted, you should have some thoughts about layout. Copy writing and layout conception go hand-in-hand. If the lead paragraph in your copy invites readers, the page layout is what *induces people to read the lead.* You review the

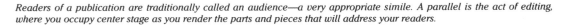

Readers of a publication are traditionally called an audience—a very appropriate simile. A parallel is the act of editing, where you occupy center stage as you render the parts and pieces that will address your readers.

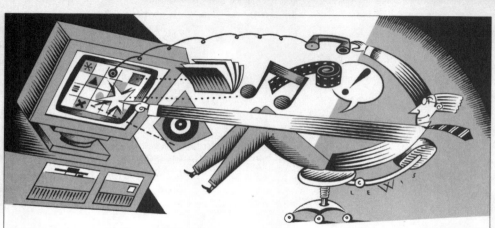

Putting More Power At Your Fingertips

Multimedia can stretch a manager's capabilities in a host of ways and help bring information alive. Some call it the biggest productivity and communications improvement since the personal computer.

How IBM managers and employees worldwide may be using multimedia, with its multilanguage capability, as a business tool in the near future.

The desktop computers around your office are going to become a lot livelier in the next couple of years.

By 1994, according to IBM's Personal Systems business unit, 42 percent of all Personal Systems sold will be multimedia machines. These are computers equipped to handle not just text but also recorded voices, music, computer graphics, still photographs, and full-motion video.

The point isn't to turn computer users into TV-gazing couch potatoes, of course. IBM's multimedia strategy is aimed at making all electronic communications more powerful.

"Our brains process audio and video information much more efficiently than they process other kinds of information," says Mike Braun, IBM assistant general manager, Multimedia. "When you combine all the media that are part of the information revolution and you add the power of the computer to let you interact with that information, you have a communication tool that's much more effective than today's computers."

Imagine, for example, a financial spreadsheet with short explanations—in voice or video—linked to various parts of the grid. When called up, these multimedia annotations would elaborate on those costs or sales figures, say, that are most likely to raise eyebrows. Says Braun, "If you're in sales and you get a written report showing that sales are down year-to-year in Hawaii or in one of our countries, the first thing you do today is get on the phone or call a meeting to find out why. With multimedia annotation, you can get additional information from behind that particular number and find out that sales were down because the weather was good and everyone was out surfing or a country was on vacation."

The Multimedia Format

Multimedia can be a liberation from the sameness of text. "But multimedia isn't going to replace all text," says Paul Evans, manager of IBM's Knowledge Systems Development in Atlanta. "It will co-reside with text." Evans points out that words are symbols that are already at least one step removed from the things they describe. Multimedia enhancements, far from being extraneous bells and whistles, he says, can offer people a more direct and more easily understandable way to communicate via computer.

"Any written material—legal documents, medical documents, sales reports, whatever—can be enhanced with multimedia," Evans says. For illustrated materials that need to be issued in several languages, multimedia versions will be faster and cheaper to produce than paper versions. "That's going to be especially useful for the new European market."

"Multimedia will help IBM managers with two of their most basic duties," says Braun. "The assimilation and communication of information. In the near future, more and more information will be deliv-

IBM Internal Use Only

Editorial content is creative and pages are smartly designed by Pentagram in an IBM newsletter that is sent to the company's management worldwide. A clever story title set in bodoni is linked to an energetic drawing.

techniques that capture readers: a provocative headline, an attention-getting picture combined with a headline, an amusing drawing . . .

F. PRODUCTION. Now you're in the throes of producing an issue. As work on the main story begins, you plan the positioning of minor stories and miscellany that will surround this editorial focal point. Think about headlines, subheads, boxed items, and the typographic plan.

A photographer whom you have assigned to the task has turned up several excellent black-and-white photos. You will

Salvador Dali's Mustache

What does this photo and headline have to do with newsletter design? Two things: 1) This illustrates the basic unit of photojournalism, a photo linked to a headline; 2) It also represents an age-old newspaper strategy of getting the readers' attention. Even though the above device caused you to read this copy, I am not suggesting that you print something outlandish to get attention. A capable editor looks for the unique twist that is eye-catching, but hopefully it's clever and at the same time respects the spirit and purpose of the publication. Remember: Humor is a rare and wonderful ingredient.

use these in strategically planned spaces on your layouts that link them with headlines or copy. You can throw away that overflashed handshake photo and the boring banquet shot. Now you can rough out thumbnail sketches on paper. The time has come to block out your layouts on the computer screen or on layout sheets. Your expectations for good-looking pages rise!

G. VERIFICATION. If other people are involved this is a point when you'll want to get further input and ideas from your associates.

H. REALIZATION. Now that all the pieces—facts, text copy, layout, and illustration ideas—are on the table, you can organize the parts, pieces, and people and craft your editorial unit. It should be ready for a final review by your publisher. Now you'll monitor copy fitting and proofing (refer to the *Chicago Manual of Style* or the *New York Times Style Book*). Both books are widely used as a "bible" for editorial style. You're ready for layout production, for the printer, and for the final moment of truth. What remains is the important matter of quality control on press. Usually, you can trust your printer for that. Your responsibilities are now over—until the next issue!

I. APPRECIATION. If all goes well, you may have a sensational issue and win appreciation from all sides!

Editing: A Human, Intuitive Art

Utilize the best software and technical methods available—which obviously help make your work routines easier. Conversely, don't allow the welter of digital equipment exploit *you*. Keep in mind that the act of editing is a human, intuitive act even though its processes may rely on technical methods. You should know and control the production activity, not as production manager but as a creative decision maker.

A flurry of feathers blew across her head. Some lodged among her notepapers and in the folds of her briefcase. As Editor of the *"Poultry Journal,"* an association newsletter, she sometimes had to go to out-of-the-way places like this processing plant in Chippewa county.

The next issue had to be in the mail in eight days and here she was out in the field, scratching around for a worthwhile lead story. Her readers—1400 processors, wholesalers, and retailers—covered a regional four-state area.

This story about a new feather-extraction technique was hardly sensational, she thought. Last-minute news-gathering seldom pays off. She completed her notes, went to her car, and in 40 minutes was back in her office, sitting in front of the PC.

She worked alone. This was solitary desktop publishing and a limited budget. Six times a year she had to fill 24 pages (72 columns!) with meaningful information. This time, her art consultant Floyd had handed her some amusing pieces of clip art—line drawings of hens, eggs, and drumsticks. Also on her desk were a rather gray photo of 12,000 chickens on the range, the shot of Intercity Poultry's new plant in Centerville, and a shot of the Association's new director, Jack Glebe, smiling broadly. She also reviewed a couple of new charts from the Department of Agriculture and some P.R. photos that arrived in the mail from a major purveyor in Abilene. Not altogether inspiring material.

She clicked on her PageMaker program, scribed the three-column cover, and indicated the logo at the top. At the center of the page she outlined a space for Glebe's picture. She would inset it somewhat wider than the middle column and let the text flow around each side, an easy job with PageMaker. She then arranged the clip art in a neat row across the foot of the page.

In the rest of the issue, she positioned one- and two-column visual items in spaces and gaps as they occurred. Twenty-four pages of news and views about the poultry field and its people set in 10 point Times Roman with Times Bold for headlines—very heavy on typematter and soft gray pictures.

Thinking Out Loud

First of all—what a boring cover idea! Rather, it's a lack of an idea. Another upfront comment—24 pages is a bit much. Traditionally, newsletter publishers have preferred to condense their content into eight, 12, or sometimes 16 pages. Their first thought is to give the reader quick access to large amounts of information. Compression is important.

We have an editor who paid little attention to the visual, except to lament the scarcity of good material. Penciled, rough thumbnail sketches of her pages might have caused some visual ideas to surface. As stories were identified with spaces, column by column, a list of visual possibilities might have developed opportunities for photos. Out in the field, a simple 35mm camera with some fast, trouble-free black-and-white film could easily provide usable photos. Almost anyone with a theme in mind can shoot interesting and usable pictures.

Those white-coated people at the plant assembly line, for example, were people with individual characteristics. In the most routine surroundings, it's possible to identify moments of human interest and capture them on film.

Everything has a history, including the world of chickens. Old prints in the public domain could illustrate a feature with visual charm. Even though her readers were looking for timely and practical information, this could lead them briefly away from the workaday world of poultry. With concentrated effort, she could have explored many other ways to relieve that gray ocean of Times Roman.

THE HERMAN MILLER QUARTERLY FOR ARCHITECTS AND

B I L L A

Or so the song goes. This issue of BILLABLE TIMES is full of people wh

would disagree with that idea. Author Walter Truett Anderson said in hi

talk to last year's conference at Aspen that designers might expand thei

kinds of things these days, including value systems and cultures. Will p

professions take up the challenge? Will they begin the daunting task of des

Talking about the future of anything is easy; there's little accountabilit

record, for example, of economists' erroneous predictions. Yet the people v

issue of BILLABLE TIMES have a real stake in what happens to designers c

themselves are designers with practices to run and livings to make. What a

friend at HOK writes that the firm faces increasing competition from o

increasing client sophistication, and non-traditional client relationships—thr

The Romans used the word respicere ("to look backwards") when they

extrapolating what we cannot know from what we do. Maybe we shoul

where we are, and decide where we want to go. Then, of course, we have t

4. WRITING TO BE READ

Thurber, Baker, Mencken, Twain? No. It doesn't require extraordinary talent to write copy for a newsletter. But readers do appreciate a perfect turn of phrase. Copy, even in the most modest newsletter, should make reading not only rewarding but enjoyable. In terms of the current cliche, it should be "reader friendly."

Ask yourself the question, Is your writing style readable? Does it exude popular appeal and still have substance? This brief chapter isn't intended to be a treatise on publication writing. It concentrates instead on three key areas of newsletter writing: headlines, lead paragraphs, and picture captions. A journalistic writing style is essential for lively and readable newsletter copy.

Your headline is the loud, clear voice that states your theme and sets the tone of the copy that follows. Daily newspapers have writers whose sole creative responsibility is to craft eye-catching headlines. It is an art and a difficult one. At the New York *Daily News,* long admired and studied for its clever headlines, one talented writer for many years wrote the heads as his principle job. He invariably looked for amusing word play, such as, "County Officials to Talk Rubbish." Because of its tone, its brevity, and its ability to sense reader interests at any given time, the *Daily News,* during its long history, has had the largest readership of any paper in America.

Typically, newspaper headline writers do their work *after* reading the article. Newsletters generally require the opposite. You draft the headline *before* writing the copy. As you begin to develop your body copy, having the headline before you is an effective way to keep on target.

A potpourri of verbal messages ornament and inform on an all-type front cover. While the effect is busy, the type elements attract attention and move readers to the inside. The two-color design is the work of Paula Kelly.

Breezy copy implanted on a clever and amusing illustration gets a weekly news publication off to a fast start. A tabloid-size page, it's an appropriate style for a media-conscious audience of communications professionals.

It also helps you coordinate the relative weights and placement of articles throughout your pages.

Here's a checklist of the qualities that go into writing an effective headline.

1. COMPLETENESS. In a very few words, does the head say as much as possible? Consider these two approaches to a story about a couple of major issues acted on by a board of directors:

Board Approves $12M Budget

It might better include two issues:

Benefits and $12M Budget Approved by Board

2. ACCURACY. As you attempt to make your words bright and appealing, have you sacrificed a degree of accuracy? Consider these two:

The Bugaboo of Current College Costs

Or,

College Tuition Highest on Record

3. SPECIFICS. Well-chosen details are important for clarity and reader appeal. Generalization can result in a boring headline:

Museum Features Outstanding Artifacts

Improved by more details:

Museum Unveils Show of Stone-Age Artifacts

4. CLARITY. An ambiguous headline is an easy pitfall that can sacrifice clarity. Here are two examples. The second gets right to the point:

Increased Tax Burden as Paving Proceeds

Taxes Soar with High Cost of Road Work

5. FOCUS. Interpret the message of your article and keep your headline strictly on target. It's easy to stray from the central idea, as shown by these two examples:

THE HERMAN MILLER QUARTERLY FOR ARCHITECTS AND DESIGNERS / SPRING 1993

TIME IS BILLABLE

Or so the song goes. This issue of BILLABLE TIMES is full of people who would disagree with that idea. Author Walter Truett Anderson said in his talk to last year's conference at Aspen that designers might expand their work to design all kinds of things these days, including value systems and cultures. Will people in the design professions take up the challenge? Will they begin the daunting task of designing their future? Talking about the future of anything is easy; there's little accountability. No one keeps a record, for example, of economists' erroneous predictions. Yet the people we talked to for this issue of BILLABLE TIMES have a real stake in what happens to designers of all sorts, for they themselves are designers with practices to run and livings to make. What are the new rules? A friend at HOK writes that the firm faces increasing competition from other professionals, increasing client sophistication, and non-traditional client relationships—three constraints on her design of the future. The Romans used the word respicere ("to look backwards") when they talked about the future, another way of extrapolating what we cannot know from what we do. Maybe we should understand where we have been, see where we are, and decide where we want to go. Then, of course, we have to go. Whatever *we decide* will be will be.

WHATEVER WILL BE WILL BE

WE ASKED SIX THOUGHTFUL DESIGN PROFESSIONALS: WHERE IN THE WORLD IS DESIGN HEADED?

That's all we asked. And the response, we think, is quite amazing.

We had decided that if we began our interviews with a gambit like, "Now that the 80s are dead and buried...", or, "Now that Clinton is in the White House...," the interviewees are the kind of people who would think we were trying to control the discussion. So we simply asked them, one at a time in separate interviews, "What's going on?" And sat back and got an earful.

What is amazing is that, different as their perspectives may otherwise be, they all see the state of the design professions in the same ambient light: They see that the old ways of thinking about design are moribund. They feel that the old ways of doing design are redundant. And they fear that the old ways of selling design are a prescription for bankruptcy. To a person, they agree on one thing: Whatever design used to be, it will not be the same again, certainly in this century.

We chose these six design professionals based on the criteria usually set forth to satisfy today's over-wrought "credentialization" mentality—but we added one rational reason of our own: We wanted people who get around. And these do. They not only see and deal with real clients but also do work that takes them out of the office and into the public realm. Thus, when asked what's going on,

Ann Chantreuil

they almost invariably prefaced their response with the qualifier, "What we're seeing is..." Take, for example, **ANN CHANTREUIL**, who heads a small and thriving architecture firm in Rochester, NY: When she says, "What we're seeing is that buildings more

and more are being designed by code," she is referring to what she's personally seeing. Her observation derives from her experience on an NCARB committee that's committed to creating a computer-administered licensing exam. "My subcommittee is developing a handicap toilet and ramp that has to meet code," she says, "and we're finding that code constraints can intrude dramatically on design considerations."

JOAN GAULDEN is an interior designer who practices in Greenville, SC. She guesses that roughly 80 percent of the ASID membership are independent designers, "just like me." Not quite. Few of them run businesses that have prospered for 30 years, and fewer know so many design professionals so well. She's gone up the ASID ladder and served several years ago as its national secretary. Plus, she knows an entirely different design crowd that her architect-husband associates with.

"What I'm seeing," she says, "are people going out of business every-day because they CONTINUED ON PAGE 2

Aimed at a sophisticated audience of architects and designers, a two-color cover on tinted stock opens this quarterly published by Herman Miller, Inc. New York designer Sara Giovanitti cleverly styled the logo for a look that suggests a traditional newspaper.

Bad Weather Troubles Meant Poor Annual Meeting Attendance

Disappointing Turnout at Annual Meeting Resulted from Heavy Snowfall and Apathy

Deadheads and Two-Faced Heads

The worst fate for a well-intentioned head is for it to leave the reader unsure what the article is all about. Consider a few deadheads:

Nice Place to Visit

Fewer Trips to Mall

Facing a Quandary

The reader has very little clue as to the subject matter of the story. An easy way to avoid this editorial guessing game is to zero in on a key word or phrase and then smoothly work it into the head as an active element.

Two-faced headlines do the disservice of giving your reader a choice of two different meanings (one meaning is enough!). Here are a few samples:

Metallurgy Companies Lead Industry Growth

Workers Strike up Acquaintances on Job

Rock Group Hit at Outdoor Concert

Science Chief Reason for Fast Growth

It's easy enough to avoid two-faced heads and other forms of ambiguity. After you've written a head, read it over for the meaning that you intended. Then read it a second time for the way-out interpretation that you may never have assumed

A sidebar in an IBM management newsletter represents the visual power of a few centered words that repeat the title of an article. Typography is by graphic designer Beth Singer.

possible! If there is any question, toss it and start over.

A Last Word About Heads

Beware of "Headlinease." This is the contrived headline that's obscure in meaning and will tax the reader's patience. Often they are amateurish imitations of city newspaper heads. Typically, these heads use commas to replace "and," use nouns in place of adjectives, and may feature a loathsome pun. There is also the temptation to use imprecise short words that try to shoehorn big ideas into small spaces. Short words are useful and desirable but often suffer from overuse. For example, the word "see" can be literal "to see" or figurative "to regard." Other overworked short words include: "name," "hit," "set," "call," and "bid," all of which may be either a verb or a noun. For years *The New York Times* has used the word "foe" in its headlines—an archaic word, but useful because in world news there are so many foes.

Short, one- or two-paragraph stories often have your highest degree of readership. When writing heads for these little gems, don't shortchange them. They need as much care and ingenuity as the longer features. It's possible that some of your readers may read *only* these short items!

Notes About Lead Power

You have a strong layout and a powerful headline. Now you need the third major element: The most important sentence in any article is the first one— which lures readers to the second one and onward into the

WRITE A LEAD

From a wire report—Ted Turner and his wife Jane Fonda have a herd of 1000 buffaloes roaming their ranch in Truth or Consequences, New Mexico. The TV leader wants a permit to graze them on public land and wants to expand the herd to 2000. Turner once said, "Buffaloes are . . . better looking than cows—they don't have all that fat on their butts." Nearby ranchers fear that buffaloes will break fences and spread disease. Al Schneberger of the Cattle Growers Association said, "I put this a little bit higher than a worm farm. But not a lot higher."

Four possible leads to this story are drafted below.

Cable TV mogul, Ted Turner faces consequences from truth about plan to graze 1000 buffaloes on public lands.

1] A lame beginning modifier and the Truth or Consequences word play is reaching a bit far. It ends up being an obscure lead that's apt to annoy the reader.

Neighboring cattlemen oppose cable TV mogul Ted Turner's plan to graze his herd of 1000 buffaloes on public lands.

2] The sentence begins with inert words and takes much too long to get to the point. A weak lead.

Ted Turner, the cable TV mogul has applied for permission to graze his herd of 1000 buffaloes on public lands. Some neighbors oppose the idea.

3] A straightforward account that starts the story in a boring, matter-of-fact way. This lead has no journalistic vigor.

Cable TV mogul Ted Turner and his wife Jane Fonda get opposition from ranchers for a plan to have their 1000 buffaloes roam on public lands.

4] The best of the four, this compact lead gains from including Jane Fonda. The subtle word play, "buffaloes roam" adds a little charm at the start of this amusing story.

Crafting a Caption

Caption writing is an exacting craft. The key is to write "into the picture." This means a carefully constructed sequence of information that helps the reader interpret. Avoid describing the obvious. In these examples,

This is a backstage photo of Deuteronomy, the star of *Cats,* in his dressing room at New York's Winter Garden Theater, reacting happily to the attentions of a group of enthusiastic visitors.

OR

Between acts in his backstage dressing room at New York's Winter Garden Theater, Deuteronomy, the star of *Cats* is happily groomed by a group of enthusiastic visitors from out of town.

text. If you're not off to a strong start, your article may be lost before it begins.

Many times, when making a writing assignment, I've asked the writer to rough out two or three lead paragraphs so that we could make a choice. It's like asking an illustrator to submit rough sketches before developing the final drawing.

There is no rule as to how long a lead should be. It can depend on your subject and your audience. If your readership is a group of learned scientists, your lead may pack more profound content than if the readership is a local marching society. Whatever your audience, don't overestimate your readers' staying power. If your lead is cluttered, overloaded with names or proper nouns, or unduly long, don't depend on fidgety people to stay with you for long. Your task is to capture your readers with a few solid details that tell

why the story was written and why it's worthwhile to read it. Don't elaborate on the reasons but persuade readers to read on by keeping them a bit inquisitive. The parts of a lead build up much as the paragraphs of your story. Pay particular attention to the final sentence in the paragraph. It should thrust the reader's attention into the next paragraph.

Whenever possible, it's desirable to have an easygoing, whimsical quality in your lead. Here's a story that is serious enough but starts with a lighthearted tone.

A fifth former premier was snagged in Italy's widening net of scandal when prosecutors told him he was suspected of extortion in the allocation of millions of lira in earthquake aid.

Ciriaco De Mita, a Christian Democrat and leading member of parliament, is from the

the left caption begins, "This is a . . . ," which is the weakest possible opening. The second-from-left caption wastes words getting into the subject. The third caption is more promising, with opening words that function like a descriptive title. The far-right caption, another winner, has a style popular in tabloid journalism: a brief and breezy editorial comment with fast pace and immediacy.

OR Deuteronomy, star of the Broadway production *Cats,* is groomed by a group of delighted visitors in his backstage dressing room at the Winter Garden Theater in New York.

OR Meow . . . cats love attention. Deuteronomy, star of the Broadway production of *Cats,* is groomed for the camera by a group of delighted visitors in his dressing room at the Winter Garden Theater.

Naples area hard hit by the 1980 quake. But De Mita, who served as premier in 1988-89, cannot be arrested or charged unless parliament lifts his parliamentary immunity . . .

The first sentence begins a note of whimsy and the reader is coaxed to continue with the hope that the account will show a crooked politician getting his just desserts.

There can be no fixed rules about writing a lead except for the general principle that you must grab the reader's attention. This involves selectivity in choosing your material as well as a sensitive choice of even the first three words in the lead sentence. Composing a lead is a creative act and should be approached in a manner best suited to the individual style and subject of the material.

P. G. Wodehouse, the late, great writer of cheerful literature, once summed up the writer's quandary: "I don't know if you have had the same experience, but the snag I always come up against when I'm telling a story is this dashed difficult problem of where to begin it. It's a thing you don't want to go wrong over, because one false step and you're sunk. I mean, if you fool about too long at the start, trying to establish atmosphere, as they call it, and all that sort of rot, you fail to grip and the customers walk out on you."*

I'll close the discussion about leads with an opening paragraph from the pages of *Time* magazine. It represents inspired and colorful reporting.

---

*P. G. Wodehouse, Right Ho, Jeeves *(New York: Viking Penguin, 1988), p. 5.*

Last week the Senate tried its level best to act like a body of statesmen. Debate on the Lend-Lease Bill opened on a plane so high that many Senators felt a little difficulty in breathing. Crowded galleries hoping for an old-fashioned quick-and-dirty scrap, with plenty of rabbit punches were disappointed. The Senate wrapped the toga of dignity and dullness about its collective paunch and gamely strove for classic words.

Picture Captions

There is little written information about the art of picture caption writing. In a newsletter setting, captions are often dashed off in a perfunctory way as a final chore before going to press.

Think about these small items of copy and their importance on the printed page. Let's assume that you, as a knowledge-able writer/editor, recognize the value of a strong photograph. There is a notion among some publication designers and writers that a good photograph needs little if any copy. Only a label will do, they argue. A strong photo explains itself. *How wrong!*

If you're working on a well-illustrated newsletter, there are two kinds of im-agery—verbal and visual. Skillfully com-bined, they work together to heighten the total effect. A photograph alone—while an exact image—falls short in expressing all that needs to be said about what it repre-sents. Don't force the reader to interpret the meaning of a photograph. Most read-ers won't stop long enough to interpret anyway or they'll come up with an inaccu-rate interpretation. This is where caption writing comes in.

English is richer in similes and met-aphors than most other languages. It's a language of images and therefore func-tions ideally in combination with pictures.

Benjamin Franklin, publisher, as a young man in 1733 was already a taskmaster who demanded extreme efforts to achieve clear, logical prose. It is written that he (Poor Richard) drafted copy over and over and over . . .

A well-written caption combined with a photo can result in communication far stronger than words or pictures alone. This basic principle of photojournalism is as true today as it was 60 years ago.

Caption Logic

The caption writer brings something to the picture—but shouldn't tell too much. As you write about the obvious externals of a photograph, you write *to* a photograph. When you deal with interpreting the inter-nals, you write *into* a photograph. While you shouldn't let the reader overlook any-thing important, the reader should bring something to the act of viewing as well.

Major magazines often have a caption writer whose sole job is to produce smaller items of copy. This visually literate person contributes much toward making the reader appreciate and enjoy the editorial content.

Many publications develop unique and creative caption styles. Note, for example, the variety of caption styles, pages 46-47, that illustrate several solutions to a given problem.

Slugs, Sidebars, Et cetera

Newsletters can and should utilize the same typographic techniques that help articulate the pages of major magazines. This is where the written word plays a dominant visual role. (See page 44.)

Quotations. (sometimes incorrectly called quotes). These blown-up extracts from the text, variously called readouts, decks, panel quotes, and pullquotes, further invite the reader into your arti-cle. If the text doesn't produce a suit-able quotation, no one will complain if you rewrite or summarize using a copy style suitable for display. This is an ideal way to break up a solid page of text, particularly if no photos or graph-ics are available.

Thoughts About Punctuation

Do you punctuate with confidence or by chance? If you're weak in this skill you're among multitudes of educated people, including many professional writers.

Punctuation as we know it is relatively new. The ancient Greeks more often spoke their profundities. When they did write, they strung out capital letters that not only lacked punctuation marks but had no spaces between words. The Romans didn't do much better. At least they centered dots between the words. Punctuation systems of various kinds developed haphazardly over the centuries. No system became universal until the 16th century when a gifted Venetian publisher, Aldus Manutius, originated a system that became standard. He is rightly dubbed, "The Father of Modern Punctuation."

A few suggestions: Punctuate with restraint. Commas are important but don't sprinkle them unnecessarily. Read your sentence over and ask "Is this comma necessary?" The colon is a commanding little symbol that's useful, but leave the semicolon to writers of scholarly prose who use it to guide readers through 90-word sentences. Beware of the three little dots instead of a dash. Leave that punctuation stunt to writers of trendy advertising copy. In general, well-constructed, concise sentences require very little punctuation.

Aldus Manutius
1450–1515

Headers. This is another way to capture the reader's attention. Newsletters often use this device, based on the tradition of book page design where running heads appear at the top of each page. Set in display type, they function as subheads that move the reader through the themes of the story. If you write them in breezy prose, they will also help take the curse off a long, intimidating text article.

Slugs. It is customary in popular newspapers to have frequent paragraphing. In fact some papers seldom have paragraphs of more than six lines. Slugs, the boldface lines of type such as you see in this book, are another way to break up long, monolithic/type columns. Ideally, they would occur at points in the copy where there is a pause—but this isn't essential. They should be placed so that they look good on the page: No one is apt to challenge their position. Sometimes, instead of occupying a full line of space, they appear as boldface words on the beginning line of a paragraph. Generally, they are preceded by a half line of space.

Labels for Information Graphics

If you're working with an artist who is resourceful and verbal, you may receive suggestions for the words that appear on maps, charts, pictographs, or tables. These labels bear half of the communication load. Brevity and clarity are essential. Information graphics almost always require a title as an immediate key to the subject matter.

Final Touches

Rewrite and rewrite again! Marvelous software programs make it possible—you make it happen. Prune ruthlessly to remove clutter and improve clarity. Is every word the right choice? Is the writing tight enough? Is any copy pretentious, pompous, or trendy? Be thankful that you can make changes before the presses roll.

He began to think it was true—writers and designers are natural enemies. Yes, she's a talented designer but what was she trying to do, control him? For two days he had labored on this 1500-word article. It's clear, he thought, and it's good. Now she has the gall to say that it had to be cut by at least 300 words to fit the layout!

He: "Crop the photo, give up some of that white space."

She: "You've got to realize that it looks right just as it is."

He: "I'm a writer. I don't know anything about art—and I have a responsibility to the readers."

She: "They won't read it if it looks too jam-packed."

He: "It's their subject. Our job is to give them information. That's what it's all about."

It was a classic disagreement. Of course, he was right—and she was right. But neither was willing to compromise.

There was the headline problem. She had the letters so tight that it was hard to read. And worse yet, the text was set in a swirl around the illustration. In a flash her computer playfully disported his copy into a ragged unreadable mass. He was wallowing in self-pity when the director of communications looked in and made a comment, "I just read your copy on benefits and you've made our readers feel like chowderheads. You forget, this is a newsletter, not literature. You've used so many fifty-cent words. How many Americans know what 'post-prandial' means? Simplify."

"I'm not writing to an audience of high-school sophomores," he said, "I'm trying to give them the whole story."

The director continued, "Your headline's too brief. Two words, 'Benefit Package,' don't say anything." His parting comment, "I don't care how many words it takes, make the title say something."

Sitting in front of his PC, our writer reviewed his copy. His choice of words sounded intelligent. He wondered if this was the right job for him. A year at journalism graduate school hadn't convinced him that journalism was a noble profession. He recalled how the noted English novelist Muriel Sparks referred to journalists as *pissoir de copie*—and that he really didn't want to be.

Then he thought about his style. It's a direct approach. He had an image of reporters slouched in front of their typewriters, banging out copy spontaneously—with little if any rewrite—then shooting it off to the editor's desk and on to composition. To labor your copy, he thought, was a waste of time. And his title—there was only space for about 15 bold characters—rang out bold and clear, even if it didn't say much.

Just then, the designer stopped by with a conciliatory idea. "I can give you space for a hundred more words, not more or less. If you tighten up your copy, it will fit into the layout. Then we'll all be happy."

Thinking Out Loud

Cool-headed mediation or arbitration needed . . .

This illustrates a typical source of tension between word and design people. It's also the age-old question of form vs. function.

As mediator, a fair-minded editor would face these sensitive egos head-on and point out that a spirit of give-and-take is the positive way to obtain results.

No layout design is unalterable and no prose is so "etched in stone" that it couldn't be tightened and compressed, which is often an improvement.

5. TYPE AND THE PRINTED WORD

Essayist John Ruskin once wrote that the main purpose of letters is to make thoughts visible. His use of the word *letters* was appropriate to the world of the 19th-century literati. For our purposes, let's substitute *Type and Typography*.

Nearly everyone knows what a typeface is—a specific design or style of an alphabet. Over the past five centuries, every typeface has had a name. In today's computer technology there are hundreds of new names. While it sounds pretty complicated, the fact is a dozen or so well-designed typefaces can provide enough choices for text copy in almost any printed piece. In fact, a noted publication designer recently remarked that he could conduct his work comfortably with as few as six typefaces.

Display typefaces—the type you use for headlines and titles—are a different story. Here, you can let your imagination ramble and indulge in a wild or decorative design to enhance an occasional special feature. However, in newsletter design, use restraint throughout your pages. Generally, a clean, classic, strong, and readable headline type style should be used consistently. It becomes the one important visual characteristic that you build into your publication's design.

What Is Typography?

This chapter will discuss the six qualities that define and determine good typography: type style, type size, line width, letterspace, word space, and line space (leading). If you are in control of these qualities, you will avoid an uneasy typographic balancing act. The result will be good typography that is readable. This

The beauty of classical Roman letter-forms is illustrated by this linear analysis drawn by a 16th-century Italian scholar, Fra Luca Pacioli.

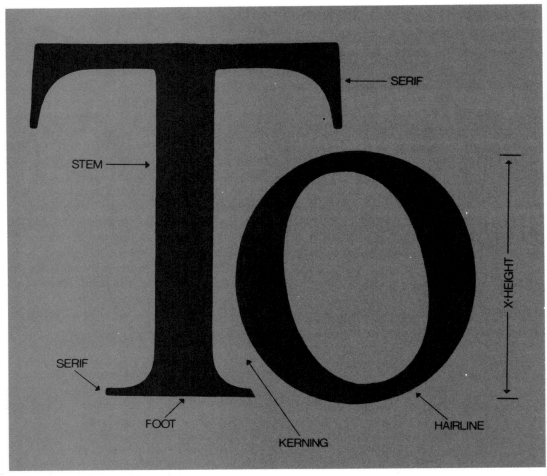

The Anatomy of Roman Letters
The principle parts of traditional Roman letterforms are useful to know as background to making intelligent selections of typefaces.

holds true if you are handling typographic decisions on your own, or it will give you confidence and better control if you are using the services of a graphic designer.

Legibility—or lack of legibility—is inherent to all typefaces. Once you've chosen a particular typeface, you are locked into its legibility. *Readability is something you can control because it's dependent on how you use the type.* You may select a very legible typeface and render it unreadable through poor typographic arrangement. The purpose of typography is to make type communicate information efficiently and look handsome on the printed page.

Many otherwise intelligent designers

Old Style

Garamond, 17th-century, is typical Old Style with heavy serifs and less contrasting strokes.

Transitional

Baskerville, 1757, forms a bridge between Old Style and Modern and has slimmer serifs.

Modern

Bodoni, late 18th-century, has even, unbracketed serifs and strongly contrasting strokes.

Sans Serif

Totally without serifs, this style's popularity began in the early 20th century.

Slab Serif

Also called Egyptian, it has heavy, blocklike serifs and strokes with no contrast.

Decorative

A vast number of ornamental faces that are available for special effects and themes.

think of text copy as just so many gray rectangles. Fill them up with sans-serif typematter,* square them off, and you'll have a splendid, almost architectural effect on the page. There is no law governing legibility. A well-known editor once said, "Send those art directors to Siberia!" Designers of newsletters should care as much about the printed word as the writers who craft the copy. More about legibility on pages 60-61.

Selecting a text typeface is the first step

in planning a printed page. Computer technology has made this a highly complex problem. Many letter shops advertise proudly that they have immediately available over 500 typefaces—a confounding richness of choice and a source of confusion to the untrained.

Unraveling the Typeface Mysteries

First, a brief note about the history of typefaces. The origin and development of letterforms has engaged artisans, scholars, humanists, and other ambitious people over many centuries. On these pages are displays of the evolution of letterforms

---

*Sans serif, simply "without serifs," came into full flower as a type style in 1928 with the design of Futura. These plain, simple type families (there are many) are excellent for headline and display uses. For text copy, they appear sterile and may go unread. You will seldom find sans-serif type in the text columns of large-circulation magazines.

from old style to transitional to modern. There is also a diagram of the principle parts of a type character. This is a subtle area, of interest primarily to typophiles. If the subject whets your appetite for more detailed information, consult one of the many excellent books on type and typography listed at the back of this book.

Scan the pages of a typical type specimen book and you'll have the uneasy impression that there's just too much. You need a guide. Most type books are alphabetical, so starting at the front of a book, I'll name and describe some favorite typefaces that I can recommend as always safe and not trendy. If you use them well, they'll cause your pages to be read and admired.

■ Baskerville. A classic 15th-century design, its contemporary versions are handsome, legible, and often used in magazines. For many years it has been the principle text face in *Harper's Magazine*.

> When selecting a typeface for text copy in a newsletter, it is essential that you consider legibility. There are many types that may look unique but pose a problem because of design.

■ Bembo. A contemporary version of a classic Roman type that dates back to 15th-century Venice where it was commissioned by the printer Aldus Manutius. It is popular with leading graphic designers who use it in periodicals, books, and in promotional literature. It is handsome and legible.

> When selecting a typeface for text copy in a newsletter, it is essential that you consider legibility. There are many types that may look unique but pose a problem because of design.

■ Bodoni. Dating back to the early 19th century, contemporary versions continue to be used frequently. In particular, a version called Bodoni Book has been used in many popular magazines, including *Vogue*.

> When selecting a typeface for text copy in a newsletter, it is essential that you consider legibility. There are many types that may look unique but pose a problem because of design.

■ Bookman. A contemporary version of this 1930s face, ITC Bookman comes in a variety of weights and is very legible. The light and medium versions are best for publication uses.

> **When selecting a typeface for text copy in a newsletter, it is essential that you consider legibility. There are many types that may look unique but pose a problem because of design.**

■ Century. This is a favorite of many prominent designers. It comes in a variety of versions. Two versions that I've often used in publications, Century Schoolbook and Century Expanded, are strong, legible, purposeful faces. Century Expanded has an elegant italic.

> When selecting a typeface for text copy in a newsletter, it is essential that you consider legibility. There are many types that may look unique but pose a problem because of design.

Many designers dedicated to the art of typography prefer to roughly sketch their type layout. For those less committed to traditional methods, any number of computer programs will deliver and modify type in countless styles and sizes. Caution—unlimited choice in untrained hands can result in poor typography.

An Old Style capital letter set in Caslon represents the elegance of a traditional typeface. It is significant that the most contemporary publication and advertising designs use type styles based on letterforms 600 years old.

■ **Cheltenham.** A 100-year-old face, Cheltenham is used to this day for secondary heads in *The New York Times*. The type you're reading in this book is set in ITC Cheltenham Book, a completely redesigned rendition that's available in many weights. This is a straightforward type—concise, unpretentious, designed for maximum legibility with a strong presence on the page.

When selecting a typeface for text copy in a newsletter, it is essential that you consider legibility. There are many types that may look unique but pose a problem because of design.

■ **Galliard.** A very recent design developed with the aid of a computer, this handsome face is based on a 16th-century type, Grandjon. The latter has long been used on the very readable pages of *The Readers Digest.*

When selecting a typeface for text copy in a newsletter, it is essential that you consider legibility. There are many types that may look unique but pose a problem because of design.

■ **Garamond.** This classic typeface has been around since the 17th century. A contemporary Linotype version called Garamond No. 3 is a popular model with a low x-height that makes it very readable. Another favorite, ITC Garamond Book, has a higher x-height and has a very round, open appearance.

When selecting a typeface for text copy in a newsletter, it is essential that you consider legibility. There are many types that may look unique but pose a problem because of design.

■ **Goudy.** An American design developed early in this century, it was unappreciated for many years but staged a comeback in the 1980s. As a text type it's slightly heavy with strong serifs that give it a commanding presence on the type column.

> When selecting a typeface for text copy in a newsletter, it is essential that you consider legibility. There are many types that may look unique but pose a problem because of design.

■ **Optima.** Designed in the 1950s, this face is popular with graphic designers. It is original and unique, being neither serif or sans serif. Thick and thin strokes relate it to transitional Roman faces. One caution: While it's readable enough as text if well leaded, it appears quite gray on the page. It's best used in a newsletter that has strong illustrations.

> When selecting a typeface for text copy in a newsletter, it is essential that you consider legibility. There are many types that may look unique but pose a problem because of design.

■ **Times Roman.** Designed in 1923 for the *Times of London,* almost everyone knows this useful and handsome face. It may be the cleanest, most legible typeface ever—and perhaps that's why it's much overused. But don't let that prejudice you. It's the classic typeface of this century. When used properly it will do credit to any newsletter.

> When selecting a typeface for text copy in a newsletter, it is essential that you consider legibility. There are many types that may look unique but pose a problem because of design.

Desktop Typography

In earlier times most newsletters simply used typewriter copy. The IBM Selectric, for example, offered few choices so you double-spaced a single column and went on from there.

Within a decade desktop publishing systems have developed techniques that are roughly parallel to the invention of movable type in the 15th century. Newsletter design has available unlimited layout, type, and typography possibilities. Today, even a modest newsletter office has microcomputer equipment that can generate camera-ready copy. Many have modem hookups that send copy from one machine to another for typesetting and layout imposition. One editor of a prominent newsletter recently said to me, "I've never even met the people at the other end of the wire. They know our style details and we get the result we're after."

Know Your Typography Guidelines

While you don't need to be a gifted graphic designer to achieve professional-looking type pages, knowing the guidelines is important whatever method you

Sans-serif type is clean-cut and can convey a contemporary spirit. Some styles of sans serif can be totally sterile and unappealing. Choose one with distinctive characteristics. You can develop your own sense of taste with the help of a well-printed type book.

Legibility and Readability

use, so let's face typography head on. Many designers devote a lifelong career to the field. Typography is a serious matter, close to the heart of communication, and it should make reading a newsletter a pleasurable experience.

Once you've narrowed the typeface selection down to ten legible styles, type size is your next decision. First, consider the reader whose reading environment may pose visibility problems such as a dimly lit subway or lurching bus or commuter train. Either of two type sizes should take care of all text copy: 10 point or 9 point (Anything smaller would go largely unread.) Leading

A handsome text type can be composed in ways that completely destroy the quality of the design. As illustrated by these two extreme examples, typography is how you arrange letters.

A handsome text type can be composed in ways that completely destroy the quality of the design. As illustrated by these two extreme examples, typography is how you arrange letters.

When you compose typematter, there are many possibilities for misjudgement. Your computer program can do almost anything. Don't let it produce unreadable copy.

(the space between lines) should be one or two points (see page 62). Your spec sheet will look like this: 9/10 (9 point type with 1 point leading), 9/11, 10/11, or 10/12. Head-

The history of   early period

When planning line length, remember that most readers scan groups of words and not individual words. Too many word groups on a line results in eye fatigue.

lines in the typical 8 1/2 × 11 newsletter may require three sizes, depending on your editorial needs: 14 point, 18 point, and 24 point. Now and then you may need a larger size for a special feature or sensational news item. Upper and lower case is

legibility

The most legible types have strong incisive serifs, a restrained design, not too bold or too thin, ample lower case x-height, and easily recognized character shapes.

easier to read than all caps. Picture captions, which are usually brief, can be set in italics or sans serif so as to contrast with the text copy.

Principles that affect legibility and readability are covered on these two pages.

Good Reading

Upper and lower case is generally considered more readable than all caps. This is easy to understand when you consider the importance of word shapes to recognition.

Techniques To Attract Readers

Many tried and proven typographic techniques help improve reader appeal. I'll describe a few that are relatively easy to achieve.

Big Initials

More than a typographic embellishment, the big drop initial (perhaps five lines deep) can be a focal point that pulls the reader into a feature story. It's a device

rn cl lo
rn cl lo

Tight letterspacing can be a deterrent to readability, especially with sans-serif type. Note the confusion that has resulted in the lower line of these comparisons.

used by many magazines. But don't overdo: One or two within the pages of an issue should be enough.

Large Text Type

Another device that will start a feature off with a bang is large text type in the opening paragraph. Try 14 point or even 18 point.

Consistently poor word spacing results in text columns that are hard to read and sloppy, unattractive typography such as you sometimes see in daily newspapers. It is easy to avoid this problem by planning your type size and column width in a ratio that makes more even spacing possible. Another way to avoid this problem altogether is to establish a flush-left style for your text copy. This results in perfectly equal word spacing and a somewhat less formal appearance.

Justified lines set in a narrow column results in eccentric word spacing and undesirable "rivers." As a rule, establish columns of from 40 to 60 characters per line.

This was an age-old technique used by Hearst afternoon papers over the years, and it still works. Another way to break typographic monotony is to run a whole opening column in 24 point type or a whole one-page article in 12 point (well leaded, of course.) This courageous act could win you widespread reader attention.

Rules

Rules, in layman's language, are printed lines. They come in a variety of widths from the slimmest hairline to as wide as 12 points. Hairlines between columns of text or outlining a full page can have a

---

Difficult to Read
This text matter is difficult to read. It has no leading, causing the lines to pinch, and the faint plainness of the sans serif typeface has a squinting effect. The

Less Difficult to Read

The lack of leading here also causes the lines to bunch together. But both the Roman (serif) typeface and the regular letterspacing

Easy to Read

This column of text reads as it should: comfortably. The Roman typeface and the letterspacing are the same as above. So the leading

Three degrees of readability: The block at the top is a problem—lightface sans serif, tight letterspacing, and lines not sufficiently leaded. The next block also has a leading problem. The third block is just right.

---

subtle structuring effect that gives a page a neat and orderly look. Oxford rules, which are simply a thick and thin rule side by side, are attractive around a boxed typographical item, a chart, or table. Most publications use rules, but don't get carried away with a complex system of rules in a newsletter. Simple is best.

Quotations

Often called readouts, pullquotes, or panel quotes, quotations are an opportunity for an eye-catching, large type element. Set them in 14, 16, or 18 point type; well leaded; and centered or flush left. They will give the reader a hint about an article and a reason to read the text.

Slugs

A repulsive name for the subheads that appear between paragraphs and signal a pause or change in subject matter. They're an excellent way to break up long text columns and may be centered within a two- or three-line space. Slugs are sometimes simply run into the first line.

The qualities that make printed material easy to read are not complicated. Largely, they are just a matter of common sense. Since legibility is inherent in the design of any typeface, simply choose one that you know is *highly* legible.

Readability is the real problem. Legible typefaces can be made unreadable through poor typography. These next two

While your in-house facilities may be adequate, the best high-resolution type composition is obtained by sending disks to an outside composition house. This will result in needle-sharp type of at least 2000 lines-per-inch.

pages discuss how you can plan for maximum readability.

We've already discussed type choices and the sizes suitable for a newsletter. Next, there are four critical areas of typographic planning that are the key to readability: line width, letterspace, word space, and line space.

Line Width

Ideally, for maximum readability, a line of type should contain between 35 and 50 characters. A narrower width will result in too few words per line and too much hyphenation when justified.

As lines become wider, reader fatigue tends to increase because of the difficulty the eye has in sweeping across long lines of type characters. Tests show that eyes do not read individual words but scan about three or four words at a time as they pause momentarily. As a rule, the reader makes about three or four pauses on a line before the eyes tire.

Individual typeface design characteristics also affect line measure. For example, since serifs help guide the eye's horizontal movement across a page, they make possible somewhat longer lines than sans-serif type. The length of a text block also affects line measure. If the text column is deep and unbroken by illustration, a shorter line width will make the copy more inviting and readable.

Letterspace

While you read lines of type in short sections, individual word shapes are the key to ease of reading. Studies have proved that the average word shape is implanted in human memory for future retrieval. We don't recognize words letter by letter. The clearest articulation of words results from tight letterspacing. Of course, this should not be carried to extremes. Text characters that touch or slightly overlap can be as detrimental to readability as loose setting.

Letterspacing that is just right will result in a pleasing evenness of "color" on the printed page. You will avoid the problem of "rivers" and disruptive dark and light spots in the text columns. Rivers are the jagged vertical formations of white space that appear as you look down a column.

Headline type, when set in capitals, can be effectively letterspaced, particularly sans-serif type. Avoid letterspacing upper and lower case headlines, which tend to fall apart and read poorly.

On the whole, skillful letterspacing not only looks better but it enhances communication and is more likely to be read.

Word Spacing

Sometimes on a justified column, you will see an extreme example of word spacing that's too open. The result is a system of visual "rivers" that is a serious hindrance to readability. It is also most unattractive. This can be avoided by keeping your line width no less than 45 characters. Equally bad is extremely tight word spacing that tends to make words run together and results in unintelligible copy. This is often the case with sans-serif text.

Line Spacing

The space between lines of type is traditionally called leading because in the days of metal typesetting thin strips of lead were fitted manually between lines of type. In the current technology, line spacing is an appropriate term. The space between lines creates thin white "guidelines" that are an aid to smooth readability. Too much space between lines can cause an interruptive gap from line to line and slow the act of reading. Leading that's too tight can merge the lines together and cause readers to strain in finding their way down a column without guiding strips of white spaces. Visually, it will also result in an unattractive text column. Choice of type style can also affect leading. For example, Garamond No. 3, which has a very low x-height, can run with very little leading. Another version of the same face, ITC Garamond, has a high x-height and requires a bit more leading. In general, two points of leading in a 9 or 10 point text will work well.

Justified or Rag-Right

Justified lines (where type is flush at both left and right) and rag-right (where lines are flush left and have a more or less random unevenness on the right) are both about equally readable. Whether you go one way or the other is very much a matter of individual choice and the style of your page layout.

A last word of advice that applies to readability on any type page is: Keep it simple. Too many type sizes or styles on any page can confuse and repel your readers. No newsletter can afford to let that happen.

In an office high above New York's East 54th Street, he was sitting slightly stooped in front of his Mac keyboard. Three months out of art school and only two weeks on the job—a one-man design department at a large textile firm. His first major assignment, to redesign and style a newsletter. Yes, the company was a bit old-fashioned but this was an ideal chance to show what a well-trained graphic designer could do single-handed to update the firm's image.

They had given him a collection of typed copy and a handful of photos prepared by the advertising staff, more than enough to fill his 16 pages. He was told to use the firm's age-old emblem, a circular affair, as a logo. Work around it, they said. Then they left him alone for a few days.

His computer program offered 120 different typefaces. First, he would make some choices. No need to restrict himself to one face for the text. Why be like everybody else? He would vary the type choice from spread to spread. He would print the circular emblem in pale gray about $6^1/_2$ inches wide on the cover behind the text. Like a bull's-eye, he thought, and readers will see it coming through the text copy.

Helvetica Regular was his choice for the cover text. Set tight. Let the characters touch. And for subtle variety he would run alternate paragraphs in italics. He would use his Mac to italicize the type at a sharp angle.

The top of the cover was clear space. Here, Helvetica Extra Light would look classy for a headline set in 120-point caps. He would ask them to do a rewrite. Two short words would do. One story with plenty of white space.

The rest of the week he worked on the inside pages. Choosing a variety of typefaces was a field day. On his three-column pages, he positioned the photos—some one-column, some two-column. He loved big numbers and decided to place 60-point Ultra Bodoni folios in the outer margins about halfway down each page. He ran three text columns on dark blue panels with type printed in reverse.

With a thrill of satisfaction he tacked up printouts of the whole issue in a row across his bulletin board. It was a knockout production, he thought. They'll be impressed.

Thinking Out Loud

Will they be impressed? Let's look at some of the problem areas.

1. A mixed variety of text and display type styles in a 16-page newsletter will be a hopeless mélange. One basic text type and a few variations of headline type would have been ideal. Typography isn't a visual playground.

2. His cover plan will never attract many readers. Printing text on top of a pale illustration—a common design gimmick—usually ends up unreadable. Helvetica set tight will cause eyestrain. Most magazines avoid this.

3. A note about italics: They are appropriate for single words, brief sentences, or picture captions, but *never* use italics for lengthy paragraphs, particularly in sans serif type.

4. Huge lightweight capitals on the cover will look stylish but will communicate weakly. The reader will be bored before turning to page two.

5. Big folio numbers are decorative but folios are intended to be functional, to be seen as needed. Calling attention to them as a design element distracts from editorial content.

6. Reverse (white) text type on a dark color panel looks fine but columns of white text type will discourage readers.

This is a designer with a self-indulgent attitude toward communication. He has used a number of pet ideas, most of which distract from editorial goals. In short, he has ignored the principle that type is meant *to be read.*

6. LAYOUT ON A SIMPLE TRACK

There was a time when almost anyone could design professional-looking newsletter pages quickly and easily. People who were computer literate but not visually literate discovered desktop. Simply summon the desktop genie out of the box and he would help you fill the spaces on the screen. So it was said. Now, all that has changed. There is more design consciousness as people have learned that there is no such thing as an "instant design."

Outstanding newsletters—and they are a small minority—result from an inspired arrangement of words and graphics on the printed page. This is not art, but it *is* a craft that involves artful combinations of well-written copy, effective typography, and appropriate visual elements. To obtain printouts you'll be proud of, you must be a well-prepared professional. That is what this chapter is all about.

Newsletters, often "read on the run," need a layout that is clear and forceful. Ideally, they should be distinctive enough to stand apart from the junk mail that clutters America's mailboxes. At a glance, they should look appealing, authoritative, and worthwhile.

Verbal and Visual Ideas

Your subject matter and available editorial material present both opportunities and limitations. On pages 107-187 a selection of successful newsletters are analyzed to illustrate design approaches aimed at a range of audiences. While extremely varied, they all share a common objective: to capture the reader's attention and communicate forcefully. Review these pages in detail for a learning experience that can have a positive influence on the success of your publication.

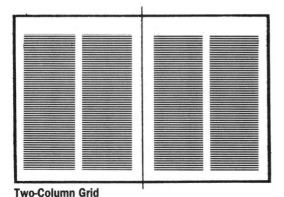

Two-Column Grid

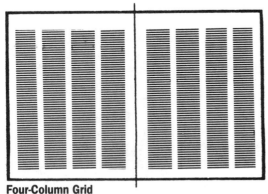

Three-Column Grid

Four-Column Grid

Three Grid Options

The two-column grid provides a simple clean layout but layout possibilities are limited within two modules. The three-column grid is popular with news magazines. It results in fast-paced copy lines and many layout options. The four-column grid slices a spread into eight narrow columns with limited words per line. Flush-left setting is essential. This grid works well for large page formats.

The Page As a Visual Structure

View the newsletter page as a structure involving many parts and pieces. All successful structures require a plan, and the plan for an editorial page layout is based on a network of lines within which content is organized. This organizing system is called a grid. At the most simple level, a single-column typewritten page with margins fits into a rectangular grid.

A single-column page doesn't offer much opportunity for layout. Therefore, the grids shown here are two, three, and four-column plans, as well as a 12-part grid that offers more challenging layout design opportunities.

Each grid option has individual advantages as well as a significant effect on the personality of your pages.

The One-Column Grid. Well-suited to a very basic newsletter where straightforward verbal information is primary, this approach represents the historical origin of the newsletter medium. Here, the burden of communication rests upon the writer. A colorful logotype on the front page would obviously be a necessity amidst all that gray typematter.

If your editorial content requires photos and other visuals on one-column pages, there is an alternative: Use a system of visual marginalia. Simply plan your pages with wide outer margins to the right and left sides of each spread. This opens up vertical spaces for visual items. While this space may be only about 1 1/4 inches in width, these graphics (and sometimes typographic callouts) will add visual interest and relieve the heaviness of solid text matter. Illustrations can be positioned adjacent to the text references.

The Two-Column Grid. This plan opens up more design possibilities and provides a text column width that's very read-

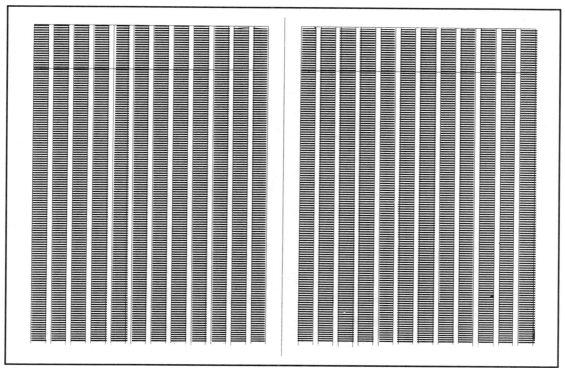

A 12-part grid is a useful plan that provides the most possibilities for creative, well-ordered layouts.

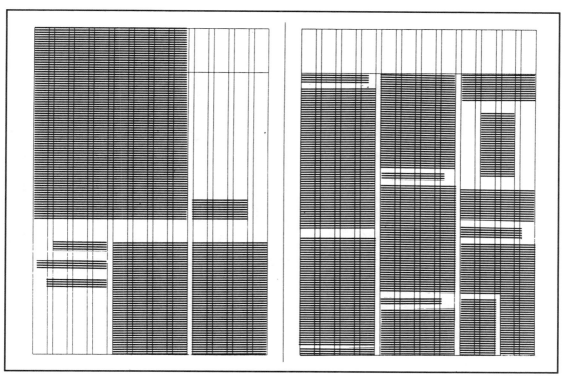

In an actual layout, the 12-part grid results in systematic modules for text, heads, captions, and illustrations.

Layout on a Simple Track

Measured Spaces

It is always useful to have spaces predetermined for the many parts of an editorial spread. The 12-part grid is used by major magazines because of its flexibility.

An Eight-part Photo

A Number-1 Head

Four-part Columns

The abc defghijklm nopqrstu

SIX POINT PALATINO DF with tino italics on eleven lead, set. The cynics notwithsta unshakable belief in the u ual man in centuries wher earth were dominated by

This is twelve on fourteen point Bembo type The decision, ostensibly made by the bers of the Russian track and field team, the meet with the U.S. in Los Angeles month because of American policy in Viet deplorable intrusion of politics into spo Russians claim the athletes themselves reso to compete, but their statements ring of par aganda. Perhaps ever more reprehensib This is twelve on fourteen point Bembo type The decision, ostensibly made by the bers of the Russian track and field team, the meet with the U.S. in Los Angeles month because of American policy in Vie deplorable intrusion of politics into spo Russians claim the athletes themselves reso to compete, but their statements ring of par aganda. Perhaps ever more reprehensib This is twelve on fourteen point Bembo type The decision, ostensibly made by the bers of the Russian track and field team, the meet with the U.S. in Los Angeles

to compete, but their statements ring of par aganda. Perhaps even more reprehensible This is twelve on fourteen point Bembo type The decision, ostensibly made by th bers of the Russian track and field team, th month because of American policy in Viet deplorable intrusion of politics into spo Russians claim the athletes themselves reso to compete, but their statements ring of par aganda. Perhaps even more reprehensible This is twelve on fourteen point Bembo type The decision, ostensibly made by th bers of the Russian track and field team, to the meet with the U.S. in Los Angeles month because of American policy in Viet deplorable intrusion of politics into spo Russians claim the athletes themselves reso to compete, but their statements ring of par aganda. Perhaps even more reprehensible This is twelve on fourteen point Bembo type The decision, ostensibly made by th

able with 10- or 11-point type. One- or two-column graphics can be used freely but there is one limitation: It is difficult to feature small illustrations without cutting them into the edges of the text.

Two-column pages have long been associated with school textbook formats, but you needn't be concerned about the academic look if your content has lively, topical subject matter.

The Three-Column Grid. Traditionally popular as the format for news magazines, this page plan can be the basis for countless layouts. The column width, akin to newspaper columns, has

A Number-2 Head

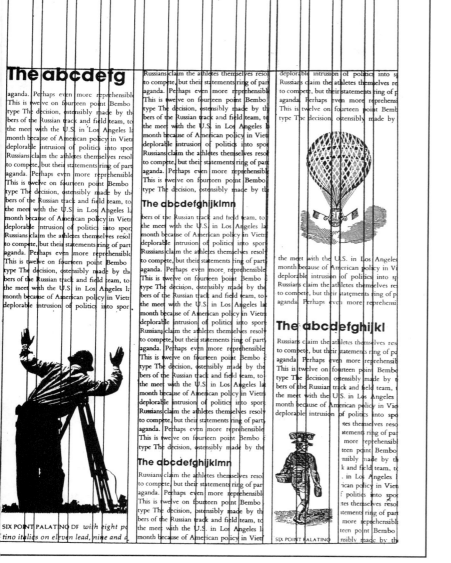

A Number-4 Head
(Center Column)

A Number-3 Head

A Two-part Illustration

a "newsy" look. These column modules allow a number of headline sizes with stories ranging in length from a few lines to several columns.

The Four-Column Grid. Generally, this division of a typical $8\frac{1}{2}\times11$ newsletter page results in columns of only three or four words on each line and may cause the reader's eyes to dance back and forth. However, with lines of text set flush left, the four vertical modules provide some intriguing layout design variations. Four columns—and often five columns—are ideally suited to large page formats, 10 or 11 inches in width.

Ideas by Pencil

Many publication designers prefer to rough out their ideas with pencil and paper in the initial stages of conceptualizing. This simple and casual approach is called thumbnailing. It doesn't necessarily require drawing ability, and the planner merely sketches type areas and indications for headlines and illustrations.

The Twelve-Part Grid. This offers almost unlimited options for the creative designer. Easily divisible into two-, three-, or four-column pages, this plan makes possible a well-structured layout that can be a challenge to any designer. Many prominent magazine designers use this grid as a standard framework for all pages. The simple spread layout illustrated on pages 70-71 is an uncomplicated three-column interpretation showing an orderly use of the modules.

The 12-part grid could result in a chaotic page if the vast number of choices are used too freely. In the hands of an experienced designer, it opens up almost unlimited possibilities for exciting editorial pages. If you're uncertain about this scheme, experiment. It's a valuable design exercise.

The Theory and Practice of Thumbnailing

For a moment, forget the CRT. Simple, thumbnail sketches on paper can never be surpassed as an effective way to firm up a layout plan. They are the best way to clarify visual thinking and visualize in somewhat primitive fashion not only page concepts but the rhythm and flow of a whole series of pages. This is your overview before serious layout work begins and it's your chance to play with visual ideas without pressure. Most designers and editors utilize thumbnails at the first stage in planning a newsletter.

The Dynamics of an Editorial Page

The grid system is ideally suited to computer coordinates. Also, grids can be constructed on paper with the traditional T-square, ruler, and pencil. Headlines, text columns, and graphic content are the components of a page. How these items merge and mingle in a layout can result in pages with visual vitality—or pages that are dull and placid.

When you're satisfied with a particular grid system and the visual plan is roughed out with thumbnail sketches, it's time to consider the next order of layout concepts. Publication designers think of two facing pages as spreads. For that reason, it's important that pages look good side by side. Many qualities affect the play-off of facing pages. For example, they may be designed to work together for a strongly unified effect, like the example at the right. For a different approach, two pages can be designed to contrast strongly and appear unrelated.

Spooks, hobgoblins, ballerinas and bumble bees swarmed the zoo on Saturday, October 24 for the Adopt-an-Animal Pumpkin Patch Party. The Discovery Zoo was transformed into a Halloween haven with over 200 pumpkins, sticky spider webs, rubber bats, and costumed keepers, docents and guests. Nearly 1,000 Zoo Parents of every shape and size were greeted with zoo-venir pumpkin yo-yos, balloons, giant pumpkin-shaped cookies, drinks, and a schedule of special events.

Here's a tongue-twister: *hobgoblins hobnobbed* with their most unusual family members, then tested their eye-hand coordination with Spider Toss and Ring Around the Pumpkin. Valuable prizes

Pumpkin Patch Party

in the form of rubber worms, bugs and bat rings were awarded purely on the basis of enthusiasm. For those without costumes, a mask-making area was stocked with all the trimmings for creating fabulous new faces. A good time was had by all, and in spite of a gloomy forecast, it didn't rain!

The Adopt-an-Animal Pumpkin Patch Party was underwritten by a second-year grant from the Houston Coca-Cola Bottling Company. Since the Adopt program began in early 1986, our Zoo Parents and donors have contributed more than $120,000 to the Zoological Society's zoo development projects. We thank you for your continuing, generous support of the Houston Zoo—and we hope to see you again next year! ▨

The Zoological Society's first annual Carolling to the Animals celebration was a resounding success. Society members flocked to the zoo on Saturday, December 12 for a morning of holiday entertainment and refreshments with madrigal singers, bell ringers, choral groups, dancers and musicians. Particularly lively entertainment was provided by Hank Amigo's Dixieland Elf Band, which had visitors stomping their feet to a variety of tunes, and Delia's Junior Jazzz, the troop of young dancers from the Delia Stewart Dance Group.

Special guests included everybody's favorite fellow in red—Santa Claus—and his most trusted reindeer,

Jungle Bells

Rudolph. A dusting of snow would have been welcome, especially for special guest Frosty the Snowman. This festive trio handed out holiday stickers and balloons to pint-sized visitors in *total* disregard of the "naughty vs. nice" factor.

A very special thanks goes to all those who volunteered their time and talents: Delia's Junior Jazzz, Cub Scout Pack #1800 of the Sam Houston Boy Scout Council, Sterling Senior High School Chorus, and St. Mary's School Chorus. And thanks again to Santa, Rudolph and Frosty for taking time out from their busy holiday schedules.

If your group would like to volunteer for next year's holiday celebration, drop us a line in mid-September or call the Society office at 529-2632. ▨

Two-page Harmony

Conceive your layouts as spreads—two pages that look good side by side. They may be visually unified as in this spread with headlines and photos in repeat pattern. When unrelated, facing pages should be strategically contrasted.

The "Key" Picture

The dominant picture on a cover or inside spread is referred to as a key picture. It visually establishes the theme of a feature in juxtaposition with a headline. This combination is the basic unit of a photojournalism layout and is followed by columns of text.

Photographs are often the visual elements that stand out strong and clear on newsletter pages. The choice and placement of photos has an obvious influence on the spirit and character of a page. Contrast is powerful communication. Small against large, lively next to quiet, dark next to light, are all qualities that can achieve dynamic results from photos or other illustrations in a newsletter layout.

Visual and Verbal Messages

Lead stories begin with strength when a dominant photo is positioned with the headline. This photo is called a key picture and thematically it identifies with the headline for a unified visual/verbal effect. Generally, a key picture ties in more successfully when played above a title as on the cover illustrated at left.

Portraits, often called "mug shots," are best used small-sized, unless you have an extraordinary photo worthy of a full page. Line drawings, charts, maps, and other graphic items provide visual variety. Try to plan graphic elements that give the reader visual information. Most newsletters try to be informational in an informal way. Purely decorative spots as space fillers don't enhance the communication value of the page. They can appear trivial, or worse yet, betray a lack of ideas.

Accent on the Verbal

While more or better visual content can be your answer for an unboring publication, many newsletters, by choice or necessity, feature no photos or any other graphics. They rely completely on printed words. This requires skillfully planned editorial content and typography. The spread shown on the opposite page is an outstanding example of creative typography. While it is hardly representative of a typical newsletter, it demonstrates how the designer, Paula Scher, used type matter with imagination. A variety of typographic ideas in this spread are well worth study.

Superior typefaces are available to almost everyone with in-house equipment. Ideally, a newsletter gains visually from the use of distinctive type styles. However, it is important that the typographic page has simplicity. There is visual power in uncluttered pages. Text matter is by nature gray, therefore your page will gain strength from the use of boldface headlines, small and large. The writer and editor always influence the typographic page. The number of words in a heading is important. A five-word heading is more likely to be read—and most often it looks better—than one of 15 words. Economy of words also applies to your logotype. A publication with one or two words as its name makes an outstanding logotype possible, and with it, a more distinctive cover.

Practical Aspects of Typography

The type sizes on your page are a key factor in well-planned newsletter design. Headline type must relate properly to text type and to the relative importance of each story. Sometimes it must also relate to a photo or other graphics. Below I describe a simple system to plan type in a news or feature layout.

Typically, a newsletter with a wide variety of stories, photographs, and other visual content will require as many as four sizes of headline type. Designers and editors of news media have traditionally spoken of headline type by a numerical sys-

Creative Typography

A striking newsletter spread with eye-catching typographical patterns was designed by Pentagram designer Paula Scher. Two factors made this design possible: the designer's talent and the fashion theme of the newsletter 7th on Sixth.

Layout on a Simple Track

Strong Promotion

Which came first, the visual or the verbal? This powerful newsletter cover in praise of a Mexican food enterprise takes its cue, much like a successful print ad, from a forceful, appealing visual image.

tem, for example: a number-1 head (30-point type), a number-2 head (24-point type), a number-3 head (18-point type), a number-4 head (14-point type). As the editorial content is evaluated at an early stage, headline sizes are planned relative to the importance of stories, the weight of pictorial matter, and the character counts possible within a given space. The layout on pages 70-71 shows a numerical system that would be standard throughout a newsletter.

A Matter of Unlimited Choice

Technology provides us with the capability to generate and manipulate images almost endlessly. This is both a blessing and a problem. Faced with unlimited choice there is often the temptation to plan a layout that veers off in complicated or unclear directions. We must recognize the difference between creativity and con-

fusion. Keep in mind that clarity should be your number-one priority in designing your pages. As any art enthusiast will attest, there is beauty in simplicity.

Blind Alleys of Editorial Layout

As your layouts are planned, editorial and design considerations will often overlap. An effective graphic composition should result in maximum editorial impact. If it doesn't, there may be some simple and obvious design difficulties that could be avoided.

A number of popular design techniques can be a disadvantage to editorial layout and should be used minimally or avoided:

1. Tilting pictures at various angles and using too many different sizes can result in visual chaos that can repel readers.

2. Don't create wild abstract arrangements of words and graphics—unless your readers are puzzle fans.

3. Avoid running typematter over photographs (except the occasional bold headline). Also, don't overlap one photo over another.

4. Use silhouetted photos selectively and with care. The background often provides useful information that shouldn't be sacrificed.

5. Do not select a text typeface for its decorative quality. Text type should be read effortlessly and readers shouldn't think "type."

6. Do not position explanatory captions at points far away from a picture. They work best at or near the bottom of the figure.

7. Avoid running caption or text type in reverse over black, over a photo, and especially over a four-color background.

Designers have a maxim that "one must learn when to break the rules." The points listed above will help you "play it safe." With continuing experimentation, you'll determine what rules to follow for your particular publication. Hopefully, it will result in forceful communication with high standards of good taste.

Mary B. was planning the first issue of a nonprofit subscription newsletter. Her promotion had been mailed out and advance responses were already coming in.

What had once been just an idea now had to become a real product. Her organization, Northwestern Timber Ltd., was providing her with a healthy budget and generous support. The editorial theme was to be wildlife—a most important concern among timber interests. She knew that a lively looking publication required the talents of a designer. Since there was no designer on staff, Mary B. desperately needed a freelance designer she could trust to do the right thing.

She was acquainted with three designers who might qualify and decided to give each one a test assignment for which she would pay generous fees. North American Mammals would be the subject. Six pages should be a reliable sampling. She put together a collection of photos and a story outline, then called in her three prospects.

Designer Number One: He had a full-time job at a medium-sized ad agency, was happy to moonlight, and took the material, saying it was a "snap" and he would be back in about a week. A few days later, he brought in some printouts. The headlines were huge. The pictures small. He announced that there was "sell" in those heads and the pictures were, in fact, attractive footnotes. "A positive approach to hammering out your ideas," he said.

Designer Number Two: In addition to her steady work as a designer of juvenile books, she was a talented illustrator. She was delighted with the wildlife theme— less enthused about the black-and-white photos. "Let's experiment with something colorful," was her comment as she left. "Lots of color is the answer." Several days later, she brought in a bundle of layout comps. Illustrations roughed out in full color covered half the space. Type-matter would be 9-point sans-serif for a "contemporary look." Photos were indicated as marginal spots.

Designer Number Three: This lively fellow designed the layout of a weekly newspaper supplement. His opinion: The newsletter needed a "strong current-events look—giant, tabloid-size pages would give it a look of importance." Two weeks later, he presented her with a group of four-column pages, 17 inches tall. A few photos were blown up, and he included a large number of one-column pictures. His approach was journalistic but overblown, she thought.

Now, it was time for her to make a choice. What had been a problem was now a dilemma.

Thinking Out Loud

Selecting a freelance designer for a complex project is never easy. Mary B. was gambling on a test based on uneducated guesswork. It had seemed logical that a workable plan could have resulted from the thinking of at least one out of three knowledgeable people. They all had track records—but they all lacked *specific, relevant accomplishments*.

Conclusion: Mary's approach to the problem was completely wrong. It was not necessary—or desirable—to run a design contest to locate an appropriate designer.

Talent scouting is an arduous task. It entails phone calls, referrals, interviews, and portfolio reviews. As you review their work, look for relevant samples and ask questions about each designer's approach.

After a likely prospect is identified, spell out in detail a *good, clear definition of objectives*. These steps would have provided Mary B. with satisfactory results.

7. THE POWER OF PICTURES

When you're working creatively with photographs, it matters very little whether you're dealing with a newsletter, a 100-page news magazine, or 300 images on a CD. Most people like pictures and your job is to use photos to attract readers and communicate. Obviously a striking photo on the front page of a newsletter will give it identity and invite interest. Well-chosen pictures throughout your pages—combined with words—will add a dimension to the editorial content.

The practice of photojournalism is a word-and-picture technique that has been around for more than 50 years. It involves a combination of skills, sometimes found in one person but more often in a group of specialists working together.

The work sequence of photojournalism follows a logical pattern:

Step 1. Think about your visual options. Then shoot or gather photos according to your editorial plan.

Step 2. Photo editing, the act of selection, identifies the best and most appropriate prints.

Step 3. Plan a layout that respects both the form and the content of the photos and supports the story content.

Step 4. Photojournalism is words-and-pictures, so the final stage is to write copy that enables the visual and verbal to work together effectively.

In the newsletter field, a single person is often editor, writer, photo editor, and layout designer—a difficult combination of skills to master. However, it's possible to develop abilities in all these related fields.

Action + Reaction = Drama

A simple equation can be the key to a compelling picture. In this school vaccination scene the camera faced a roomful of students. Instinctively, the photographer selected one whose facial reaction to the kindly doctor was most intense and beamed the camera full force into that expression. Selection and timing combined to result in a dramatic, storytelling picture.

Within the budget constraints of a typical newsletter, it's possible to shoot or obtain photographs that will add drama to gray, typographic pages. Exceeded only by the Japanese, Americans carry more cameras and shoot more photos per capita than any other race in the world. We are visual to an overwhelming extent. While researching this book, I reviewed hundreds of newsletters and was struck by the bland quality or complete lack of photographs in many of them. People working in this field are either unwilling or feel unable to use a camera. I've never developed a photo negative or printed a photo, taken a photography course, or subscribed to a photo magazine, but I've shot many photos in response to editorial needs, some of which appear on these pages.

Reportage by Camera

The camera can be a "faithful witness" with a view of the world far more penetrating than the human eye. "In seeing, you use a kind of visual shorthand, whereas your patient camera takes in everything within its ken in laborious, literal longhand . . . The camera is always a stranger; it takes nothing for granted."* But the needs of photojournalism go much further. We expect the camera to catch a fleeting facial expression that provides a rare insight into a complex human personality. It must also stop the drama of human activities at the instant of highest emotions. These are some of the marvelous powers of film behind a lens.

Working with your camera, you must be selective and shoot with keen judgement and an understanding of editorial needs. If you are directing a photographer, be firm, be decisive, and be specific. It is always wise to overshoot (film is cheap), which is a common practice in photojournalism. (continued on page 88)

---

*Thomas H. Miller and Wayne Brummitt, This Is Photography (Garden City, NY: Garden City Publishing Co.) p. 11.

Frankly Posed

A posed picture can be effective depending upon how it is planned. The faces of these Andean children clearly mirror pleasure as they react to the personality of a skillful photographer.

Posed/Unposed

The people have been arranged for picture taking and are obviously aware of the camera. The photographer used a technique called posed/unposed where he asked them to relax and ignore the camera.

The Warm Smile Principle

Look at the covers of countless magazines on a newsstand and you'll notice the ever-present power of the winning smile. Magazine editors and their marketing staffs know that people are interested in *people* and they rely heavily on the appeal of a radiant face.

Obviously, photos for editorial or documentary use should avoid the prevailing style in fashion photography that emphasizes sad or hostile expressions. Most readers with normal sensibilities will react favorably to faces with sparkle and animation. Within a very few pages, newsletters must capture the reader's attention. Even with the limitation of black-and-white printing on modest stock, the winning smile will come through.

The Tell-Tale Background

Beware of blank backgrounds. Ideally, the effective editorial photograph will disclose something about time, place, and the uniqueness of the setting. Except for the bare-bones portrait, it is almost always possible to plan a revealing background. Ansel Adams, the great master of backgrounds, once commented that you don't "take" a picture, you "make" a picture. Sometimes subtle, sometimes not so subtle, backgrounds are a prime part of picture planning. Even in the everyday, sterile environment of an office, backgrounds can vitalize your picture: a vista through a window, attractive bookcases, poster displays on a wall, and sometimes a glimpse of other people will provide a touch of drama in the background.

Eyes: On-Camera

Like the "winning smile," eye contact can rivet your reader's attention whether the subject is close-up or far away. It is ideal for the personality picture and for portraits.

As a communication medium, photography involves three people: subject, photographer, and viewer. The photographer interacts with the subject, consciously or unconsciously. Eyes have boundless expressions and the photographer, working with the subject, can achieve eye-to-lens contact that results in a picture that is emotionally expressive. The reader reacts, frequently assisted by a well-written picture caption.

Eyes: Off-Camera

Depending on the circumstances and your editorial needs, eyes off-camera can result in a believable scene when that is important. People reacting to a situation—even when carefully posed or staged—can be directed to appear spontaneous and not betray camera consciousness. After a minute or two of shooting, people in front of the camera will lose the self-conscious expression and a photo can result that appears candid and credible—like the one above. An important point: Avoid using direct flash, which is disconcerting to the subject and creates blank faces and inky shadows. Fast black-and-white film, ASA 400 or faster, will produce believable, journalistic pictures of most newsletter subjects under most any lighting condition.

The Power of Pictures

The Ubiquitous Photographer

This affable photographer could just as well be you, capturing a scene as it unfolds. Whoever is behind the camera, part of being an effective journalistic photographer is being at the right place at the right time. It also means carrying a three-pound camera around your neck, or if that's too much, a one-pound one. Better yet, if your budget permits, assign a capable free-lancer. More about this on page 88.

Sequence: One-Two-Three

My computer can generate more than 400 different colors. Even the good, gray *New York Times* is now sporting color pictures. However weak and muted, *it is color.* And I've become totally jaded by the colorful pyrotechnics of TV ads and titles. Color, color, everywhere! Despite all this, black-and-white still photography continues to be a magical medium.

Take the heartwarming sequence shown here, for example. Modest in scale and form, it

is a creative act of photography, very much an attention-getter. With minimal 35mm equipment, it's possible to capture a sequence in almost any setting. A picture act such as this can enliven your newsletter page.

Develop a repertoire of visual ideas for other photography "acts." For example, there is visual drama in contrast. Watch for a chance to play off two unlikely pictures side by side that result in a "third effect."

The great photographer, Phillipe Halsman,

had a unique way to humanize his subjects. During every assignment with a prominent person, he would persuade them to jump as high as possible before the camera. His collection of jumpers included such unlikely gymnasts as Richard M. Nixon, The Duke and Duchess of Windsor, and J. Robert Oppenheimer. This was a workable way to loosen up his subjects. Whenever possible, try to get people to relax and look alive.

Cropping: An Artful Act

Late afternoon, the camera was pointed west. Writer Michael Crichton was surrounded by a group of admirers. Strong sunlight and deep shadows gave the figures a "snappy" quality that projects on the printed page.

But look! Tight, literal cropping took away something that the photographer had captured skillfully—a dramatic shadow display that, at right, made a literal crowd scene an extraordinarily dramatic picture. What does this prove?

Cropping is an important act of design and editorial judgement. Unless the photographer is a genius who composes through the viewfinder, most photos need to be cropped.

Often, you crop only to remove extraneous, unwanted clutter. But cropping can be an art form that brings out unique qualities in a picture. It can also emphasize an editorial theme in a story. There are no hard-and-fast rules, but it is important always to have cropping in mind and take time to experiment.

Cropping Hemingway

The portrait at the left is self-consciously too close up and "arty" as a standard approach. The middle portrait is too centered. The right-hand portrait is cropped just right, with a bit more background space front of his face.

(continued from page 81)
Quantity assures that there will be a good number of usable shots at the moment of truth when picture selection takes place on the editor's table.

The Crucial Act of Selection

At Time-Life, where I worked with pictures, the Photo Editor was in charge of the picture supply but didn't necessarily make the decision as to which photos would be used. The final authority on picture selection was the Managing Editor. This person had the ability to react almost instinctively to a photograph that had the quality of good journalism.

For our purposes, what makes a good picture or what makes a picture good? It may not be artistic or technically perfect but the *right* picture can make the editorial page expressive and the task of writing easier. The ability to use pictures effectively is an important resource. The illustrations, ideas, and principles on these pages should inspire you to produce effective editorial pages. Each picture was chosen to define specific principles of photojournalism as they apply to the creative act of planning newsletter pages. In the hands of a prepared photographer, editor, and designer, practically any subject can result in drama on the printed page.

Making Photographs Happen

Shoot your own photographs, if you can. Otherwise, you'll need to find a photographer who will understand your editorial needs. Here are a few tips:

1. Try your local newspaper as a source. Credit lines on published photos will give you the photographers' names. A moonlighting arrangement is always possible.

2. Photographers who specialize in weddings and other celebrations are located in almost any city or town. They are generally expert at shooting spontaneous pictures.

3. Many colleges and art schools have photography courses. An instructor or advanced student may be available.

When you review portfolios, avoid catalog or still-life specialists. They may show marvelous prints but you don't want your pictures of people to be still life. Also be wary of direct flash that dazzles the eyes, flattens facial features, and throws inky shadows in the background. Look for photographers who use "bounce light" reflected off ceiling or wall or no auxiliary light at all. After you've identified the right photographer, you will need to come to an understanding not only about fees but about your objectives and requirements. Freelance photographers own the negatives and copyrights unless you make other arrangements ahead of time.

Directing a Photographer

If you are covering an event, be specific about your editorial needs and draw up a simple list or shooting script. It is also useful to show examples of the kind of results you're after. A handful of prints or clippings can do much to clarify what you have in mind. If this is a black-and-white assignment, specify in advance that you'll need strong, contrasty prints that will scan and print vividly.

Establish a rapport with your photographer. Try to be present during the shooting. I have worked with countless photographers, including Alfred Eisenstaedt, the "father of photojournalism." They all need and welcome some editorial direction if it's done with tact. Stay in the background and, to avoid confusion, let your photographer call out instructions to the subjects. Unless you are shooting on a busy street or in a crowd with many people in view, you'll need a signed release form that gives you legal rights to publish photos of people. (See page 189.)

Dialogue: A recent graduate from journalism school discusses his career plans with a family friend, a seasoned newspaper editor. The discussion revolves around techniques of reporting, writing style, page makeup, the subject of pictures in news media, and the use of the computer to modify images.

Seasoned Editor: Did they give you a course in photojournalism?

Recent Grad: No. It wasn't in the curriculum. My professors didn't believe that photos are important to journalism. Actually, we didn't get into visual images at all.

Seasoned Editor: Do you agree?

Recent Grad: I'm not sure.

Seasoned Editor: Let me answer that with a proposition. I'm amazed at what people can do to combine or change images with the computer. They're photo illustrators. But, the new imaging media won't affect the craft of photojournalism. If you're a journalist in the classic sense, you use photos linked with words to document a story.

Recent Grad: I believe you. It sounds simple enough—but here's my situation. This week I got a job offer to start up a newsletter for the employees at MidCentral Electric . . . 3500 people, office and maintenance. They want a lively paper that'll interest everybody. My budget would be limited. Standard desktop equipment and no staff. So, assuming I believe in the power of pictures—what can I do? I don't shoot pictures.

Seasoned Editor: Don't mention budget. But go into the job with determination, ready to make a huge effort.

Recent Grad: Such as?

Seasoned Editor: Here's my one-minute lecture. Get an SLR camera. Cover every event with your notebook and camera. Almost anyone can use a camera with fast film. Let everybody get used to seeing you with the camera. If you're the journalist I think you are, you'll know what to shoot.

***

June 3: Started work at MidCentral Electric. Right away, began to plan and organize material for first issue. Made a story list and did some page layouts for practice. The desktop outfit included a Page-Maker program.

June 5: Made a decision. Bought a secondhand Nikon with my own money.

June 8: Tried some test black-and-white shots. The camera is working well. Three weeks to go before the first issue goes to press.

June 13: Took the camera along to cover a lively labor-management meeting. A spirited discussion. Shot two rolls. Surprised at how easy it was.

June 15: Contact prints of the meeting pictures look good. Will have the lab make 8×10's.

June 17: Well worth all the effort. Blowups are really quite good. Tried a few different layouts for the labor story. A cover shot and a full page of pictures inside.

The camera is a constant companion as I rove about the offices and out in the field. People expect it.

July 2: First issue is off the press. Pictures look great. Praise comes in from all sides. The company supplies a brand-new Nikon.

Thinking Out Loud

Bravo!

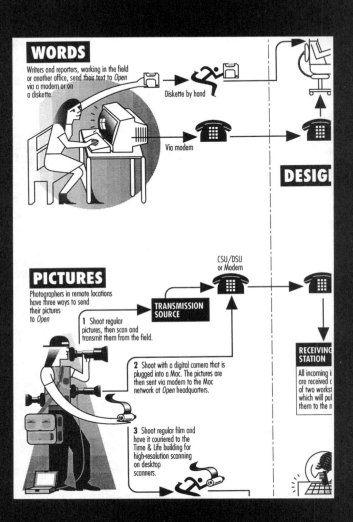

WORDS

Writers and reporters, working in the field or another office, send their text to *Open* via a modem or on a diskette.

Diskette by hand

Via modem

DESIGI

PICTURES

Photographers in remote locations have three ways to send their pictures to *Open*

CSU/DSU or Modem

TRANSMISSION SOURCE

1 Shoot regular pictures, then scan and transmit them from the field.

2 Shoot with a digital camera that is plugged into a Mac. The pictures are then sent via modem to the Mac network at *Open* headquarters.

3 Shoot regular film and have it couriered to the Time & Life building for high-resolution scanning on desktop scanners.

RECEIVING STATION

All incoming i are received c of two workst which will pul them to the n

8. INFORMATION GRAPHICS

On a sandstone cliff in southern Utah there is a remarkable work of information graphics. Hundreds of years ago, a primitive people carved pictorial images that recorded with considerable detail the activities of a hunting and gathering way of life. These petroglyphs, called "Newspaper Rock," may be North America's earliest examples of information graphics.

Today, information graphics occupying small spaces on a printed page carry sizable loads of information. This is an ideal way to achieve editorial impact within the restricted space of a newsletter.

At times complex and sometimes basically simple, minor graphic works can be produced by most any newsletter. Creative thinking and some determination are all that's required. The approach can be quite logical, based on familiar graphic elements such as a pie or bar chart, a table of facts or figures, a visual sequence, and a map or some sort of diagram.

The proper use of information graphics requires clearheaded editorial ideas. What is the message? Does the information enhance the story? Identify the facts that will be the substance of this word-and-picture idea. Also, evaluate what is workable and attainable in terms of your idea and resources. Information graphics, in its microcosm, requires creative effort parallel to what goes into the overall planning of a lively visual newsletter. As a method of transmitting information, small works of information graphics are often as effective as an elaborate drawing, diagram, or chart. Their simplicity won't intimidate your reader.

Thomas Bewick, the noted 18th-century woodcut artist, created a whimsical work of information graphics that would be controversial in today's world.

Information Graphics

Visual Guidelines

You'll need to block out sufficient time to perform step-by-step planning, just as you would when outlining columns of text content. If you're working with an artist, you must emphasize: "Think small, compress ideas, think clarity." Avoid self-consciously overblown art styles that place art media ahead of the message. There are many ways of achieving novelty but there is also the hazard of overstepping the bounds of logic or good taste. Avoid novelty for novelty's sake. Conceivably, a small work of information graphics could stand the test of enlargement to poster size or projected image six-feet wide.

listening to his master's voice, a steel engraving of George Washington, and the Eiffel Tower itself are all symbols."*

The information graphics displayed in this chapter are reprinted from various successful, lively newsletters. Even the most simple and basic examples resulted from editorial brainstorming. Someone felt the need, developed an idea, and had the determination to make it a reality.

The late, great media theorist Marshall McLuhan once wrote that it is misleading to suppose that there is a basic difference between education and certain entertainment content. While information graphics may be minutely detailed, technical, statistical, and of serious intent, at times it

Pen-and-ink cartoons, lively, freehand, and nonmechanical, illustrate an incident in British economic history. Note the frame-by-frame consistency of the images combined with the simple flow of running caption information.

Words, Symbols, Visual Effects

The ingredients of information graphics are words, numbers, and visual symbols. This formula suggests a meaningful combination whose design possibilities are as infinite as the subject matter.

Paul Rand, the famous graphic designer, wrote about visual symbols: "The fact that some of the best symbols are simplified images merely points to the effectiveness of simplicity but not to the meaning of the word per se. In essence, it is not what it looks like but what it does that defines a symbol. A symbol may be depicted as an abstract shape, a geometric figure, a photograph, an illustration, a letter of the alphabet, or a numeral. Thus a five-pointed star, a picture of a little dog

can be witty, dramatic, and entertaining. The sequence above was designed by me in the late 1950s for a newsletter called *United Nations World*. This visual feature began with a well-written headline, a sequence of captions, and a time frame. I assigned a cartoonist to animate the events in a lighthearted way even though we were dealing with sober economic facts. Note the freehand pen-and-ink style of the animated figures, the movement and visual consistency accentuated by black triangles. This little strip encapsulated the theme of a lengthy text feature.

The language of information graphics has many voices and a vast visual vocabu-

(continued on page 96)

*Paul Rand, Paul Rand: A Designer's Art (New Haven: Yale University Press, 1985) p. 7.

Small in Dimension, Large in Message

You don't have to be a trained artist to direct and orchestrate the creation, styling, and even the design of information graphics. Editors need to know the criteria on which "design" is based. As stated earlier in this book, *"It all begins with the editor."* Without exception, all the graphics shown here resulted from editorial imagination. The visual concepts followed.

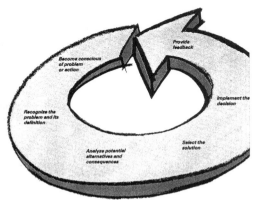

A hefty arrow symbol is about as basic as it can be—simply a sequence of words that follow the arrow's pathway. A verbal concept became a graphic statement in *FSD Manager,* an IBM publication.

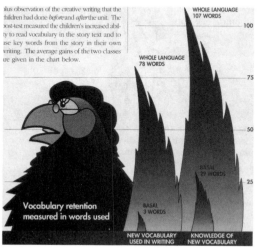

Decorative and functional, a bar graph takes the form of a hen in a newsletter, *The Whole Idea.* Aimed at teachers, it uses tail feathers as bars to report on the results of a vocabulary test.

Many of the most amusing cartoons in popular magazines have no "gag lines." Likewise, information graphics can communicate without words as in this elegant food pyramid in the newsletter, *5 a Day.*

GETTING THE FACTS ON **5 A DAY**

Eating at least 5 fruits and vegetables a day may help lower a person's risk of getting certain cancers.

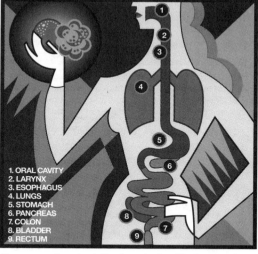

1. ORAL CAVITY
2. LARYNX
3. ESOPHAGUS
4. LUNGS
5. STOMACH
6. PANCREAS
7. COLON
8. BLADDER
9. RECTUM

Human anatomy, stylized and simplified to make a point, is the technique in this decorative diagram rendered by computer. Skillfully symbolic, it was produced by the Washington group, Porter/Novelli.

Human Imagination
Aided by Computer

The computer has made high-quality information graphics available and possible for almost any publication. A graphics artist with *USA Today* recently commented, "The computer has given us . . . more time to come up with good ideas and more time to do proper composition." Whether your publication is large or small, there is no longer any reason for a newsletter to be visually boring.

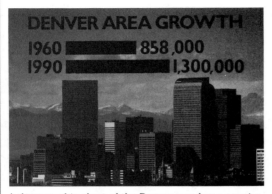

A demographic chart of the Denver area has a concise, clear message. The photo, obtained free from the Chamber of Commerce, was scanned and the type and bars composed on computer in a matter of minutes.

Stock market performance around the world (in U.S. $)			
Hong Kong	+33.7%	Japan	-31.6%
Mexico	+26.3%	Canada	-10.8%
Malaysia	+18.1%	Denmark	-10.8%

A simple, small tabular chart doesn't provide much opportunity for dynamic graphics—and it needn't. The skillfully designed, tiny arrow symbols add a welcome note of distinction.

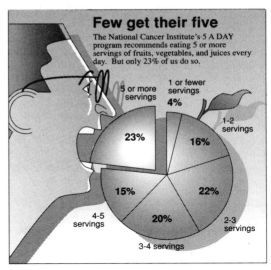

The pie chart mode, designed as an edible piece of fruit in sections, tells the story with directness. It was rendered with linear smoothness by computer for the National Cancer Institute.

A fantastic figure that is a takeoff of a known work of fine art vividly represents the fears of children. Illustration and words were combined effectively by The Wright Group, Seattle.

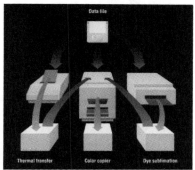

This diagram of a color copy system, featured in the *Step-by-Step Electronic Design* newsletter, has visual elegance. Before computers, rendering such refinement took hours of laborious effort.

Nutrition Action, a subscription newsletter, often illustrates food and health principles with amusing cartoon characters and lettering drawn in a traditional hand-crafted, pen-and-ink style.

Self-reliance in Learning is the subject of a chart that uses a currently popular flathead comics style. The chart was rendered by computer and ran on the cover of *The Whole Idea* newsletter.

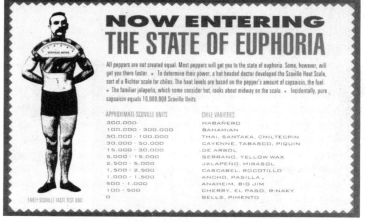

Tables and lists, by nature visually boring, can be dressed up to look appealing. Facts about the relative "heat" of peppers were written in clever tongue-in-cheek copy. The designer added handsome typography, a decorative border, and a funny figure in 19th-century style.

Information Graphics

(continued from page 92)
lary. As you read this you may be uncertain about how to get started with a plan for information graphics. Where to begin? If you have a proven talent for originating and producing editorial content, you're already on the right track. Think about form versus function. You want graphic features that (1) are vivid, appealing, and colorful, and (2) will express information clearly. Even though you may be a word person you'll need to consider the visual equally as important as the verbal.

After you locate a suitable artist/designer, be prepared to give direction, armed with facts, figures, and objectives. A rough thumbnail sketch will be helpful.

Over the years, the major news magazines have developed all kinds of ingenious charts, diagrams, and maps. This is the ideal source for models to follow. Many newsletter editors clip and file examples of graphics for use in planning visual content. You can avoid misunderstandings when making an assignment if you show examples of styles you want to emulate.

Whatever the subject matter of your newsletter, there is apt to be an occasional topic that would benefit from a map, an appealing and inviting graphic feature that can attract and inform readers. Unless you have an audience of geographers, maps for our purposes are not cartography. All maps are "pictures." Whether you illustrate a city block or a whole continent, there are a vast number of styles, from outright pictorial to sparse outline. Decide what style best illustrates your story.

Computer map programs, with some limitations, are a ready-made answer. If you're inclined to create a map, there are drawing programs such as Adobe Illustrator and Aldus Freehand that can be used by your artist. If you need base maps for tracing there is no better source than an up-to-date atlas. Excellent maps in the public domain can be obtained from the National Geological Survey in Denver, the CIA, and the Defense Mapping Agency in Washington, D.C.

Type style is important. I recommend sans-serif type, all caps, not too bold or condensed. On broad land masses and waterways, letter space widely. Avoid running type over lines or deep shading. Most maps have a subject, therefore you'll need a well-written title. A compass rose showing North and South and a scale of miles is often necessary. A variety of map symbols are available for the computer in the Carta Program by Adobe Systems. The symbols can be accessed from the keyboard just like a type font.

Your Mental Approach

Planning and designing information graphics is a creative act that involves a unique outlook. You must cultivate an almost instinctive feeling about visual information. Call it "visual thinking."

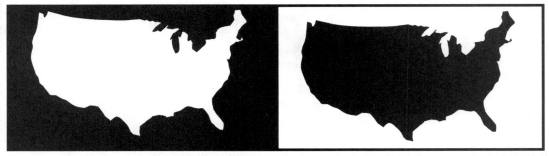

Negative and positive space is related to map design. Should land areas be dark or light? Humans are land-oriented, so land areas are more satisfying in darker tones; the sea and other adjoining areas light.

Here's a hypothetical situation: You're the editor of a monthly newsletter that's read by 8000 real estate agents nationwide. You work alone, doing the idea work, writing, editing, and page makeup—everything but the printing. Much of the editorial content consists of facts and figures about housing, the economy as it affects the housing market, construction trends, personalities, and population data.

You have a top-notch desktop system—a Mac, Quark 3.3, a scanner, and a laser printer. As a one-person staff, with a good deal of trial and error you've learned most of the system's editing and production techniques. However, your creative efforts and imagination are usually channeled in words. In every issue you try to feature spot illustrations that come in on disks from a clip-art service. Infrequently, you use a freelance illustrator. Now and then some acceptable photos land on your desk. Quite a good-looking newsletter, you think.

Lately, your bosses have mentioned a number of times that they want you to start running some information visuals. They weren't very specific. Subject matter wouldn't be a problem. Plenty of data comes in each day but you hate sacrificing word space. In terms of visuals, you know what you like—but you're not a designer. Most of your visual ideas are about as appealing as a warmed-over TV dinner. Your problem: How do you turn facts into graphics that effectively tell a story?

Thinking Out Loud

First of all, learn to value information graphics even though it displaces word content. Nigel Holmes of *Time* magazine, the acclaimed designer of charts and diagrams, wrote: ". . . a writer might understand he or she is not losing precious lines of delicious prose to some unneces-

sary graphic, but instead be pleased that the attractiveness of the illustration will lead the viewer into reading the words. In the process he or she will be free to write unhindered by the statistics which are necessary for the argument but which get in the way of the article's flow."*

Now, let's review this month's batch of incoming material—facts, figures, and photos—about new housing starts. Good idea material. But there's one problem: You (and your computer) are totally without design talent.

Here's a glossy photo—a vivid air view of a huge low-income housing project that stretches off to the horizon. There must be more than a hundred units underway or completed. It might be an effective background for statistics—say, the number of housing starts over the past decade.

Scan the photo into the computer. Gray the image down to about a 30% tone value so that you can overprint it with black type and your second color—royal blue. A bold line graph (sometimes called a fever chart) will look good on the photo and it's easy to render with the Mac. The pattern of houses will show through just fine. A bold title in the sky area can be set in 18-point Helvetica Bold Caps and the numbers along the sides in 10-point. The grid lines can be hairlines. The ascending line, scribed a heavy 10-points wide, can be printed in blue. This simple scheme becomes an easy answer to a colorful and professional-looking graphic chart. Definitely worth two columns.

Don't overlook clip-art possibilities. Explore ways of integrating a line drawing with facts and figures—it can be done easily on your marvelous Mac. As you can see, with a little experimentation, the way is clear for a variety of functional graphics using your own resources.

---

*Nigel Holmes, Designer's Guide to Creating Charts & Diagrams (*New York: Watson-Guptill Publications, 1984*), p. 10.

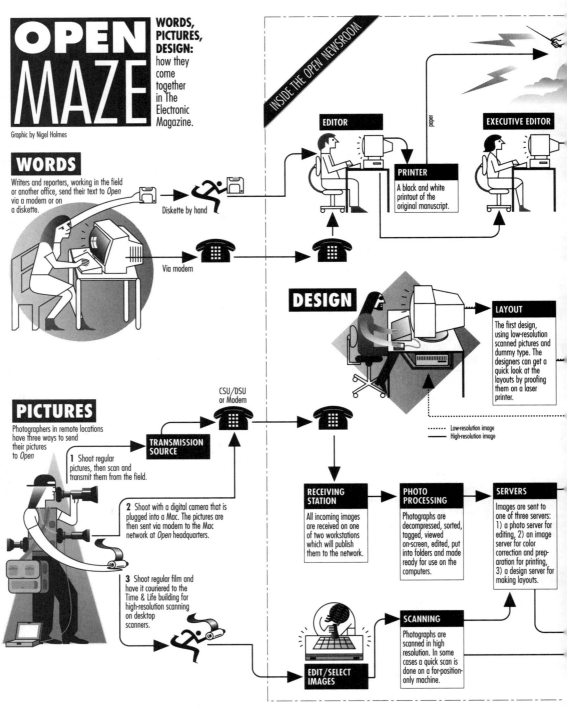

OPEN MAZE

WORDS, PICTURES, DESIGN: how they come together in The Electronic Magazine.

Graphic by Nigel Holmes

INSIDE THE OPEN NEWSROOM

WORDS

Writers and reporters, working in the field or another office, send their text to *Open* via a modem or on a diskette.

Diskette by hand

Via modem

EDITOR

PRINTER
A black and white printout of the original manuscript.

paper

EXECUTIVE EDITOR

DESIGN

LAYOUT
The first design, using low-resolution scanned pictures and dummy type. The designers can get a quick look at the layouts by proofing them on a laser printer.

········· Low-resolution image
——————— High-resolution image

PICTURES

Photographers in remote locations have three ways to send their pictures to *Open*

1 Shoot regular pictures, then scan and transmit them from the field.

2 Shoot with a digital camera that is plugged into a Mac. The pictures are then sent via modem to the Mac network at *Open* headquarters.

3 Shoot regular film and have it couriered to the Time & Life building for high-resolution scanning on desktop scanners.

CSU/DSU or Modem

TRANSMISSION SOURCE

RECEIVING STATION
All incoming images are received on one of two workstations which will publish them to the network.

PHOTO PROCESSING
Photographs are decompressed, sorted, tagged, viewed on-screen, edited, put into folders and made ready for use on the computers.

SERVERS
Images are sent to one of three servers: 1) a photo server for editing, 2) an image server for color correction and preparation for printing, 3) a design server for making layouts.

SCANNING
Photographs are scanned in high resolution. In some cases a quick scan is done on a for-position-only machine.

EDIT/SELECT IMAGES

Graphic Information On a Huge Scale

Words, pictures, design—it all comes together in this remarkable chart by Nigel Holmes, *Time* magazine's noted designer of information graphics. It is useful to study both as a chart and for its information content. It describes an

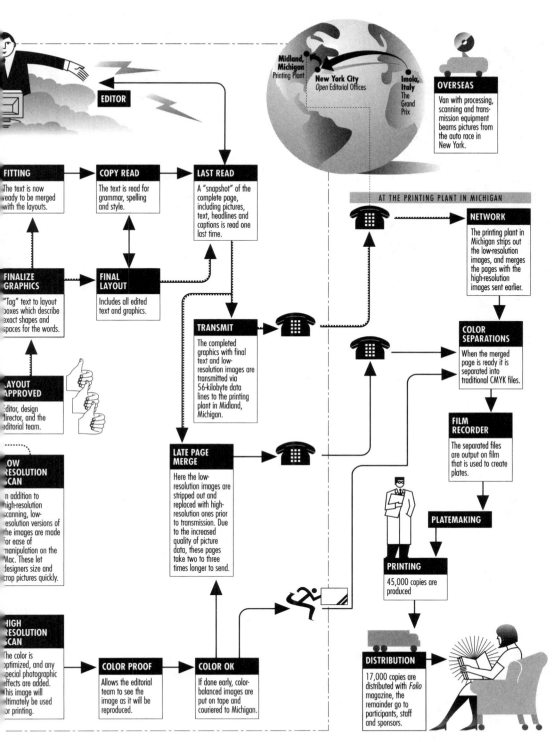

actual project in which 99 magazine designers, writers, editors, and photographers from all over the United States cooperated to produce a 92-page experimental magazine. The task was to utilize the latest state-of-the-art hardware and software for a totally electronic publication. Equipment was provided by sponsors such as Kodak, Apple, and Quark Inc. The chart style is timeless—the system described was cutting edge in 1993.

9.
PRODUCTION AND PRINTING

If you are a computer maven or are quite computer literate you may want to skip over the next two pages. They are intentionally very basic and directed at readers who have had little contact with desktop publishing.

Digital technology has dramatically changed the way people work and the way they think. Whether you work alone or with a staff of editorial and design helpers, an interactive work flow all comes together on the screen with a merging of the verbal and the visual points of view. As one editor said, "You have more time to concentrate on what you're doing, not on how you're doing it."

Most of the editorial, design, and production tasks that prepare a publication for printing are made easier with a desktop publishing system. Your facility need not appear like mission control, but basic desktop equipment is necessary as well as some understanding about what happens when the offset press begins to roll.

A Desktop System

Hardware and software make up a basic desktop publishing system. Hardware, in addition to the computer, includes a keyboard, mouse, monitor, and printer. Software is the program and information stored on disks in digital form.

The *keyboard* is used to type in the copy and the *mouse* is an attachment that may be moved on a flat surface to call up programs; select typefaces; and enlarge, reduce, and position all design and typographical elements of your layout. The mouse eliminates most keystroke commands and, as a result, speeds up your page design.

The *monitor* is the viewing screen on which you see your page design and typematter. Newsletter layout is best viewed on a screen large enough to include the image of an entire page.

The *printer* produces "hard copy," which is your final output. A dot-matrix printer delivers a coarse image that is only suitable for office tasks such as letters. For our purposes use a laser printer that produces fine type and graphics quality (300–600 lines per inch), which is suitable for a typical newsletter. If you wish to produce type of even higher quality, send disks to a commercial typographer whose equipment can deliver a screen of more than 2000 lines per inch.

Software is the information and programs stored on a disk that controls type composition, layout design, production, and other procedures. Software is available that will accomplish all phases of a newsletter project. You can keyboard manuscript copy using programs such as Microsoft Word or Claris MacWrite. These programs can be used in conjunction with page-layout programs such as Aldus PageMaker or Quark XPress.

The ability to do a vast number of graphics techniques just short of the turning of the press is within your reach. If you need to draw diagrams or illustrations, programs such as Adobe Illustrator and MacDraw have line and shading capabilities. New programs are continually being developed that combine many of the above functions all in one program.

If you want to delve more deeply into state-of-the-art technology, sophisticated programs are available to interface with desktop and pre-press equipment.

The Miracle of the Disk

Among the outstanding capabilities of desktop publishing is the ability of the disk to store keystrokes. Once your text copy is satisfactorily keyboarded there is no need to "rekey." Copy can go directly into type composition. This can be accomplished in your own office or the disk can be sent to the printer. For even faster turnaround, disk contents can be delivered by modem directly over telephone lines. By eliminating many of the traditional steps, the desktop method helps avoid possible errors.

Page Layout Design

After your written copy has been keyboarded onto a disk, you can "call it up" on the screen and use the mouse to start layout design. Your design program provides many options, which are spelled out in the menu on your screen. To start, choose your column grid; select a typeface, size, and style; place your graphics; and view your efforts actual size. You can experiment freely and view many layout options. One caution to have in mind: Easy-to-use desktop procedures in the hands of an untrained user can result in eccentric layouts and poor design.

After you have settled on a workable page design, do a printout on your laser printer. For checking purposes, a relatively coarse 300-line proof is satisfactory. After final corrections and approval, the disk can be turned over to a professional type house for high-resolution output of type and strong black-and-white images of artwork on photo paper, ready for printing.

Preparation for Printing

As virtually all newsletters are printed by offset, it's important to understand the principles of the process. Offset presses come in a great range of sizes from a small office duplicating machine to a huge web-fed perfecting press that prints thousands of impressions per hour in eight colors on both sides of the sheet simultaneously. Few newsletters exceed 16 or 24 pages in two colors, so we'll concentrate on smaller equipment and press runs.

In order to keep it simple, we will discuss black-and-white printing. The material you prepare for printing originates in either of two categories: line copy or continuous-tone copy. Line copy is solid black such as a pen-and-ink drawing or the type you are now reading.

Continuous-tone copy—called halftone—has a full range of tone gradations such as in a photograph. Since the printing process can only reproduce line copy, continuous-tone copy must first be converted into line copy. This is accomplished in the form of solid dots that result from a process called screening. The art or photo subject is photographed through a screen that can break the image into anywhere from 55 to 300 dots per inch. The finer the screen, the closer the reproduction will resemble the original photo.

Fine-screen printing requires smooth-coated paper such as used in quality magazines or books. Line copy prints successfully on a relatively rough surface such as newsprint pulp paper.

The Traditional Mechanical

Over the years, the mechanical has been the critical step between layout and printer. The line and typographic parts of a page are pasted in exact position on a firm board or layout sheet and halftone copy is precisely indicated for position by outline or photo copy. Using this mechanical, the printer screens the halftones and "strips" them together with the line copy onto a single film negative called a flat. The printer uses this negative to make the printing plate.

Nowadays, many people still prepare mechanicals but this step largely has been supplanted by desktop programs that make preparation for offset printing an easy matter. A quality program such as Quark XPress can provide a clean image with all components screened and assembled in position.

Offset: True to Its Name

While printing your newsletter, the offset plate never actually contacts the paper.

The Offset Process

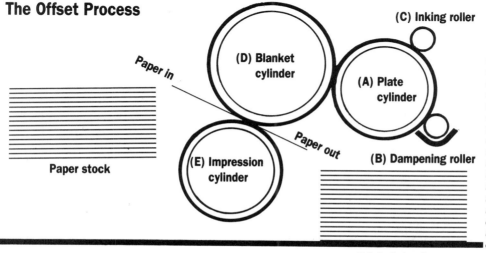

The printing plate is clamped to the plate cylinder (A). It contacts the dampening rollers (B), then the inking rollers (C). The dampeners wet the plate so that the nonprinting areas will repel ink. The inked image is then transferred to the rubber blanket on the blanket cylinder (D). Paper never contacts the original plate and is printed as it runs between the blanket and impression cylinder (E).

Printed sheets

The process involves three revolving cylinders called *plate, blanket,* and *impression.* The printing plate etched with the image of your page is dampened with a solution that the image areas reject and the nonimage areas accept. The plate then contacts an inking cylinder with an opposite effect: The image areas accept the ink and the inked image is then transferred onto the blanket cylinder, which offsets the image onto the paper surface.

Mind Your Paper Choice

Your choice of paper can greatly affect the visual and tactile quality of a newsletter and the impression you make on a reader. All the editorial and design effort that goes into producing a newsletter can be compromised if you use an inferior or inappropriate paper stock.

If your print run is relatively small—say, 5000 or under—choice of paper isn't a significant budget item. It would be false economy to use anything but the best. Your printer may have a stock of paper "on the shelf" that could represent a saving. If your print order is large, printers will order a shipment from a jobber.

Five characteristics you should consider when specifying paper:

1. *Weight.* Also called basis weight, this is designated in pounds. As the word suggests, weight affects the thickness and firmness of your newsletter. It is also a factor in printing quality as well as the cost of mailing. Most newsletters are printed on a 60- or 70-pound stock. Anything heavier would be pretentious. Although, if you publish a simple four-pager, 80-pound stock could be desirable for firmness.

2. *Size.* Your printer will choose a sheet size appropriate for the size of your publication and the shop's equipment. A standard size that avoids waste is important. For example, a typical 8½×11

newsletter of 16 pages could print on 23×35-inch sheets.

3. *Finish.* The paper's surface can be coated or uncoated. If you run photographs and illustrations, coated stock is preferable because it will provide maximum contrast and vividness. Coating may be glossy or dull, both of which print equally well. Dull coating is considered best for comfortable reading of text copy. Uncoated paper is excellent for text readability but is less satisfactory for pictures and illustrations. Fancy paper textures and patterns are not recommended.

4. *Color.* Tinted stock, which is generally uncoated, can have a further dampening affect on photos and other graphics because highlights will lose their strength. If you have an all-type newsletter, colored ink printed on colored paper can be quite attractive if you choose colors that complement and a deeply muted color for type. However, white paper stock has many advantages for a newsletter with photo illustrations.

5. *Bulk and Opacity.* The thickness of your publication depends on bulk. High-bulk paper is usually uncoated and has a heavy buildup of fibers that can make a newsletter look and feel more substantial. Generally, high-bulk stock doesn't print as well as low-bulk.

Most paper stock is rated for opacity. To avoid having type and other images showing through, be certain to emphasize high opacity when selecting a paper stock.

Even though your press run may be small, it is important to consider environmental safeguards and specify recycled paper.

Thoughts About Ink

Most people don't think much about ink. It's the medium that carries your message and it can vitalize or subdue words and pictures. All inks are not alike. Superior black-and-white printing requires ink with specific qualities, among them, strong pigmentation and a proper degree of tack. Tack is the quality of stickiness that causes ink to transfer effectively onto paper. Offset inks must be tacky to print sharp images.

Varnish content in ink can make your pages glow, especially when printed on dull-coated paper. Ink is not a big cost factor in printing, so be sure your printer uses the best ink for your purposes. Also try to use soy-based ink for environmental considerations.

Ink color is another story, chapter, and verse. Planning a two-color newsletter can be a creative challenge. On pages 140-143, a newsletter, *Osprey,* is a prime example. Editor/Designer, Carl Herrman used no black ink but combined tints and overprints of two colors to give, as he says, "the effect of three to six colors."

Recommendation: Do not print photographs in red, blue, purple, or green, which can detract from striking black-and-white photography. Black is best for photographs or, if you must, dark brown. If your printer has developed the skills, try duotones. This is a technique where a photo is printed in black and overprinted with values of the second color.

A Binding Decision

Any newsletter printed in multiples of four pages can be bound by saddle-wire binding, which is staples through the fold. This is the most elementary and common method used by newsletters and most printers have the necessary equipment. A tabloid-size newsletter of eight or 12 pages can have no binding at all and simply fold the sheets firmly and accurately. If you have an eight-page publication, you can also avoid the binding step by simply planning a gate fold, a roll over, or even an accordion fold. This means that a single broad sheet of paper becomes multiple pages. Your printer can show you examples of various folding methods.

Quality Control

No printing project is so minor as to allow you to overlook quality control. Larger printing plants usually have a quality-control person on duty during all press runs. Smaller shops should have a dedicated pressman who is responsible for quality standards. Basically, quality control involves watching for evenness of inking on type columns, whether photos are over-inked or underinked, and if a second color is in register (fitted perfectly in position). Also watch for unexpected imperfections such as "hickeys"—black dots of ink in unwanted places or white flecks on a photo.

After the difficult and demanding efforts in planning a publication with high standards, the final reward is high-quality printing and production.

10. DESIGNS FOR STUDY

A procession of noteworthy newsletters that define and illustrate a variety of editorial and design principles.

The most successful newsletters are not necessarily winners of design awards. However, a large number of outstanding publications do receive design honors because they show a well-edited blending of visual and verbal content. A few of the newsletter designs on the following pages may shock the sensibilities of sophisticated art directors, but they are designed to attract a large body of readers. They are definitely *not boring*.

Some of the following examples deserve study because they display a happy combination of editorial vitality and story-telling photos. The pages are lively, documentary, and journalistic. Though they may appear simple and uncomplicated, their appeal results from a strong combination of dramatic pictures and well-crafted words.

Other examples show the results of a content-oriented designer to whom telling the story is important. The designer and editor are in sync and the result is a handsome and engrossing newsletter. Lastly, there are those examples that are simply outstanding works of graphic design, conceived with so much originality that they rivet the reader's attention.

While making this selection of 20 newsletters, I reviewed hundreds of publications from all corners of the country. The examples on the following pages display various individual qualities.

Marginal annotations point out specific features that make the pages distinctive. Some of the points are subtle, but altogether they illustrate the qualities that result in unboring newsletter pages.

Time Inc.

FYI: FIFTY YEARS LATER, THE 1990s VERSION

Art Director
Beth Power
Publisher
Time Inc.
New York, NY
Text Type
Goudy Old Style (88% condensed)
Display Type
Helvetica Extra Compressed
Page Size
$8\frac{1}{2} \times 11$
Printing
Two Color
(sometimes four)

"FYI" is a classic among classics. Also, it may be the oldest in-house newsletter published in the United States. When it first began more than 50 years ago, Time Inc. was a vigorous and growing company. The "FYI" logo was designed to mimic the scrawl of cofounder Henry R. Luce who, it is said, routed urgent papers and editorial leads to staff members with "FYI" pencilled across the corner.

Originally produced by typewriter and mimeograph, "FYI" is today a live-wire publication with graphics and breezy copy, completely in tune with the 90s. Belinda Luscombe, its editor, describes her publication: "Because of the media-saturated nature of our employees' workday we try to create the expectation that if they don't read "FYI" when it lands in their inbox, they'll be missing out on the most interesting take on what the company is doing. So we're as cheeky and disrespectful as we can get away with being. Time Inc.'s corporate culture is pretty healthy and the chiefs don't mind laughing at themselves now and then."

Belinda has a "gem of a full-time art director, a cache of prized freelance photographers and illustrators, and a substantial amount of computer equipment. The format is flexible, which permits a change of paper stock, trim size, and number of pages when occasion calls for it."

The logo—settled on after an experiment with hefty block letters—is once again a scrawl that's a handsome reminder of the 1940s model. The typographic style is clean, readable, and contemporary—a sound background for content that's churning with editorial ideas.

"FYI" is a model to follow. Even a trace of its influence could help liberate conventional newsletter planning in some of America's otherwise fast-moving institutions.

f.y.i.

TIME INC. MARCH 15, 1993

CAROLE SEGAL

I AM NOT A TARGET MARKET

Sara Ruffin, 24
MARTHA STEWART LIVING

THE NEW HUMAN BEINGS

TIME INC. ZEROES IN ON GENERATION X

by Belinda Luscombe

Boomlets. Busters. Slackers. Thirteeners. Twentysomethings. *Shin jin rui*. Generation X. Call them what you will, but it's no longer possible to ignore them. In case you haven't noticed, there's a siren blaring in advertising agencies and magazine offices across the country, signaling the emergence, virtually overnight, of 46 million people—make that 46 million *consumers*—who everybody is dying to reach. The generation famous for the catchcry "I am not a target market" has become just that—with a vengeance.

"In my 15 years of marketing, I don't think there's been a phenomenon this dramatic," says **Scott Kauffman**, di :tor of marketing, promotion and development for ENTERTAINMENT WEEKLY and Time Inc.'s resident Generation X-pert. "And I think we're just in the early stages of it."

FORMER SPY MEISTER LANDS JOB AT TIME...P4

109

Designs for Study

Marketing is invariably news around a vast publishing empire. Generation "X" as a target is the subject of this incisive feature, illustrated with specially set-up photos and two pictographs. "FYI" is published fortnightly (or thereabouts).

In a way, it's all TIME's fault. In July 1990 it ran a cover story on twentysomethings that was the first to paint a portrait of the age group born after the end of the Baby Boom in 1964. The article described a skeptical bunch brutally realistic about its future, but also constantly at odds with the boomers for always defining what that future would be. In 1991 Douglas Coupland gave the group its catchiest epithet, Generation X, in a novel/lexicon of the same name. He emphasized the group's media savvy and concomitant weltschmerz. A new species was catalogued.

The real trouble started in Bermuda last year when Karen Ritchie, VP-director of media services at McCann-Erickson Worldwide, Detroit, announced at the American Magazine Conference her "discovery" of a vast un-reached audience—the "purple-. haired people"—Xers. The spontaneous generation of 46 million individuals with economic power (Xers are said to be worth $125 billion) and—gasp!—still largely unformed brand loyalties was enough to make any marketer jump. "Think of the Generation X phenomenon as an ambulance screaming down a crowded Fifth Avenue," says Kauffman, who read about the speech in the trades. "Well, we got behind it." He realized that Ritchie had unwittingly defined a large portion of EW's readership for media buyers. "It really was a godsend," he says. "And we intend to help articulate, accelerate and exploit an understanding of this group for all it's worth." Although Xers are a big part of EW's readership (40% of which is age 18-29), Kauffman didn't want to forget the boomers either. He rallied the sales force and put together a new brochure to show how EW reaches both boomers and Xers. "Popular culture is one of the the only things boomers and Xers have in common," says Kauffman, "and that's why we can run ads for diet cola as well as diamonds."

EW isn't the only magazine concerned about the twentysomething generation. TIME has an unofficial new bureau called Newgen, made up of reporters in their 20s who meet regularly to discuss story ideas. At the suggestion of society editor Nancy Gibbs, the group also functions as the X bureau, and its first assignment was reporting on how Xers view God for a planned package on religion. "We started something with the twentysomething cover," says Sophfronia Scott Gregory, who co-authored the "twentysomething" cover with David Grose. "And we're in the best possible position to continue the dialogue."

The publishing side is happy about Newgen's existence too. AT&T is currently deciding in which newsmagazine to place a series of X-targeted ads, and Scott Gregory was called on to explain TIME's approach to her generation to the agency. Even the culture section, long the domain of revered but hardly twentysomething critics, is getting a younger look. A recent profile of Denis Leary was written by 26-year-old reporter Chris Farley, who says he doesn't believe in age classification.

Eric Schrier, Time Inc. Ventures VP, says he looked over a number of proposals for Xer-type magazines even before Ritchie became the generation's Delphic oracle. "A lot of them were focused on music and fashion," he says. "The basic premise was that Xers have a different attitude to life from the boomers, but that doesn't mean they don't have a brain. We've stayed in touch with one or two of the groups, but we obviously

A storytelling table of comparative "facts" is designed as a visual/verbal focal point. The title type style is in keeping with the copy's tongue-in-cheek tone.

boomers VS. xers

Bought house paint within past six months	Bought condoms within past six weeks
Remembers where they were when Kennedy died	Remembers where they were when Gary of *thirtysomething* died
Wants to retire at 65	Wants to get a job before 65
Saw man land on the moon	Saw space shuttle blow up
Likes *Star Trek*, hates *Deep Space Nine*	Likes *Star Trek: Next Generation*, hates *Deep Space Nine*
Post-Elvis	Post-Elvis Costello
Has house, wants life	Has life, wants house
"Layla"	"Layla Unplugged"
Free love	$2.50 the first minute...
Knows there's light at the end of the tunnel	Knows it's a train

The four-column page layout, averaging five words a line, has a fast pace. While there is abundant copy, the columns are smooth, unbroken, and inviting to the reader on the run.

Pages are boxed in with subtle hairlines that give structure to the spreads. Photos cleverly sustain the cover theme and display a terse legend, making caption copy unnecessary.

weren't interested in any proposals that leaned toward music." Obviously, because that readership is already going to be more than adequately served by VIBE.

Launching VIBE could be considered Time Inc.'s strategic initiative for penetrating the X market. If VIBE's newly appointed 29-year-old chief operating officer **Keith Clinkscales** gets his way, then his peers will soon have a new handle. "I want them to be known as the VIBE generation," he says. And, while he's not totally convinced that his generation can be so easily pigeonholed, he feels VIBE is the perfect vehicle

The X-iest Magazines
Percentage of readers aged 18-29

Entertainment Weekly	40%
Sports Illustrated	36%
Fortune	32%
Life	30%
People	25%
Time	22%
Money	14%

FLY BOYS

John Rollins, the new publisher of VIBE, and **Keith Clinkscales**, its COO, are both 29, right on the cusp of X-ness and boomerdom. And although their résumés look distinctively get-ahead funky, their attitude is very X.

Rollins was with *Rolling Stone* and *Spin* before he joined VIBE on Monday, so he maintains he's always been with the music magazine that defined its era. Clinkscales completed his Harvard M.B.A. and turned his full attention to the magazine he had started in college, *Urban Profile*, for which he was publisher and editor-in-chief. "It was a very in-your-face type of publication," he says of his outspoken magazine, which attracted media attention for its "Black in Iraq" issue and its

Elliot Morales, 23
Library

I'VE POSTPONED MY REBELLION

for picking up X readers. "The African-American influence on this generation is more prevalent because the generation is more diverse," he says.

Xers are so familiar with marketing ploys they are not easily swayed by hype. "They have less and less time to read magazines, which are considered conservative anyway," adds Clinkscales. "So you have to make sure you're delivering something genuine and something they can't get elsewhere. God bless *Rolling Stone*. They don't cover black music well. They left it wide open for us."

As the future unfolds, a big

cheeky service feature on "How Black Men Can Avoid Trouble with the Police." "I'm very proud of what I did at *Urban Profile*, but it always boiled down to: If only I had more money, I could ... So coming to VIBE was a rare business opportunity."

VIBE's first regular issue is due out in September. It will be followed by three more in 1993 and 10 in '94. Both Rollins and Clinkscales say they were surprised when they heard Time Warner was going to produce a hip-hop magazine. They were equally surprised when they saw VIBE's test issue. "It wasn't a magazine you could laugh off," says Clinkscales. "It was frightening."

VIBE will work, says Rollins, because "every gen-

Clinkscales and Rollins are the new suits at VIBE.

question remains. Will this new generation of readers stay a cohesive group with the same needs and attitudes all their lives, or are they just future boomers in disguise? "The deep dirty secret is that if you give an Xer a good job and a great AV system, then just like the boomers, you've got a sellout waiting to happen," says Kauffman, who will chair a two-day $1,000-plus seminar on Generation X in May. "But whether Xers remain self-contained or become like the generation before them, the people themselves are here to stay, and we need to reach them."

eration of young adults has turned to music as the most potent expression of their difference from the generation before them. I fully expect that in 10 years there'll be a new form of music, and we won't get it." —BL

EDGE
BY BELINDA LUSCOMBE

Do they know something we don't? A recent issue of *a.m.e.b.a.*, the publication of the Association of Magazine Editors of the Bay Area, mentions a radio interview that featured president/CEO, Time Inc. magazines ...**Robin Wolaner**.

Is there a leak on the 24th floor? In a bizarre coincidence, TIME and *Newsweek* ran virtually identical cover billings for their coverage of the World Trade Center bombing. TIME's line: TERROR HITS HOME: THE SEARCH FOR THE TOWER BOMBER. Brand X's: TERROR HITS HOME: THE SEARCH FOR THE BOMBERS.

Hepburn lives! Last Wednesday in a ceremony at the U.N., PEOPLE publisher **Ann Moore** and M.E. **Lanny Jones** donated $100,000 of the newsstand revenue from the Audrey Hepburn commemorative issue to—what else?—UNICEF.

On Monday, March 1, WHO turned one and its éminence grise, PEOPLE international editor **Hal Wingo**, 58. The Sydney staff celebrated in a beautiful park in the sun, while the New York crew settled for the conference room on the 29th floor.

3

A one-column feature is capped by a logo in a second color that stands out loud and clear. The letter "E" bleeds off the top of the page. Note the subtle positioning of the byline.

Top to bottom, the column feature stands crisply typographic and self-contained in its regular right-hand position in each issue.

A smaller feature, a close-up of two individuals, is illustrated by a single photo in which both men are posed in parallel stance. Caption type is reverse on a black band, the standard style throughout "FYI."

Short black bands pick up the massive strokes of the column's logotype and are used in place of headlines to separate brief story items.

111

**American Institute
of Architects Foundation**

VISUALLY SUCCESSFUL FOR VISUAL READERS

Architects, by necessity, are concerned with eye appeal. Their practice often involves graphics and at times they utilize printed items so, understandably, they have strong feelings about layout and typography. While architects are the primary audience for "Forum," it is also aimed at nonarchitects to stimulate public awareness and discussion about American architecture.

"Forum" is a much-praised newsletter that, for obvious reasons, must look serious, purposeful, and visually lively. Printed modestly in black and white, typographically it has an admirable quality of understatement. Headlines are small and tidy, set in Helvetica Black, condensed 10%. The small logotype, centered on the cover, beckons for attention—and it succeeds, proving that placement and white space can be almost as forceful as large, bold type. The designer has planned the cover in three vertical panels to function as a visual table of contents. Appropriate to the subject matter, the cover design has "architecture."

The three-column grid structure, set in unpretentious Century Old Style, makes no attempt to be trendy. The design of type and pictures on these pages deserves close study. It is a sophisticated design that doesn't carry sophistication to the point of visual sterility. Washington designer Marilyn Worseldine, commenting on the one-color limitation, said, "I love the challenge of black and white."

Published by the American Institute of Architects Foundation, "Forum" has attracted national attention and was included in Graphic Design USA #7, the annual, highly prestigious New York show of the American Institute of Graphic Arts.

Art Director/Designer
Marilyn Worseldine
Publisher
AIA Foundation
Washington, DC
Text Type
Century Old Style
Display Type
Helvetica Black
Page Size
7 × 12
Printing
One Color

FORUM

The quarterly newsletter of
The Forum for Architecture
First Quarter 1986

A Forum Exclusive Report:
America's Architects
Select the 10 Best Buildings
in the United States,
1885 and 1985

Designs for Study

The pages display functionally elegant typography and illustrations strategically placed to give the layout a visual persona. The design lends integrity to the content. Form and content are one.

White space in the column is occupied by three disparate, well-placed type elements, all flush left. The ample head margin, suited to these tall pages, is abandoned on the page opposite, then repeated again on the page at far right.

WE'RE PROUD... to announce that Forum has been chosen to be included in Graphic Design USA #7, the annual, highly prestigious New York show of the American Institute of Graphic Arts. ■

WOULD YOU HIRE THIS MAN TO DESIGN YOUR BUILDING?
Even if your taste in architects doesn't run to large, bearded men in monks' habits, had you been looking for a designer during the 1870s and '80s, you would have been well advised to select this gentleman. He's Henry Hobson Richardson (1838–1886), one of the greatest architects this country has ever known, and the only person to have designed a building that was voted among the country's 10 best in 1885 and again in 1985.

This photo was taken by George Collins Cox in 1883, a decade after Richardson designed his masterpiece, Trinity Church in Boston. For more on Trinity Church and this remarkable man, see Page 10. ■

WHAT IS A JERKINHEAD? No, it's not an epithet heard around the house in the heat of sibling rivalry, but you could have one on your house right now and not even know it. To find out if you do, turn to Page 12.

EVERYTHING YOU EVER WANTED TO KNOW... about architecture is included in *A History of Architecture*, the new, lavishly illustrated landmark text covering the entire scope of humanity's efforts to build human environments. This 788-page book, featuring 950 illustrations, was written by noted architectural historian Spiro Kostof, and is available to Forum members at the special price of $47.50 plus 5 percent for shipping and handling. To order, send a check to the AIA Service Corporation Fulfillment Service, 44 Industrial Park Dr., Box 753, Waldorf, Md. 20601. Order book #R333, and be sure to indicate that you are a Forum member. ■

FORUM
Executive Editor: Kevin Fry
Creative Adviser: Tom Murphy
Art Director: Marilyn Worseldine
Copy Editor: Jo Anne Moncrief
Editorial Advisers: Sherri Lee, Ray Rhinehart, Tony F. Wrenn

FORUM (ISSN 0756-0560) is published quarterly by The American Institute of Architects Foundation. Receipt of the newsletter is a benefit of membership in The Forum for Architecture. Of each member's annual dues, $9 is for a subscription to FORUM. Suggestions for articles, corrections and comments are welcome and should be addressed to the editor, or made by telephone by calling (202) 626-7496.

Opinions expressed are not necessarily those of the AIA Foundation or the Forum for Architecture. All rights to published material are retained by The American Institute of Architects Foundation. ©1986 by The American Institute of Architects Foundation. Vol. 86, No. 1, 1755 New York Avenue, N.W., Washington, D.C. 20006.

A look at the way architects view American architecture

A FORUM EXCLUSIVE POLL

THE 10 BEST BUILDINGS IN THE UNITED STATES: 1885 AND 1985

The perception of what is good—or bad—architecture changes over time. What's renowned today may be tomorrow's eyesore; a building disparaged yesterday becomes today's precious architectural treasure. It is safe to say that few structures have been beloved for every moment of their existence.

Tastes and perceptions are in a continual state of flux, providing, ultimately, the great variety and rich mixture of architecture that dots the landscape. Changes in historical and intellectual perspectives alter what we build *and* the way we see and evaluate the built environment. What we find worthy and unworthy in our own architecture and in the architecture of the past, tells us much about ourselves.

It is an interesting—and valuable—exercise, then, to reflect periodically on the accumulated architecture around us and evaluate it, not only to determine how what we have created in our own time fits into the grander scheme, but to hold a mirror up to our values, to take a hard look at what is important to us.

It can be even more interesting and instructive to compare our perceptions with those of our predecessors.

In 1885, American Architect and Building News, a magazine primarily for the rapidly developing architectural profession, asked its readers to send in a postcard with nominees for "the ten buildings which the subscriber believes to be the most successful examples of architectural design in this country."

Though the response was disappointing (only 75 architects participated, 31 of whom were from Boston, New York City, Chicago or Philadelphia), 175 buildings were nominated. The 10 top vote getters were overwhelmingly from the East Coast; one architect, Henry Hobson Richardson, a contemporary of the voters, designed half of the winners.

Interestingly, the 1885 poll almost totally ignored America's early history. Only the U.S. Capitol, whose great cast-iron dome was added during the voters' lifetimes, in 1865, was considered worthy of mention. To further demonstrate the narrow vision of the era, no building in the top 20 was located farther west than Albany. The results, though somewhat tainted by the small response, tell us a lot about the point of view of American architects at that time. It sheds light not only on how they perceived architecture, but on how they perceived the country, as well.

One hundred years after the 1885 poll, FORUM asked the members of the College of Fellows of the American Institute of Architects to answer the same question their 19th-century counterparts were asked. We received 170 responses, naming a total of 339 buildings.

The exclusive FORUM poll results show that the West and South (Virginia excepted) remain unrecognized, although good architecture apparently has moved as far west as Chicago. And, it seems, a much broader historical perspective has been achieved. As in the 1885 poll, one architect stands out: in this case, Frank Lloyd Wright, who designed three of the top 10.

What conclusions can be drawn from the poll results? That's for you to decide. For one person's perspective, turn to Page 9.

So that you can assess the changing perceptions of a century of American architects, we present a pictorial record of the 10 best buildings in America: 1885 and 1985.

THE ARCHITECT: 1880s

A.J. Bloor, FAIA, in his office. Courtesy: AIA Archives.
From "United in Fellowship" exhibit, 1981.
Photo: Walter Smalling Jr. Courtesy: AIA Archives.

THE ARCHITECT: 1980s

2

3

The inside cover is dominated by an arresting photo of a great architect of the past and a provocative headline. This is a brief story but intriguing enough to get readers into the mood for the pages that follow.

Two small photos, depicting then and now, align at left and right to form a pleasing horizontal pattern. Vertical type elements located at the edge of each photo provide caption information.

A lengthy text story is relieved by bold leads and informal, freehand pen illustrations that lend a light touch to heavy subject matter. The page is visually attractive and easy to read.

Functional type elements are positioned in the top margin. Column-width black panels with reverse type, uniformly located in the right-hand corners, stand out strong and clear.

They go into people. Researchers are beginning to identify a wide range of pollutants that can make indoor air unhealthful, especially in buildings that are not sufficiently ventilated. Some of the contaminants are from bad outside air that is infiltrating the building and not being adequately ventilated or diluted with clean indoor air. Other pollutants are generated by things inside—by people themselves, machines, chemicals, natural elements, or by the very materials with which the building is constructed—creating the frightening reality of a building polluting itself.

Some of the most common pollutants of indoor environments are:

Radioactive radon gas. Radon, which comes from radium, is naturally present in soil and groundwater, and is found in concrete and stone building materials. Under normal conditions it dissipates and is harmless. But if radon is trapped in a building in sufficient quantities, some believe it could pose a health hazard. In very large doses it has been shown to cause lung cancer. No one knows its long-term effects in amounts common in "tight" modern buildings.

Microorganisms. More than half of all diseases are respiratory, and most respiratory diseases can be transmitted through the air on tiny particles expelled when people breathe, cough, sneeze or even talk. Everything from colds and flu to tuberculosis, measles, mumps and chicken pox can be caught from airborne particles. While everyone recognizes the threat of airborne contamination, there is growing concern that modern ventilating systems may actually be spreading, if not fostering, contagious disease. A case in point was the outbreak of legionnaires' disease in Philadelphia.

6

Asbestos. Asbestos has been used in virtually every kind of building in America in insulation, fireproofing substances, floor and ceiling tiles, spackling compound, cement and other materials. Asbestos fibers released into the air from these products can cause a variety of cancers and lung diseases.

Tobacco smoke. A major source of indoor pollution, and one of the hardest to eliminate, is cigarette smoke. Aside from the smokers, who are well known to suffer ill effects from smoking, nonsmokers are subjected to carbon monoxide, nicotine and other pollutants, which cause irritations of the eyes, nose, throat and respiratory tract. Long-term consequences for nonsmokers have not been fully determined.

Indoor combustion byproducts. Whenever fossil fuels are burned indoors, whether in gas stoves, fireplaces or kerosene space heaters, there is a danger of contamination from carbon monoxide, nitrogen dioxide, sulfur oxides and large particles if the area is not sufficiently ventilated. Carbon monoxide in moderately severe levels can accumulate in an average kitchen after only an hour of cooking on a gas stove.

Organic contaminants from household products. Some of the most common potential sources of contamination of the air in homes are the everyday products used to clean, paint, polish or deodorize. Insecticides, aerosol products, adhesives and disinfectants can all produce a variety of harmful pollutants if they are used improperly or used without sufficient ventilation.

Formaldehyde. Even in low concentrations formaldehyde can cause eye, nose and throat irritation; nausea; diarrhea; headaches; skin rashes, and other irritations. People with respiratory diseases are particularly susceptible. Urea-formaldehyde foam was a widely used form of insulation in the energy-conscious '70s. Of more concern are formaldehyde resins, which are used as the adhesive that keeps plywood and particle board together. Formaldehyde gas can be emitted from these building materials for years following installation.

What can architects, engineers and builders do to reduce the hazards of indoor air contamination?

One obvious approach is not to use building materials that emit hazardous contaminants like formaldehyde or asbestos. Another is to separate smokers from nonsmokers. In areas where office machines may be producing harmful contaminants, localized exhaust systems could be installed. For example, hoods could be put over copying machines that emit gases that have been shown to alter DNA.

Contaminants can also be removed by employing a variety of air cleaners or can be diluted by mixing outdoor air with polluted indoor air. Better design of ventilation systems and a more flexible approach to energy efficiency that recognizes the dangers of indoor contamination from excessively tight buildings are also important.

Architects are facing the new challenge of designing buildings that satisfy both our need to breathe clean air and our desire to save energy. Until now these goals have frequently been at odds. One of the major issues in architecture in the coming years will be how buildings can be made safe *and* efficient so that we will be able to go inside for a breath of fresh air.

CLERESTORY WINDOWS

The clerestory, or clearstory, of a building is the portion of a multi-story room that extends above the single-story height. It often contains windows for lighting and ventilation. These are *clerestory windows*, and they have been used in architecture for over 3,000 years.

1. The first recorded use of clerestory windows was in the Great Temple of Amon-Ra at Karnak, Egypt, built around 1290 B.C.

2. The Romans used clerestory windows in great public buildings like the Basilica of Maxentius, built in A.D. 306.

3. The most prolific use of clerestory windows has been in churches from the Middle Ages to the present.

4. Gen. Montgomery Meigs' design for the old Pension Building in Washington, D.C., built in 1885, uses clerestory windows to provide more than light. The windows permit hot summer air to escape and warmth from the winter sun to get in.

5. Modern clerestory windows are now an integral part of energy-efficient design.

2. From *Architecture of the Western World*, ed. Michael Raeburn.
Courtesy: Rizzoli International Publications Inc.
3. St. Paul's Cathedral, London, 1675–1711, Christopher Wren, architect.
Photo: Kevin Fry
4. Shelly Ridge Girl Scout Center, Miquon, Pa., Bohlin Powell Larkin Cywinski, architects.
Photo: ©Otto Baitz Inc.

IN THE VERNACULAR . . .

Some of the most interesting architecture in America hasn't come from the drawing boards of architects—it has sprung from the imaginations of everyday people. All across the country, in neighborhoods and along highways, the art of architecture has been practiced by people seeking personal expression or maybe just a way to grab attention. We call it vernacular architecture.

Some people take architecture into their own hands out of necessity. Some do it for fun. Vernacular architecture can be a form of advertising. Or it can be a personal statement. Whatever its motivation or purpose, it is a reflection of the spirit of the people who create it.

If you have an example of vernacular architecture in your area, take a picture and send it to us. Be sure to tell us what and where the structure is. Black-and-white 35mm photos are preferred.

"Lucy, the Margate Elephant," Margate, N.J. Built by James V. Lafferty, 1881. One of the most serious "monumental follies" of the Victorian era, it was originally designed to be offices, but later became a hotel, which it would operate with six stories set to feet long, weighs 90 tons.
Photo: Peter McCabe

7

Two stories neatly occupy a page. A picture story at the top is keyed by numbers to the text reference. The photos are tightly juxtaposed for effective contrast of architectural patterns. At the bottom, a bright little story is accented by a slim, black shadow.

Inter-American Development Bank

STRIKING WORD-AND-PICTURE REPORTAGE

Editor/Designer
Roger Hamilton
Publisher
Inter-American Development Bank
Washington, DC
Text Type
ITC Bookman Medium
Display Type
ITC Bookman Demi-bold
Languages
English, Spanish, Portuguese,
and French
Page Size
8½ × 11
Printing
Two Color

"I plan each new issue by making a thumbnail sketch of my pages," says Roger Hamilton, Editor of "The IDB." "From that point on, the layouts evolve with the text. The articles suggest graphic approaches. Visual elements determine editorial content. I guess this is to be expected where the editor is also the writer and designer."

This stylish, journalistic publication, combining a newsletter's immediacy with the scope of a magazine, is published in four languages. The subject matter of "The IDB" is economic and social development in Latin America and the Caribbean, in particular the investment projects financed by the Washington, DC–based Inter-American Development Bank. Its audience includes leading figures in government, business, science, and education in the bank's 44 member countries.

In words and pictures, "The IDB" takes readers to a rubber tapper community in the Amazon, a beach conservation program in Barbados, a massive hydroelectric project in Brazil, and scores of other locations. The striking cover and well-written, graphic pages demonstrate effective photojournalism. The publication looks significant, insightful, and believable.

Most issues are mailed together with four-color supplements and newsletters targeted at specific readerships. While different in format, all share common design elements.

Recently, the editor sent a survey to its 40,000 subscribers to gauge their opinion of the publication. The response was not only large, but also overwhelmingly positive. In particular, the readers appreciated the effort to explain economic development in human terms. The quality of the photos was frequently mentioned.

"The IDB" uses ITC Bookman for both headlines and text, giving the pages typographic integrity.

Costa Rica report

THE IDB

Inter-American Development Bank • July 1993

Powerhouse crew
P. 2

Farmers and free trade ▪ Energy conservation
Financial reform ▪ Barbados protects its beaches

Designs for Study

The approach is documentary. Words and pictures describe and define economic and social trends in Latin America and programs financed by loans from the IDB. There are 40,000 readers worldwide.

At the head of each page, department slugs in reverse type are printed on color bands.

Bullish on the region

The jury is in on Latin America's long-awaited economic recovery, and the verdict is positive: a marked upturn is indeed under way, as evidenced by key economic indicators for the past year.

According to this year's IDB report *Economic and Social Progress in Latin America* in 1991:
▶ Total regional GDP rose by 3.2 percent, compared with a 0.1 percent drop in 1990.
▶ A net $36 billion in capital flowed into the region, mostly in the form of private investment.
▶ Unemployment declined and wages increased.
▶ Consumer demand rose by 4.1 percent.
▶ Inflation declined in all but a handful of countries.

The report takes a bullish stance on the region, whose economic performance contrasted with the continuing slowdown in the world economy. International prices for several of the region's major agricultural exports reached historic lows in 1991. But even that failed to seriously dampen the overall picture. By the end of 1991, nearly every Latin American country showed stronger growth than in the previous year.

Resource inflow. The region's sweeping reform efforts deserve most of the credit for the impressive economic performance, according to the report.

"Favorable expectations generated by the reform process stimulated private investment, encouraged a boom in the equity markets, and attracted substantial capital flows from abroad," the report notes. This inflow, coupled with low U.S. interest rates, "completely reversed the transfer of resources in Latin America's favor."

Unlike the pre-1980s capital inflows that financed growth but also fueled the debt crisis, the new inflows "seem to be directed almost exclusively to the private sector, with hardly any impact on foreign debt."

The largest component of capital inflow was foreign direct investment, most of it concentrated in Argentina, Chile, Colombia, Mexico

The challenge will be to translate the region's new resources into a higher standard of living for all its citizens.

and Venezuela. These countries were perceived "not only as having stabilized their economies, but also as being the most advanced in the structural reform process." As much as one half of the foreign direct investment was attracted by privatizations.

Stocks and bonds were the second most important source of capital, as regional capital markets

increasingly opened up to foreign investors. Latin America boasted four of the world's five top-performing stock markets in 1991: Argentina, Brazil, Chile and Mexico.

Dilemmas of success. The inflow of resources has posed a special challenge to the region's policymakers. It has, on the one hand, helped to improve exchange rates, thus contributing to lower domestic prices. But it has also caused an expansion of the money supply, presenting "an embarrassment of riches, entailing potentially destabilizing effects on the financial markets."

Restrictive fiscal and balanced monetary policies helped most countries handle the inflows. But another challenge remains: translating the new resources into a higher standard of living for the region's citizens.

Real wages in the region rose in 1991, but not as fast as GDP. "This gap between expected and actual gains in living conditions may explain some of the social tensions that continue to characterize the situation in many countries," the report notes.

If countries persevere with their policy reforms and the private sector successfully channels the new resources into productive capacity, the current trends are likely to continue. However, if policymakers yield to "adjustment fatigue," confidence could wane and the resource transfer cease.

"The political challenge of the 1990s consists therefore of generating broad-based social support for the reform process by spreading the benefits of renewed growth more equally over all groups of the population."

— *Donna Eberwine*

The four-column inside cover has illustrated contents columns, the masthead, and a statement of purpose. Photos from the field tie in with features and enliven the content listings.

The type style is consistently ITC Bookman, 10 point medium for text and demibold for titles. A somewhat extended letterform, it has unusual strength and readability as well as a topical character.

A large photo extends across the gutter for a "gutter bleed." There is an effective contrast in photo sizes in which the farm family is a key picture.

The choice was to crop the photo with or without the cow. A skillful editor chose to include the animal for a subtle touch of human interest.

THE BANK IN ACTION

Farm families in Uruguay have received credit through the IDB's Small Projects Program.

ARGENTINA
Scouting foreign food markets

Export-minded farmers in Argentina are scouting out new international markets with help from an IDB-financed program to promote nontraditional agricultural exports.

The program, called Promex, provides assistance to members of agricultural export consortia, cooperatives and chambers of commerce, as well as to individual producers. Their nontraditional agricultural exports include asparagus, kiwi fruit, organic garlic and onions, Belgian endive, trout and rabbit.

Last year, Promex took groups of Argentine exporters to the United States, Spain, France and Brazil to meet with market researchers, international trade experts, and potential buyers.

In Denver, Colorado, U.S.A., a Promex group

visited the 43rd Annual Produce Marketing Association Convention, met with international marketing and trade experts, and investigated potential new ports of entry for counter-seasonal produce.

In Madrid, a Promex group opened negotiations with a major supermarket chain and took orders for shipments of asparagus, garlic and honey. In Paris, a group attended the biennial International Food Fair. The most recent group attended a meeting of the International Federation of Organic Agricultural Movements in São Paulo.

In addition to organizing the foreign marketing trips, Promex also provides exporters with consulting services and access to a database with information on pricing, markets, local and international consultants, and leading importers.

Asparagus for export.

BOLIVIA
Sewerage system starts up

Bolivia's minister of urban development and housing, Fernando Kieffer, was on hand recently for the inauguration of a long-awaited sanitary sewerage system in the neighborhood of Villa Mexico, Cochabamba.

The $650,000 system will serve some 26,000 families in one of the city's most densely populated areas, which until recently had among the least developed public services.

The new sewerage system was constructed with funds from an IDB-financed global credit program for urban development and sanitation that is being carried out by Bolivia's National Fund for Regional Development and the national Potable Water and Sewerage Service.

Residents of Villa Mexico provided some $150,000 on their own to complete the project.

COLOMBIA
Making it big in bags

Colombia has long been known by foreign tourists for high-quality leather goods at moderate prices.

But for natives Gabriel and Leticia Echavarrya of Barranquilla, Colombian leather goods seemed overpriced, especially, they say, for the amount of labor involved.

The couple decided to turn their consumer frustration into entrepreneurial drive. They set up their own small business, Glamour Bags, to manufacture leather purses and bags.

The couple teamed up with a local expert on morocco (a specialty leather) and received a loan and technical assistance from the Mario Santodomingo Foundation, a nonprofit nongovernmental organization that has received financing from the IDB's Small Projects Program.

As Glamour Bags perfected its products, it entered samples in the foundation's annual Microenterprise Fairs. After participating four years in a row, Gabriel Echavarrya, as company owner, was honored with the foundation's Outstanding Microentrepreneur of the Year award.

Glamour Bags has since shown its leather goods in New York City, most recently, at the world's largest leather goods fair, in Milan.
— *Dalia Losada de Franco*

Bags by Glamour.

URUGUAY
Small successes

Small-scale farm settlers in the department of San José, Uruguay, have raised their output and incomes with help from an IDB-financed credit program.

Members of the Settlers' Association of Uruguay, the farmers raise crops and dairy cattle on small parcels of land in settlements created under a government-sponsored land distribution program. Prior to the program, some two thirds were earning less than the national minimum wage.

Through a revolving credit fund financed through the IDB's Small Projects Program, the farmers received loans to finance working capital, irrigation and erosion

control works, machinery and vehicles. More than 500 loans have been made to groups and individual farmers.

Three years into the program, dairy farmers participating in the project reported an average increase in output of 15.6 percent, and an average increase in yearly income of $909.

Farmers growing feed crops reported an average rise of 38.8 percent in forage production, with one colony, Galland, reporting an increase of 161 percent.

A report on the program points out that one of its major successes was in "keeping the families firmly established in their farms." In the face of the rising cost of living, "the program has, at the very least, maintained the buying power of the nuclear family."

REGIONAL
Sustaining the savanna

Agronomists at the International Center for Tropical Agriculture (CIAT) in Cali, Colombia, have developed a method for growing rice and grazing cattle on tropical grasslands without exhausting soil resources.

The technique uses a variety of rice developed at CIAT that grows well on the highly acidic soils of the South American savannas. Called rice pasturing, it entails simultaneously planting rice in rows and broadcast sowing grasses and legumes on the same fertilized pastureland.

The rice is harvested four months later, and cattle are then let loose to graze on the forage.

"On-farm experiments show that the system is

profitable and protects the savanna environment," says José Ignacio Sanz, of the CIAT Savannas Program, which is financed by the IDB. The project currently has some 6,000 hectares under cultivation.

The rice harvest more than pays for the establishment of the pasture, which flourishes from fertilizer applied to the rice. The rice, in turn, benefits from nitrogen produced by the legumes.

The system is far kinder to the environment than traditional pasturing, which often depletes soil nutrients, encouraging ranchers to encroach on new lands.

The system is also better for farmers than other forms of pasturing, which require major investments in land preparation, fertilizer and seed, and take two years to start turning a profit. Rice pastures can support six times more cattle than native savanna.

Applied elsewhere, rice pasturing could help save some of the four to five million acres of rain forest throughout the region that are razed each year for use in farming and cattle ranching.
— *Thomas Hargrove*

Sanz in the field.

A spread of short news stories has two-line titles with one-word lead-ins that indicate countries of origin. Picture captions are in italics to contrast with text.

Headlines and text are set flush left throughout. This not only gives the text a welcome informal quality, it also results in clean typography that avoids erratic word spacing.

Art Center College of Design

DRAMATIC PAGES FOR DESIGN EDUCATION

Design Director
Kit Hinrichs
Design Group
Pentagram Design
San Francisco, CA
Publisher
Art Center College of Design
Pasadena, CA
Text Type
Bodoni Book
Display Type
Futura
Page Size
11 × 17
Printing
Six-color press

It is not surprising that one of America's most prestigious colleges of design has an outstanding newsletter. "Review" is rich in color and makes a virtue of its large (11x17) format with design and graphics replete with invention. Designed by a noted graphic designer, Kit Hinrichs—who is an alumnus—it is a costly production supported by donations.

Most newsletters would find the design of "Review" excessive in color and design pyrotechnics. For an art school it is eminently appropriate. Also, it provides a regular showplace for student and alumni art.

There is much to learn from these pages that can apply to any newsletter in any field. The cover, for example, is a masterful organization of design elements. It illustrates the strength of a single-word logotype that is a powerful horizontal pattern. The inside pages have unusually long text blocks, sometimes five columns, sometimes six, skillfully interspersed with distinctive graphics.

The text type is Bodoni Book slightly condensed—a favorite old classic in a contemporary setting. Hinrichs respects the reader and never allows type to veer across and be obliterated by design elements. Rarely do the columns have jagged or complex runarounds. Clearly, the designer is influenced by elegant corporate design, which makes up much of his year-round activity at Pentagram. With this newsletter, he has a continuing font of graphics and photography produced by the school. The design is executed on a Mac with the QuarkXPress program. Hinrichs prefers to rough out his thumbnail layouts on paper for presentation purposes. He enjoys a smooth collaboration with the writers. "They'll edit the copy to fit and sometimes we modify the design for copy purposes."

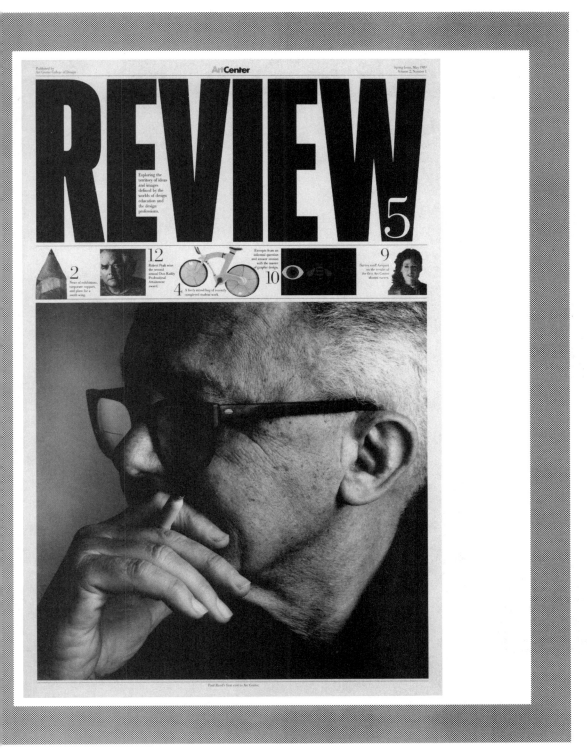

Designs for Study

Echoing the strength and boldness of the cover's logotype, the news feature has a giant title that is in perfect balance with the powerful graphic display on this 22-inch-wide spread.

A daring eight-column illustration, simple and brutally strong, provides a leitmotiv for the visual communications theme. It bisects the spread so that no text column becomes unduly long.

On a five-column grid, the president's letter spans two columns of space. A forceful, five-line drop initial calls attention to the column. Headlines for individual news items are set in small, bold caps that stand out strong and clear, underscored by a bold rule.

NEWS

"Old ideas, once valid, are the hardest things in the world to change," said Jack Telnack, the speaker at Art Center's Spring graduation, Vice-President for Design at Ford Motor Company. Telnack (TRANS '58 has garnered numerous awards this year, including *Automotive Industry*'s coveted Man of the Year and an honorary doctorate from Art Center. "I read that a couple of years ago, the U.S. spent $150 million for Radio Free Europe to beam propaganda broadcasts into Eastern Europe," he said. "In the same year, the Soviets spent $300 million to jam the broadcasts. So in total, the two countries spent $450 million and nobody even talked to anybody."

HORACE BRISTOL AND MARY ELLEN MARK EXHIBITIONS

In the 1940s, just before the omnipresent eye of television first opened and before we celebrated the concept of instantaneity, the first evidence of a global village unfolded in the pages of magazines such as *Life* and *Fortune*. These magazines expanded our cultural consciousness via the backstage labors of a pioneer breed of photojournalist. One such individual was Horace Bristol, now 80 years old, who traveled the world framing its drama during the '30s and '40s. He was present when John Steinbeck interviewed migrant workers prior to publishing *The Grapes of Wrath*; when downed World War II pilots were rescued from the sea; and when traditional cultures in Asia seemed unaffected by the twentieth century. Bristol's work was the subject of a retrospective at the main campus gallery, January 28 through March 4, 1989. The exhibition was supported by the Virginia Steele Scott Foundation, and a video interview with the photographer was funded by the Fellows of Contemporary Art.

If Bristol was a reporter of the human condition, then Mary Ellen Mark might be described as one of its visual poets. Mark's efforts are surrounded by the visual clutter of our time, the onslaught of instant information that punctuates our daily lives. Her work slows the pace delving into the psyche of her subjects, revealing more than reporting. Her ongoing series America was exhibited at Art Center's downtown gallery January 16 through 28, 1989. Mark was the William A. Reedy Memorial Lecturer at Art Center in November 1988. The exhibition was made possible by the Eastman Kodak Company, Professional Photography Division.

HONDA ENDOWS SCHOLARSHIP

"We are not interested in bricks and mortar—or in this case steel and concrete—as much as in student opportunity," says Charles Allen, assistant vice president at Honda R & D North America and an Art Center alumnus. Acting on that philosophy, Honda has established a $1 million scholarship fund at Art Center. The income from the endowment, which will be paid to the college over five years, will be used to provide scholarships for students in all majors. The scholarships will be awarded on the basis of academic achievement and financial need.

The broad nature of the gift reflects Honda's wide-ranging concerns within the design community. "It's clear that Honda is a company with vision," says C. Richard Spiegel, Art Center's vice president for development. "They wanted the assistance to go directly to students." Spiegel also notes that every dollar of scholarship money that comes from outside sources reduces the amount Art Center must budget from internal sources to fund its ever-increasing commitment to scholarships, now running at an annual rate of $1.2 million.

Honda has sponsored a number of projects at Art Center in recent years, most notably a design competition for a sculpture installation at the company's headquarters in Torrance, California. In addition to Allen, who has played a major role in the design of several Honda vehicles, including the sporty CRX, the Torrance office currently employs 11 Art Center graduates.

PRESIDENT'S LETTER

There's a lot going on at Art Center these days, some of which you'll read about in this issue of *Review*. But recently, in the midst of the customary crush of daily events, I was brought up short by a reporter's question. She asked me, "How much of your time do you spend on *education*?" Since we had been talking about fund-raising, corporate involvement, the building addition, and Art Center (Europe), her question was a logical one.

My answer was, "*All* of it," because that's the way I look at what I do. "Administration" has two roles, and two roles only. The first is to support what happens every day between dedicated teachers and talented students, and to enable the educational process to occur at Art Center. The second is to see to it that this process can and does continue into the deep future at a level of quality equal to or even higher than the present.

Since these two responsibilities are often in conflict, we constantly need to make artful choices. But the focus is and must always remain teachers and teaching, students and learning. So my answer is "*All* of it" because I try to look at all of what we do at Art Center with an eye toward how it will help the quality of teachers and teaching, of students and learning.

DRBrown

SOUTH WING PLANNED

Art Center is once again stretching its boundaries—this time, physically. Construction of a 47,000-square-foot addition to the college's existing 166,000-square-foot structure is expected to begin this summer. The purpose of the expansion is not to accommodate more students but to create more specialized learning areas. The new facility will be located on the south end of the current building and will house six multipurpose studios, three lecture classrooms, three project rooms, two computer classrooms, a gallery and studios for graduate students, a 90-seat lecture hall and projection room as well as offices and storage areas.

The addition, which should be ready for occupancy by fall 1990, was part of the original plan for the campus conceived by Craig Ellwood Associates but was never completed because of limited funds. "We take great pride in this building," says Art Center President David Brown, "and look forward to completing it according to its original and powerful concept."

While enrollment has remained stable since 1981, the college's educational programs have expanded considerably, reflecting changing professional requirements in the fields of art and design. Areas that were originally used as classrooms have been converted to computer labs, a printmaking workshop, and studios for graduate students. Since 1986 Art Center has leased additional space in downtown Pasadena.

Working drawings for the new wing have been prepared by James Tyler, who served as project architect for the original building. William T. Moran, Art Center's vice president for facilities, is overseeing the project.

The process of obtaining permits was well under way by March but hit a snag with the passage of a slow-growth antidevelopment initiative in Pasadena. Says Brown, "We feel that the project is well within the spirit of the new law, but the test will come when we apply for the building permit." Stay tuned.

ArtCenter

...TER ABSTRACT

...entieth-century modernism, like ...ry other art-historical move-...nt, has evolved its own set of ...umptions. This is ironic, since ...st of its doctrine has revolved ...und the notion of radicalism, ...ich evaluates art primarily on ...e basis of whether or not it ...aks new ground. About a ...ade ago modernist radicalism ...s supplanted by postmodern ...iction, which embraced the ...st as a way to look new.

A number of artists working today regard modernism as a language largely depleted of its ability to create meaning, a metaphor for the failed utopian ideals of this century. Others, however, have recultivated its pictorial field, regarding its familiar vocabulary as a language that retains a capacity for nuance and substance. This fork in the modernist road has created two paths, one leading to an art that is a critical, deconstructive examination of modernist tenets, and the other to an art that is about expression, one that perceives modernism as a positive

source of imagery that has yet to be exhausted.

These concurrent paths were explored in *After Abstract*, an exhibition of 28 paintings by nine Los Angeles-based artists presented in Art Center's main campus gallery from September 24 through October 29, 1988. The show was organized by Stephen Nowlin, director of exhibitions. It was accompanied by a 50-page color catalog whose publication was supported by the Pasadena Art Alliance. Catalogs are available upon request.

FORD CHAIRMANSHIP ESTABLISHED

Ford Motor Company has pledged $1 million to Art Center to endow the Ford Chairmanship of the Department of Industrial Design. The income from the grant, which is payable over five years, will help underwrite the salary of the chairman of the Industrial Design Department.

"This gift acknowledges the commitment to design and design education that Ford and Art Center share," says Ford's Vice President for Design Jack Telnack, an Art Center alumnus who led the team that developed the innovative aerodynamic design of the automaker's highly successful Taurus and Sable cars.

Ronald C. Hill, chairman of the Industrial Design Department at Art Center, describes the gift, which will continue in perpetuity, as "an expression of confidence in the future of the transportation and

product design programs at Art Center, and one that we will strive to measure up to."

According to C. Richard Spiegel, Art Center's vice president for corporate and foundation relations, the gift is significant not only because of its size but also because it underlines the importance of Art Center's industrial design program in training designers for the automotive industry: "It is a major gesture of support and respect." Spiegel also acknowledges the key role played by Telnack in encouraging Ford to make the gift: "He was the advocate of the idea at Ford."

The Ford endowment comes at a time when automakers, having spent more than a decade adapting their products to meet stricter federal regulations, are placing renewed emphasis on design in an effort to be more competitive in the world market.

Art Center has had strong ties with Ford for many years. Ford Chairman Donald Petersen was awarded an honorary doctorate by the college in 1986. Vice Chairman William Clay Ford serves, along with Telnack, on Art Center's Council of Executives. The company has contributed substantially to Art Center's industrial design program, scholarship fund, and construction of the college's facility in Pasadena and has sponsored many transportation design assignments at the school.

60-YEAR BOOK PLANNED

Leon Whiteson, architecture critic for the *Los Angeles Times*, is currently at work on a book about Art Center's first 60 years. Whiteson's commissioned text will be illustrated with images from Art Center's past. He and designer Kit Hinrichs request submissions of all kinds from alumni. If you have written records, recollections, personal anecdotes, memorabilia, photographs, or artwork produced at Art Center, especially in its early days, please send them to Jean Parry at the college's Alumni Office no later than July 1, 1989.

PARTNERS IN EDUCATION

Sponsoring the publication of *Review* are ColorGraphics, Inc., and Kirk Paper, who have donated in part the costs of printing and paper. These gifts continue a long tradition of partnership between Art Center and the business and design communities, a hallmark of the college since its founding in 1930.

COLORGRAPHICS/Los Angeles
150 North Myers Street
Los Angeles, California 90033
(213) 264-7171

COLORGRAPHICS/San Francisco
1221 Tennessee Street
San Francisco, California 94107
(415) 821-7171

KIRK PAPER COMPANY, INC.
6550 East Washington Boulevard
Los Angeles, California 90040
(213) 685-7460

ColorGraphics

...BALL TO I-BALL

...magine yourself as anyone or ...ything that you've ever wanted ...be..."

Many of the guests at Art ...nter's first annual Imagination ...all took the invitation literally, ...ming as, say, Marie Antoinette ... a jailbird, a "scientifically ...ccurate" insect or a Las Vegas ...nge lizard. (Evidently, not ...eryone's fantasies are upwardly ...obile.) In fact, virtually all arrived ... costume or "creative black tie."

The gala, which took place ... June 11, 1988, in Art ...nter's Sculpture ...arden, revived ...e grand tradition ... the Beaux-Arts

ball. The event was organized by the Art Center One Hundred, with trustee Alyce Williamson serving as chairman. All of the proceeds from the ball went to the college's scholarship fund.

Among the 500 guests were many Art Center students. Cash prizes were awarded for the most inventive costumes. Best of show

went to Allen Tam for his elegant samurai warrior getup. Cheryl Pelly's black lizard outfit, which included a shiny plastic headdress that zigzagged all the way to the floor, won the prize for the most innovative use of materials. Four students—Beth Fielding, Todd Grant, Dennis Juett, and Mona Weir—came as a table set

for a formal dinner for four and walked away with the award for the best group costume. The prize for the sexiest guise went to the couple from outer space, Kirk Demorest and Kathryn Nanney, and the winner for the funniest costume was lounge lizard Robert Moore, whose outfit was topped by a monumental pompadour.

The Wayne Foster Orchestra kept the dance floor packed, and additional entertainment was provided by a magic troupe. Dinner was catered by Rococo. Williamson, who reigned over the festivities as a glittering, beneath-ered, white-clad Snow Queen, described herself as "overwhelmed" by the response from guests, many of whom called or wrote to thank her in the days following. Perhaps the ultimate kudos came from *Town and Country* magazine, which featured the Imagination Ball prominently in its January 1989 roundup of the best parties of 1988.

For those who missed out on the fun the first time around, the second annual Imagination Ball will take place on Saturday, June 24, 1989. Last year's was a sellout, so alumni who would like to attend are advised to reserve their tickets early. To order tickets for this year's bash, see page 13.

Crisp, vertical hairlines and bold horizontal rules combine to give a clean architectural structure to the spread. Type-matter is consistently flush left. The text type, Bodoni Book, has a fast-paced journalistic quality. A neat running title crowns the top of each page, slightly off center.

The exceedingly tall outer column is interrupted by a tilted rectangular element strategically placed at a distance from the large illustrations. The contrast, large to small, results in effective visual dynamics.

An elaborate group picture taken at the school's gala costume ball is silhouetted and is a forceful free-form shape. Bleeding off the foot of the page, the group picture, with no distracting background, brings out the animated faces vividly.

International Apple Institute

PALATABLE GRAPHICS FOR APPLE EATERS

Here's a welcome relief from the press releases that fill the mailboxes of food editors. "Two Apples a Day" is a striking newsletter that is clearly a P.R. medium. Its colorful content is planned to support the healthful habit of apple eating. Sponsored by the International Apple Institute, its readers are urged to freely pick up and publish the stories and graphics in newspapers and magazines.

There is also an unusual twist. The publishers will furnish full-color graphics on Macintosh 3 1/2" disks to editors anywhere. And for immediate pickup, materials will even be dispatched by modem.

Pages are enlivened with whimsical illustrations and colorful infographics that are executed on a Mac with the Adobe Illustrator program. Page layouts are executed on the Quark XPress program using as text the Bitstream type Sabon set on two-, three-, and four-column grids. The text is definitely designed to be read with ease. Information graphics are designed by John Sherlock, a former *USA Today* illustrator. The logotype has an eye-catching apple motif with a blending of apple colors. It is unlikely that this newsletter could be overlooked.

The Washington publication group, Porter/Novelli, is a computerized shop from A to Z. After page designs are completed, the customary procedure is to have the client sit with the monitor and work out corrections and approvals.

The group produces similar publications for a number of nonprofit clients that use the newsletter medium to communicate with the press.

Creative Director
Dan Snyder
Art Director/Designer
Gary Ridley
Illustrations
Mike McConnell
Design Group
Porter/Novelli
Washington, DC
Publisher
International Apple Institute
Washington, DC
Text Type
Sabon
Display Type
Many styles and
hand lettering
Page Size
8½ × 11
Printing
Four Color

TWO APPLES A DAY

GETS THE DOCTOR'S OK!

PUBLISHED BY THE INTERNATIONAL APPLE INSTITUTE • VOLUME F2

5 a Day – for Better Health!

2 Apples a Day is Good Start for "5 a Day"

In July of this year, the National Cancer Institute (NCI) launched a $2 million public education campaign called 5 a Day to encourage Americans to eat five servings of fruits and vegetables daily. According to IAI president Ellen Terpstra, apples offer a convenient and tasty way for many Americans to get their minimum two servings of fruits a day.

Bernadine Healy, director of the National Institutes of Health, said at the launch of the 5 a Day campaign, "An apple a day keeps the doctor away" was a step in the right direction, but only a step. The importance of diet in the prevention of major killer diseases like cancer and heart disease is paramount. The 5 a Day message — to eat five or more servings of fruits and vegetables daily — is positive, easy to carry out and will not be overturned by the food fad of next week."

According to Terpstra, the 5 a Day message reinforces the apple industry's theme that Two Apples a Day Gets the Doctor's OK. Terpstra said, "Eating two apples a day gets a person almost to the halfway point of 5 a Day."

One medium-sized apple counts as a serving of fruit. So does 3/4 glass of juice or a 1/2 cup of applesauce.

Terpstra said that apples offer the convenience and selection consumers find important when choosing fruits to eat. In addition to the many varieties of fresh, whole apples available year round, consumers can select apple cider, apple juice, applesauce, canned and frozen sliced apples or dehydrated sliced apples.

According to Terpstra, apples' health attributes, the wide selection of apple products and the convenience of eating them probably account for why *The Packer's* 1992 Fresh Trends survey found that Americans bought apples more than any other fruits during 1991.

At a recent NCI press conference, Health and Human Services Secretary Louis W. Sullivan said, "Research clearly shows that a diet with plenty of fruits and vegetables is good for health." Terpstra adds, "Two apples a day

continued on page 6

ALL COPY AND ARTWORK ARE AVAILABLE FOR MEDIA USE. COLOR VERSIONS OF ALL ILLUSTRATIONS AND INFOGRAPHS APPEARING IN THIS NEWSLETTER ARE AVAILABLE ON MACINTOSH 3 1/2" FLOPPY DISKS OR CAN BE SENT VIA MODEM. FOR MORE INFORMATION PLEASE CALL ANNETTE ANDERSON AT PORTER/NOVELLI, 202/342-7000

Each page in this three-panel, six-page newsletter is designed to ride alone or combine harmoniously with others as the pages unfold. This spread resembles a magazine feature story with a decorative display headline linked to a forceful illustration.

Short features about apples occupy small text blocks, each of which has a theme and a headline. The pictograph, below right, tells a story independently. Editors who receive this newsletter are urged to pick up and freely publish the content.

A special text feature printed on a pale color panel has a calligraphic headline and an incisive four-line drop initial. Strong and simple, this feature succeeds in being prominent on the page.

Two single-page units work independently to provide a fund of information. The title type on the feature below links up and is in complete harmony with the three-column illustration. All illustrations and graphics are in full color.

A lyrical page of news items has a rustic, hand-hewn headline followed by a casual, non-mechanical sans-serif body type. The unusual page-wide columns don't exceed 12 lines in depth.

Tabular matter and short bits of information are set in sans-serif type. Captions about recipe ideas are introduced with titles in free-flowing script. The colorful "Carmen Miranda Fruitful Hat" pictograph is a clever way to spell out statistical information.

Rollicking, animated spot drawings are positioned for balance and visual rhythm. Headlines are staggered right and left, down the page. This is a news page that will grab the reader's attention.

National Geographic Society

AN AUDIENCE OF WELL-READ READERS

Designer
Kay Hankins
Photo Editor
Caitlin Wargo
Publisher
National Geographic Society
Washington, DC
Text Type
Galliard
Display Type
Franklin Gothic
Galliard Italic
Page Size
$8\frac{1}{4} \times 11\frac{1}{4}$
Printing
Black only on 100%
Post-Consumer Waste
Recycled Paper

It is not surprising that an organization with a 106-year tradition of editorial and visual excellence has a newsletter with high professional standards. The design of the "Insider" is distinguished by compelling photographs and a clean, clear layout that supports its informational character.

Its editor, Catherine Healy, sums up the design objectives in a few words: "Make 'Insider' look so spontaneous and natural that it's no effort to get through. We have a lot of busy people here, and we want them to read the publication. Pages have to feel open or the articles will look too heavy to read."

An experienced editor and one-time novelist, Ms. Healy plans her issues to appeal to all levels of the Society's 2700-plus employees and retirees.

Although Ms. Healy is a one-person staff, she receives part-time support from ambitious editorial, photo, and production employees who want to move ahead professionally. "Since many 'Insider' staffers work after-hours and on weekends, we simplify every way we can to keep their hours reasonable," she says.

Simplicity means short articles, which the editors style on Quark XPress with Galliard text for a classic look and Franklin Gothic heads for a topical touch. Articles flow one after another in three-column grids. Photos and boxed photo stories give variety.

"We also always have one or two features where everyone involved can really stretch themselves to put fine writing and great photos together," says Ms. Healy. "Simple is efficient, but it's not as much fun as tap dancing. Our audience appreciates a really well-executed flourish."

□INSIDER

NOVEMBER 1993

FOR AND ABOUT THE STAFF OF THE NATIONAL GEOGRAPHIC SOCIETY

MARK THIESSEN

Skirts a swirl, dancers give lunchtime diners at Headquarters a taste of Hispanic culture. Page 20.

Inside the Insider

The single word "insider" is an appropriate logo for this in-house publication. The content is topical. The layout design is simple and elegant, as it should be.

A close-up story opens with a Galliard Italic headline that flows gracefully across the page. The happy, emotional photo captures a momentary glimpse of reality.

AWARDS

Charlene Valeri Wins Photographic Staff's Gilka

GUMPTION, INTEGRITY, Loyalty, Know-how, Awareness—these qualities add up to Bob Gilka, a former director of Photography who retired in July 1985. In January of that year he was presented with the first Gilka, an award created to honor him and other Photographic staff embodying the characteristics spelled out in his name.

Each year Photographic staff members cast secret ballots nominating the co-worker they feel most merits the award; this year Charlene Valeri, senior administrative assistant, was so honored on January 7.

"It was nearly unanimous," said Susan Smith, assistant director of the division. "The Gilka, along with Editorial's Ethel, is one of the neatest awards presented at the Society. Both are from colleagues honoring colleagues."

Charlene, who worked with Bob Gilka for 18 years, said, "This is the high point of my career here. I thought very highly of Mr. Gilka. I was stunned to receive it, and am very honored."

"Charlene was given this accolade because she has been so wonderful over the years with the photographers," commented Tom Kennedy, senior assistant editor and director of Photography. "She takes care of details, deals with problems as they come up, is always cheerful and positive, and keeps a cool head in a crisis. She knows a tremendous amount about how the Society operates and

"Me?!" Charlene Valeri, flanked by colleagues in Photographic, discovers she's the 1993 Gilka winner.

the things that have happened over the years, so when history comes into the picture, Charlene knows what to do."

As Kent Kobersteen, associate director of Photographic staff, summed up in his nomination: "Charlene knows what's going to happen, who it's going to happen to, and what to do when it happens, long before anyone else. She has GILKA if ever I saw it."

KRISTINA D. EIDE, *Typographic*

Detroit Honors Advertising's Andrea Vaughan

A PANEL OF LEADERS in Detroit's advertising community chose the Society's Andrea Vaughan for their sixth annual Award of Excellence. Adcraft PM presents the award to honor "an exceptional advertising professional who has demonstrated outstanding leadership qualities and a dedication to the pursuit of excellence," both in the workplace and in the advertising community itself.

Andrea was hired as an account manager in Advertising's Detroit office in November 1990, with primary responsibility for the Ford Motor Company. Since then, she has brought five new clients or divisions to the Magazine, and the Ford business has grown from an annual level of some $270,000 to more than $5 million.

Among those nominating Andrea for the award was Susan Kiltie, vice president at J. Walter Thompson, Ford's advertising agency, who said, "Andrea combines a superior knowledge and passion for GEOGRAPHIC with an educated understanding of Ford's marketing goals, demonstrating her professionalism with consistent assertiveness. Outside of the office, Andrea tirelessly dedicates her time to volunteering and supporting advertising community events."

Andrea's service to the community includes work on the Boy Scouts Croquet Tournament committee, which last year raised $52,000 for the Scouts. She was cited for her "heroic patience and grace" in scheduling more than 400 players on 145 teams—"all advertising types with meetings and travel"—to appear on time and ready to play.

ASSOCIATE EDITOR CATHE BALLAY, *Typographic*

INSIDER • MARCH 1993

An inset portrait with eye contact pulls you into a news story from the field. The flush-right headline, set in Franklin Gothic Condensed, combines with the photo for a strong, visual verbal unit.

Note the subtle typographic styling of bylines located in a sign-off position: caps and small caps combined with italics.

AWARDS

WORLD WON TWO AWARDS FOR EXCELLENCE in recent months. Parents Choice Foundation, an organization that reviews and comments on children's media, named WORLD a 1992 gold medal winner. WORLD also received an Ozzie Award for Design Excellence from *Magazine Design & Production.* In addition, the magazine was one of five children's publications cited as "Great Magazines for Kids" in *Parents* magazine, which said, "...the editors [of WORLD] have obviously thought long and hard about what sparks middle-school kids' curiosity."

FOUR ED MEDIA PRODUCTS are among approximately 30 to receive *Technology & Learning* magazine's Award of Excellence. NGS winners are: *THE PRESIDENTS: It All Started With George*; the Kids Network units, "What Are We Eating?" and "Too Much Trash?"; and GTV: *Planetary Manager.* Also, *Mammals: A Multimedia Encyclopedia* has been awarded a 1992 Reader's Choice Award by *Multimedia World* magazine, and *Dinosaur Babies,* one of the titles in the Set 6 Action Books, won a silver award in the Dimensional Illustrations Awards show. Selected from more than 1,400 entries worldwide, the winners were exhibited at the Art Directors Club in New York last fall and will be displayed in London in the spring.

TOP CABLE HONORS FOR EXPLORER Two CableACE awards—cable television's equivalent of the Emmys—went to National Geographic EXPLORER at the annual ceremony held in mid-January. For the third year in a row, the Society's weekly cable series won an award for the best Magazine Show. And, for the first time, EXPLORER won for having the best Magazine Host, Robert Urich. Larry King and Leeza

Gibbons were among the television hosts competing for the award. Urich began his acceptance speech by noting his college bachelor's and master's degrees, then said, "But I never realized how stupid I was until I

Best cable host in 1992: EXPLORER's Robert Urich , on location in England last year for "Apes and Humans."

started working for the National Geographic Society." He went on to say, "National Geographic EXPLORER celebrates the diversity of our planet. Perhaps from such information will come knowledge, from knowledge will come wisdom, understanding, respect, and perhaps love." In closing, Urich mentioned how much he has always wanted to be on the best series on television.

THE SOCIETY OF ILLUSTRATORS' 1993 EXHIBITION of editorial art opened in New York in late January with nine NATIONAL GEOGRAPHIC pieces included in the display. Senior assistant editor Allen Carroll, head of Magazine Art, said, "Given that there are several thousand entries but only about 200 pieces chosen for the show, I think we fared unusually well this year." Artist Jerry Pinkney won a gold medal for his September 1992 painting of a slave market "scramble auction." Staff artist Christopher Klein's July 1992 depiction of life on a wharf piling, designed with art director Mark Holmes, also appeared in the show. Other illustrations on display included Herbert Tauss's February 1992 spectacular battle scene for the Pizarro story, one of Burt Silverman's August 1992 paintings for the article on Jing Di's tomb, and two from the October 1991 issue—Richard Schlecht's whaling scene and Jack Unruh's Mohawk ambush depiction.

Artist Jerry Pinkney's prize-winning NGM illustration: slave market auction.

Horizontal dotted lines printed in a halftone screen unify the layout and add a discreet decorative note. Typematter in the top margin is widely letter-spaced to contrast subtly with other display type.

Photos and art are well separated. Viewed as a spread, the visual elements seem to revolve and give the layout a lively, kinetic quality.

Four brief stories take on individuality with run-in bold headlines. Flush-left lines give the text a welcoming look of informality.

Children's Television Workshop

BURSTING WITH VISUAL VITALITY

Here's a newsletter that's exploding with visual vitality. The "Ghost Writer Newsletter" has a history.

In 1992, the Children's Television Workshop began a series of TV programs designed to encourage reading and writing skills among inner-city children. The producers wanted their enterprise to have the highest standards of design excellence and be able to eventually produce it in-house. For that reason they assigned the prestigious New York design group Pentagram to style the graphic features of the program as a package. Pentagram then trained the CTW's in-house department to continue, following the system.

The centerpiece is a distinctive logotype that also appears as the TV title on the air as well as on various print items. Teachers and prospective financial supporters find it hard to resist reading this lively publication. The tumbling figure on the cover is an inspired and memorable image. The designers organized the inside pages using a Mac and the Quark program.

A four-column grid system uses Garamond for text combined with Franklin Gothic for headlines, subheads, and picture captions. Stories are short and concise. Readers can scan the narrow columns quickly and easily. When asked if the text was written to fit the layout, designer Paula Scher said, "No, we were handed the copy."

After the start-up phase, Pentagram turned over the design guidelines to the CTW designer Michele Weisman, who continues to follow style.

Designer
Paula Scher
Design Direction
Pentagram Design
New York, NY
Publisher
Children's Television Workshop
New York, NY
Text Type
Garamond No. 3
Display Type
Franklin Gothic Demi-bold
Page Size
$8\frac{1}{2} \times 11$
Printing
Two Color

A Quarterly Newsletter from Children's Television Workshop | Issue One — Spring 1992

Ghost writer™
Newsletter

• Target audience is seven to ten year-olds, with emphasis on minority and economically disadvantaged kids

• GHOSTWRITER is breakthrough children's programming. It tailors traditional drama to kids' unique perspectives by incorporating MTV-style graphics, music and editing.

Ghostwriter Team Takes Its First Case; Production Under Way

LITERACY PROJECT GRABS KIDS WITH ENERGETIC, CONTEMPORARY ATTITUDE AND LOOK

What's GHOSTWRITER? Here are some clues:

• The new literacy project from Children's Television Workshop, designed to make reading and writing exciting and relevant to kids, and to bring new viewers to public television stations

REMINDER: FOR FULL UPDATE AND SCHEDULING INFORMATION, REFER TO THE GHOSTWRITER VIDEO REPORT AS FED BY PBS ON MAY 5TH AT 2:00 PM ET (REPEATED MAY 6TH AT 1:00 AM).

Mayteana Morales (Gaby) has been in Presumed Innocent, Prince of Tides, Mo' Better Blues and Jungle Fever. She speaks and reads Spanish fluently.

The distinctive logo is made further distinctive as a vertical element in the margins left and right.

Issue One — Spring 1992

ghost writer Newsletter

Impressive Research Statistic #1

When asked how they liked GHOSTWRITER compared with their own favorite TV show, 94.5% of the kids who viewed the test episodes said that they liked GHOST-WRITER as much as or better than their favorite.

Source: Comprehension Study, Maguire Associates, February 1992

• All of the pieces of the GHOSTWRITER puzzle were created to fit perfectly with public television stations:

TV — Making Literacy Fun and Exciting

The television component of GHOST-WRITER is a mystery-adventure series with a unique twist —

three boys and three girls solve neighborhood mysteries with the help of a secret teammate they call "Ghost-writer," an invisible character who can

Sheldon Turnipseed (Jamal) has appeared in the films Mo' Better Blues, Jungle Fever and Cadillac Man.

only communicate with the kids through the printed word. They read his messages and write back to him.

Shot on the streets of Brooklyn, NY and in a New York studio, each mystery takes place over four half-hours, with cliffhangers building anticipation and loyal viewership as the kids on the team and viewers at home "rally" with Ghostwriter and together get closer to the solution.

Clues can show up anywhere — like on a billboard whose letters Ghostwriter rearranges into a message seen only by the team members or on a computer screen, for example. While the kids go about their sleuthing, they're demonstrating everyday opportunities to read and write, like

Todd Alexander (Rob) has appeared in numerous theatrical, TV and film roles, including Kate and Allie, Lean on Me and Saturday Night Live.

writing a persuasive letter to get an interview with a police lieutenant and keeping a casebook where they list their clues and suspects.

GHOSTWRITER uses engrossing, compelling social issues to grab today's kids. Its "hot"

contemporary style and format help GHOST-WRITER promote literacy in an off-beat and entertaining way. The series' appealing cast, state-of-the-art effects and original music are sure to draw an audience that crosses age, gender and racial lines. GHOST-WRITER's production

David Lopez (Alex) speaks Spanish fluently, and pitches for his Little League team.

team includes an executive producer with ten years' experience at MTV and directors who have worked on M*A*S*H, L.A. Law, ABC Afterschool Specials, Roots and Clarissa Explains It All.

Entertaining, Full-Color and FREE

Kids don't like to read? Wait until they get their free copy of GHOST-WRITER magazine! They'll get a preview of what's coming up on GHOSTWRITER, puzzles, short stories, polls and reading-and-writing activities. And they'll be encouraged to write in often.

Twenty million copies of the magazine — two million each issue — will be distributed during GHOSTWRITER's first season to schools, after-school centers and other places where they're sure

to reach our target kids. Copies will be given free to PBS stations for local outreach.

GHOSTWRITER Goes to School

More than 350,000 copies of teacher's materials will be distributed through a variety of channels, including CTW's Creative Classroom magazine. Copies will be available to stations upon request.

GHOSTWRITER Stays Afterschool

CTW is reaching out to youth-serving organizations who are including GHOSTWRITER in their afterschool activities. Millions of kids in our target will be introduced to GHOST-WRITER through the efforts of:

• Boys and Girls Clubs of America

A free use of photo silhouettes catch the character of the TV audience. There is a spark of animation in the figures. The silhouette shapes have been skillfully executed with sensitive details.

Ten-point Garamond text type is set flush left on 8½-pica columns for an open, informal quality. Notice that copy was edited for staggered line breaks with minimum hyphenation.

Issue One — Spring 1992

- 4-H Extension Service
- Girl Scouts of the U.S.A.
- Girls Inc.
- YMCA of the U.S.A.

We'll be sending GHOSTWRITER magazines and activity guides to leaders of these groups and encouraging them to work with public television stations to make the most of local opportunities.

Impressive Research Statistic #2

On a scale of interest in seeing the next episode, ranging from one ("no, not at all") to five ("yes, a lot"), 99% of children said they want to see the next episode — and 88% said they wanted to see it "a lot." (Mean score of 4.9 on a one to five scale.)

Source: KRC Research and Consulting, Inc., GHOSTWRITER In-Home Test Show Study, January 1992.

Blaze Berdahl (Lenni) was featured in Stephen King's Pet Sematary and appeared in Last Exit to Brooklyn. She'll do her own singing in GHOSTWRITER.

The Case of the GHOSTWRITER Promotion Plans– Bring on the Co-Conspirators!

CTW is planning a wide range of promotional activities and materials to help stations get the most out of the launch and first season of GHOST-WRITER.

The Case of the GHOST-WRITER Promotion Plans comes your way later this spring, offering ideas for activities that won't take a lot of time or money, but can have big payoffs in community outreach, press coverage and viewership. Many of them include tie-ins to groups that are committed to supporting GHOST-WRITER, including the ALA and the U.S. Postal Service.

Also included in the package will be customizable promotion and advertising materials and an order form for an assortment of promotional items that will arrive in plenty of time to plan for GHOST-WRITER's premiere.

Watch! Read! Write!

GHOSTWRITER IS BEING PROMOTED THROUGH:

- A national awareness campaign, including two national sweepstakes, promoted in part by public television stations.

- A national publicity campaign reaching target kids, their parents, adult decision-makers and schools. Stations will receive customizable press releases and photos for local use.

- Awareness and tune-in campaigns in conjunction with:

- The American Library Association, which will promote public and school libraries as "GHOSTWRITER Headquarters," GHOST-WRITER posters, bookmarks and other materials for school and library use.
- The U.S. Postal Service, which will feature GHOSTWRITER displays as part of its Stamp Out Illiteracy program in over 35,000 post offices this fall. GHOSTWRITER materials included in the Postal Service's Wee Deliver newsletter will reach an estimated 10,000 schools.
- A series of GHOST-WRITER books by Bantam, published this fall and through the next year,

ghostwriter Newsletter

Trem Anh Tran (Tina), like her character, is a Vietnamese immigrant whose background will be the basis for an upcoming GHOST-WRITER story.

NIKE's Just Do It Fund Helps GHOSTWRITER Materialize with $5 Million Grant

GHOSTWRITER is off and running with a $5 million grant from NIKE, Inc., the world's leading athletic apparel and footwear company.

"GHOSTWRITER is truly breakthrough programming for kids, and the most exciting method of dealing with literacy issues that we've ever seen," said Richard K. Donahue, NIKE's President and Chief Operating Officer.

The grant from NIKE's corporate giving program, the "Just Do It Fund," supports the company's stated goal of funding "unique educational opportunities for low-income, urban youth," according to Virginia Hensen, NIKE's Director of Public Affairs.

"The chance to become involved with an innovative new project like GHOSTWRITER, which addresses our own philanthropic objectives so perfectly, doesn't come along every day," Hensen said, "and when you add CTW's track record for producing excellent children's programming, it was simply too good an opportunity to pass up."

NIKE, based in Beaverton, Oregon, will help the GHOST-WRITER launch by participating in national sweepstakes, publicity events featuring the company's endorsement athletes and promotional products.

Additional funding for GHOSTWRITER has been provided by PBS, the Corporation for Public Broadcasting, The John D. and Catherine T. McArthur Foundation, The Pew Charitable Trusts, the Mary Reynolds Babcock Foundation, and Children's Television Workshop.

Picture captions printed in red harmonize with the silhouette shapes and are written with an economy of words.

Following the series of brief news items, a single large Franklin Gothic head stands alone and boosts interest in a special item at the end of the spread.

A special news item set two columns in width, printed in red, stands out even though the text is smaller in point size. The box is outlined with a delicate hairline.

AIGA Washington Chapter

A STUDY IN SUBTLE ELEGANCE

Yes, the two designs at the right are newsletter covers. Subtle, aren't they?—and elegant, too. With all the talent within its membership, it isn't surprising that the American Institute of Graphic Arts, Washington Chapter, has a newsletter that's truly unique.

Covers are designed by members, under the guidance of Editor and De-signer Pat Taylor. No need to embla-zon the name on the cover (see also page 23)—the members are an "in" group and all this newsletter attempts to sell is fraternal solidarity. In some respects it educates, too.

Content roams the field of local de-sign activities. It's a guide as to who's who in the design community and it keeps members in touch with the AIGA Board. Each issue carries a close-up of a prominent member and displays the design accomplishments of members and others prominent in the field. Each year, this publication continues to be recognized for its design excellence in both local and national competitions.

In Washington's vital design commu-nity, the AIGA is prestigious. As you might expect, the printing, paper, and mailing service are all donated to this nonprofit organization.

What can you learn from this un-complicated publication?

1. A subtle cover can make your newsletter stand out and it can also be refreshing. You may consider this ex-ample excessive but, whatever your field, you're not aiming at newsstand display.

2. This tall, $4\frac{1}{4} \times 11$ format is handy, palm size, and its one-column grid is easy to design. Also, the size and shape are distinctive.

3. If your editorial content is gener-ally limited, this format is one way to avoid a thin, diluted look.

4. And, of course, the simplicity of the page layout design is well worth study.

Editor/Designer
Pat Taylor
Publisher
American Institute of Graphic Arts
Washington, DC Chapter
Text Type
Univers No. 55 & 56
ITC Cushing Book and Cushing Heavy
Display Type
Bold versions of text type
Page Size
$4\frac{1}{4} \times 11$
Printing
Two Color

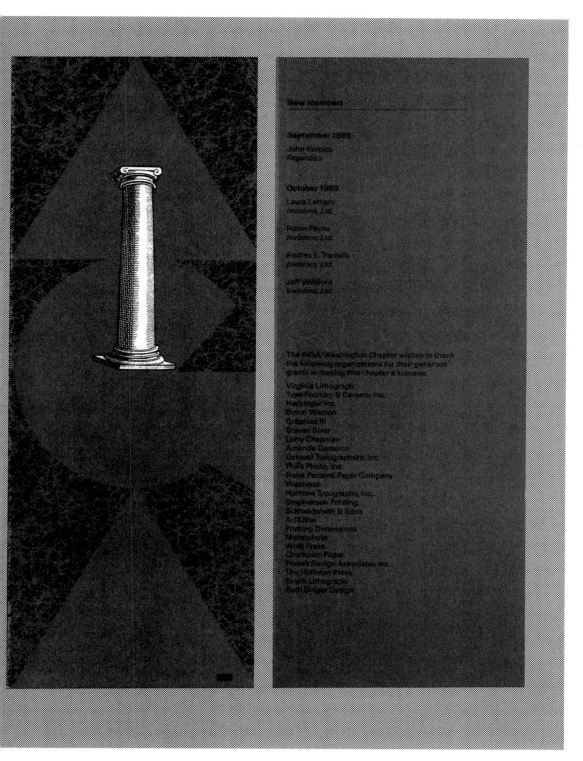

New members

September 1989
John Korpics
Regardie's

October 1989
Laura Latham
Invisions, Ltd.

Robin Payne
Invisions, Ltd.

Andres E. Tremols
Invisions, Ltd.

Jeff Williford
Invisions, Ltd.

The AIGA/Washington Chapter wishes to thank the following organizations for their generous grants in making this chapter a success:

Virginia Lithograph
Type Foundry & Camera, Inc.
Harbinger Inc.
Byron Weston
Graphics 111
Steven Biver
Larry Chapman
Amanda Cameron
General Typographers, Inc.
Phil's Photo, Inc.
Frank Parsons Paper Company
Westvaco
Harlowe Typography, Inc.
Stephenson Printing
Schneidereith & Sons
Art Litho
Printing Dimensions
Metrophoto
Wolk Press
Champion Paper
French Design Associates Inc.
The Huffman Press
Smith Lithograph
Beth Singer Design

Two tall spreads display a wide assortment of graphics. The Member Profile feature utilizes the wide side margin for a small portrait. Text is brief and the visuals dominate.

Member Profile
Kathleen Wilmes Herring

Kathleen Wilmes Herring is a native of St. Louis. She earned a B.F.A. with honors from Washington University School of Fine Arts in St. Louis. She is married and lives in the District of Columbia.

Kathleen joined Soghigian and Macuga Advertising in 1985 as creative director/collateral. In 1986 she became a partner and creative director of Yankee Doodles, the design division of the agency. Prior to joining the firm, she was vice president, creative director at MDB Communications, Inc. and also spent four years with Walczy Brown Design, a division of the Earle Palmer Brown Companies, leaving there as vice president, designer.

Kathleen has been active in the design community in Washington, D.C. since 1973. She has won numerous awards for her design work both on a national and international level. These awards include Graphics, CA, Print, AIGA 50, and gold and silver awards from the New York Art Directors Club, Strathmore Paper Company and the Art Directors Club of Metropolitan Washington. She had a one-woman show of her work in St. Louis in 1986. In 1989 Kathleen was elected to the Board of AIGA/Washington.

Photo by Earl Zubkoff

Poster

DECEMBER

Westland Printers

Button

Banners

The Cafe

Logotype

Compactness is characteristic of all 24 pages and white space is used effectively to complement the graphic content.

Two large illustrations bleed into the gutter and visually tie the right-hand page to the opposite page.

Brevity, typical of this publication, is emphasized by an unusually narrow flush-left type
column. The content of the column supports the premise of
simplicity in typography.

**Tricky
Type**

**Pat
Taylor**

Is the type
readable?

Is the type
large enough?

Is the type
spaced in a
proper way?

Who cares?

We all should
care!

The best
typography is
easy to read,
comfortable to
the eyes;
therefore
it's not noticed.

In my opinion,
the following
pages illustrate
the power of
communication
and are highly
creative exercises
in typography
that work.

deəp

deəp

deəp

deəp

deəp

deep

deep

deep

deep

deep

deep

Gene Federico

Vaclav Kucera

break up

Otto Storch

Gerry Rosentswieg
HARP

MOTHER
CHILD

Herb Lubalin

Frances Ullenberg
Overcrowding.
Shortages.
Frances Ullenberg

tERRoRsm

Herb Lubalin

Gisela Cohrs

ALVIN AILEY

Steff Geissbuhler

Inspirational graphics are
featured with no
explanatory captions,
only credit lines. The
bottom right-hand
illustration bleeds into
the gutter and its top
edge aligns with the
left-hand rectangle for
a strong horizontal pattern.

Outstanding examples of typography from the writer's collection surround the text block
in a simple, orderly arrangement.

University of North Florida

TOP HONORS FOR ORIGINAL GRAPHICS

Designer
Carl Herrman
Mac Production
Fred Elliot
Publisher
UNF Office of Admissions
Jacksonville, FL
Text Type
ITC Garamond Book
Display Type
Garamond Book Condensed
Page Size
$8\frac{1}{2} \times 11$
Printing
Two Color with Duotones

A warm invitation to enroll at the University of North Florida is the theme of the lively newsletter, "Osprey." It is a recruitment publication and an exuberant promotion for the school. Eight times a year, it is mailed to high school juniors and seniors.

Director of Information Carl Herrman, who is its designer, also teaches design at the university. He has worked previously as an art director at *Newsday* and at Doubleday, Inc. It is easy to identify in these pages the influence of sound publication experience. There are live-wire editorial ideas and an ensemble of graphic features that fill the pages with youthful vitality.

Where do all these graphics come from? Some are produced by students who are paid as professionals. Some are created or collected by the designer. Another continuing source is a quality subscription clip-art service. Layout production is done on a Mac using the Quark XPress program. Text copy is generally written to fit the layout.

The designer has developed a special production technique that gives the pages a rich variety of color: Printing is done on a two-color press and the secret lies in choosing two ink colors that, combined in various screen tones, will result in a third color. For example, in this issue a deep blue—which is used for text—is combined with a light red. Overprinting these colors in different screen combinations produces a third color, a variation of purple. When a 100% value of one is printed over a 100% value of the other, the result is a deep eggplant color (used here on the logotype).

"Osprey" is edited and designed part-time by a small staff with high standards. Their efforts have been rewarded by a number of top awards.

OSPREY

UNIVERSITY OF NORTH FLORIDA   JACKSONVILLE, FLORIDA

YOU'RE NUMBER ONE!

Social Security Number? Student Number? It seems as the world gets busier, we become our SS#. Quite often we are statistics instead of students. At UNF people remain individuals. See, UNF is small, with an enrollment of about 9,300. This means classes are small, averaging about 30 students per class, so you don't get lost in the crowd. UNF cherishes the individual tastes of its students by offering something for everyone.

Sports are Alive at UNF

UNF has teams or clubs for a variety of sports. There are facilities available for playing tennis, racquetball, volleyball, soccer, basketball and baseball. The UNF gym is fully equipped with free weights, Nautilus equipment, stationary bikes, steppers and a treadmill. Throughout the year, daily aerobics classes also are available. All facilities and classes are offered free to UNF students and full-time faculty.

Sounds of Music

UNF's music building is filled with beautiful sounds throughout the day. Year-round concerts on campus present UNF's student performers, local bands and popular artists. However, if your appetite exceeds even UNF's diverse choices, Jacksonville clubs cater to all tastes. Clubs around town promise alternative, Top-40, jazz, blues or heavy metal. It's all here, provided by club DJs or local bands.

Fun with H$_2$O

UNF is only 11 miles from the sparkling Atlantic Ocean. School

A Newsletter for New Students / September 1992

Stand Out in the Crowd...

UNF will cater to your individual tastes. Read all about it.

Countdown to College...

Here are some helpful hints to help you plan your college career.

Coming Soon...

The Electrical Engineering Program and the Physical Therapy Program will debut at UNF this fall! UNF now offers 45 undergraduate and 24 master's level programs.

Designs for Study

The page grid is a uniform three columns. The typeface is ITC Garamond Book set 10/12, printed in deep blue. Lines of text type are set flush left and there is *no* hyphenation. The result is clean, smooth, and easy to read text.

Titles composed in Garamond Book Condensed have a classic, noncommercial look. The larger headlines and the vertical hairlines are printed in red. Paper stock is ivory.

A no-nonsense column of dates is punctuated graphically at the bottom by an amusing playing card drawing printed in red. The vertical band at right is printed in combination screens of red and blue.

The Trials and Tribulations of Ozzie Freshman:
The First Day of Classes

stress is easily released with a day of surfing and sunbathing. The St. John's River, Jacksonville's lifeline, provides a premium playground for water-skiing, swimming and sailing. And right here on campus, UNF's Aquatic Center offers a relaxing environment for swimming, exercising and water sports.

On-campus clubs

Whatever your hobby, sport, or favorite academic pursuit, UNF has a club for you. If you like to write, the Writers' Guild will provide you a sounding board for your prose. For those with interests a little out of the mainstream, UNF has clubs for jugglers, lacrosse players and karate enthusiasts. For adventure lovers, UNF offers the Rapid-Transit Club, which engages regularly in white-water rafting and canoeing. Plus, there are a variety of special interest groups, such as the Sawmill Slough Conservation Club.

The Art of UNF

The University Gallery presents a variety of exhibits throughout the year, including the Annual Juried Student Art Show, a faculty show, and exhibitions and lectures by local and national artists.

Nature is Everywhere

In the courtyard, he sits quietly eating his Reeses peanut butter cup. The squirrel watches with interest for a moment and then proceeds to crawl closer and closer waiting for a chocolate treat. Nature lovers are in heaven at UNF. Squirrels, armadillos, foxes, rabbits and the rarely seen deer keep the surrounding area alive with activity. UNF harbors miles of marked trails and 10 beautiful lakes.

The diversity is what makes UNF so special. There is something for everyone. At UNF, you aren't just a SS#, you're a person with thoughts, opinions and dreams.

—*By Kristina Kuehler, a junior majoring in communications*

"Well, what's your name, son?"
"Ozzie Freshman, sir." Did my voice just go up an octave? Now I'm a late freshman who sounds like Michael Jackson.
"Take a seat, Ozzie."
And the only seats left are right up front. I am the most unlucky person that has ever entered college.
"Pass these down, please."
Oof, these are heavy. "Is this the book?"
He's laughing at me. "No, this is the syllabus."
It's going to be a long semester.
"When you acquire a text, begin with the first assignment. Look over the syllabus and we'll discuss any questions Wednesday at the beginning of class. Today we'll cut it short. Thank you."
Can we go? Already? Cool.
"Hey Ozzie...Ozzie..."
Someone is calling me. I can't believe it, it's her, Kim, calling me. Thank you...Thank you.
"Hi."
"Isn't the first day great. You get out of all your classes after about 20 minutes."
"Yeah, cool, huh."
"A few of us are going to the Boathouse for lunch. It's the campus restaurant. Um, the food's really good and, uh, well, would you like to go with us?"
I can't believe it. She's nervous.
"Yeah, sure, that sounds great. I'm starved. I skipped breakfast because I was late to class."
She's smiling at me. She's walking with me, talking with me. YES! Oh, things are really looking up.

—*By Kristina Kuehler*

"Oh, NO! I'm in the wrong room. Can I just sit here? Do I get up and look REAL stupid? Oh, everyone is staring. Stop, don't look at the dumb freshman. I'm almost to the door...salvation. I feel like such a moron.*
Oh, boy, now I'm really late. Why did I ever decide to go to college? Geez, this campus is big. Education building? No, um, sciences. Well, shoot, where is the computer building?
"Hey, you lost? You look sorta confused," she asks.
"Um," *She's cute, say something.* "Uh, I'm looking for Computing Sciences and Engineering."
She's really cute. Geez, why can't I say something witty? Do you think she can she tell my underwear is pink because I'm doing my own laundry?
"Come on, I'll show you. I'm Kim..."
"I'm Ozzie." *Brilliant conversationalist here, HELP.*
"Well, nice to meet you, Ozzie. That's the computer building, what class are you taking?"
"Uh, Freshman Core I..." *Great, just tattoo it on my forehead, Freshman.*
"Don't worry, it'll get easier to find your way around. I've been here all summer, you'll like it."
I will if I can see you again. So speak, you fool.
"Um, thanks for your help."
"No problem, see you around."
Wait, don't leave me! I don't know anyone here.
"Room 1303, great, found it."
"Thanks for joining us. Your name?" *the professor is asking someone.*
What, me? Is he talking to me?

"This is Organic Chemistry 101. Is everyone in the right place?" the professor announced.

Ozzie Freshman takes a break. (By the way, "Ozzie the Osprey" is UNF's mascot.)

SO YOU'RE GOING TO COLLEGE...

September is here. Your acceptance letter and housing assignment are in hand, but one question lurks in your mind: *What can I expect as a college freshman?* At the University of North Florida, we want your transition between high school and college to be smooth, with as few surprises as possible.

Five Colleges to Choose From

UNF has five colleges—the College of Arts and Sciences, the College of Business Administration, the College of Computing Sciences and Engineering, the College of Education and Human Services and the College of Health. You will spend most of your freshman and sophomore years in the College of Arts and Sciences because your required core, or general education, classes are in this college.

A Solid Foundation

The College of Arts and Sciences provides the University's liberal arts base. This college offers the widest array of subject areas—graphic and fine arts, natural, political and social sciences; economics; history; communications; literature; mathematics and foreign languages.

UNF's required classes will give you an education with breadth as well as depth. Dr. David Courtwright, chairman of the Department of History, Philosophy and Religious Studies, says students who are liberally educated find it much easier to change career directions than do students who concentrate on one subject area.

A+ Academic Advising

Most freshmen are undecided about their majors. That's perfectly normal. UNF's advising program helps students choose a major. Our advisers are full-time professionals, and our program won two national awards for "excellence in advising."

The process starts at the freshman level when every student is assigned to an adviser, given a personalized program of study and provided with one-on-one counseling. Follow-up advising is required each semester, and then the process continues with advisers in the college of your chosen major.

Popular Areas of Study

Eventually everyone will decide on a major, and UNF makes it easy with a wide range of choices. The most popular choices among National Merit Scholars who applied to UNF are medicine, law, communications, business, computer science and political science.

Medicine and law are two of UNF's pre-professional programs. Aspiring physicians can complete pre-med studies at UNF as biology majors. According to Dr. Darwin Coy of the Department of Natural Sciences, "Students who finish our program have a very good success rate (at least 75 percent) of admittance to medical school."

UNF offers a variety of majors that serve as pre-law programs. "Our students have gone on to successful careers in medicine, veterinary science, dentistry, optometry, pharmacy and law," says Arva Leath-Sufi, coordinator of academic advising.

UNF also has strong programs in many other areas, including business, computer and information sciences and engineering. For those interested in communication, a rapidly growing field, programs in advertising, public relations, journalism and broadcasting are available.

—*By Elena Campbell, who graduated in 1992 with a BA in communications*

Dates to Remember...

The UNF admissions staff will be visiting high schools and community colleges on these dates:

September 21
H.B. Plant High School, Tampa

September 22
Land O' Lakes High School, Land O' Lakes

September 23
Zephyrhills High School, Zephyrhills
Chamberlain High School, Tampa

September 24
Jesuit High School, Tampa

September 29
Edison Community College, Ft. Myers

September 30
Bishop Verot High School, Tampa
Collier County public schools, Ft. Myers
Collier County public schools, Naples

October 2
National Merit/Achievement Semifinalists Dinner at UNF

October 3
Alpha Kappa Alpha Meeting, Orlando

October 12
Volusia County Schools, Deland

October 13
Valencia Community College, West Campus, Orlando

October 14
Seminole Community College, Sanford

The UNF mascot, "Ozzie the Osprey," is photographed by the newsletter's editor, Sandra Reid—an indication of the editor's involvement in visual media.

Silhouettes are a strong graphic device. This symbol of sailing was conceived to integrate neatly with the title. The type is blue, the drawing is an overprinting of red and blue that appears almost black.

A column about the city of Jacksonville, as described by the Chamber of Commerce, opens with a strong red title, tied into a vintage line engraving with a blazing red sunset.

The Zen of Sailing

Odysseus. Bligh. Blackbeard. Columbus. Porter, Pearson and Purser. Sailors all.

What is it about sailing that fuels a passion in men and women strong enough to leave hearth and home (if only for an afternoon sojourn on the St. Johns River)?

The editors of *Osprey* conducted a survey to find out. Fortunately, a few sailors were right here on campus.

The sailors—Nils Pearson, a senior majoring in computer science; Becky Purser, UNF recreation director; and Dave Porter, associate professor of graphic design and photography—are all members of the UNF Sailing Club.

What attracts them to the sport? Sailing is a "type of Zen experience," says Nils, who has been sailing a mere year and a-half, yet races in local regattas and last year was elected UNF's Sailing Club commodore (president).

"The boat becomes an extension of your body. You are one with the boat. It takes all your concentration, yet it is effortless," Nils explains.

With 25 years of sailing experience, Dave is a true "salty dog" (seaman's jargon for "seasoned sailor"). "To me, sailing is an escape. To be out on the ocean with balmy breezes and no telephone—there I'm captain of my own world," says Dave, who is also the club's faculty adviser.

Becky, one of the more experienced club sailors, says, "Sailing is a fascinating sport. You learn something new every time you go out on a boat." She didn't know how to sail until she came to UNF six years ago and learned on the *Lasers* with other club members.

The club—with a membership of about 50 sailing *aficionados*—owns six *Lasers*, 13-foot, one-person boats; one *Laser II*, a two-person boat; and three sailboards. The boats are kept in a boathouse on the grounds of the Bolles School, a private school on the east shore of the St. Johns River, about 12 miles from campus.

Because of UNF's location—midway between the Atlantic Ocean and the St. Johns River—sailors on campus are ideally situated to enjoy the pleasures of off-shore and river sailing. The St. Johns River bounds approximately 60 miles of milewide navigable waters between Jacksonville and Palatka to the south.

"Breezes are constant, and the waters are sheltered, creating an almost ideal situation for sailing," according to Dave. Year 'round Sunday races, annual regattas and traditional trips to such points north as Cumberland Island are sponsored by local sailing clubs and yachting associations. Off-shore ocean sailing is best appreciated during the milder summer months.

"The club provides an excellent opportunity to learn how to sail," says Becky. "We provide the instructor and—through funding from the Student Government Association—the equipment."

Throughout the year, club members conduct sailing clinics to teach one another how to sail. Intraclub regattas add a competitive edge to club camaraderie.

"The focus of the club is to teach sailing, but we have contacts in the Jacksonville sailing community for the more advanced students who want to race on big boats," says Nils.

Each spring the club takes a "safe-break" spring trip. In the past, students, faculty and alumni have traveled to the Dry Tortugas, the Florida Keys and Captiva and Sanibel Islands off the west coast of Florida.

During the four years he has captained boats for spring break trips, Dave says, "We have never had bad weather, no serious problems, no injuries. We sail along rather comfortably. There's an opportunity for everyone to snorkel and scuba dive, too."

"The sailing club has been a UNF institution for almost 18 years," says Becky, who will captain a boat this March on the spring trip along with fellow club member and big-boat racer Pete Silva, a senior majoring in mathematics and former club commodore.

By the way, Becky owns a boat. It's a 25-foot *Venture*, which she bought from Dave, which he bought from Jack, which has been to the Keys and back with Ray and Dave... [It's a long story—just the type sailors love to swap!]

The UNF Sailing Club is one of more than 40 clubs, organizations, academic honoraries and social clubs at UNF. Among them are the French Club, Sawmill Slough (a conservation club), the Maclab (for Macintosh users), the Potters Guild, Phi Theta Kappa (academic honorary), the Institute of Electrical and Electronics Engineers, the Inkwell Club, the Baptist Student Union, the Surf Club and seven national fraternities and sororities.

By Sandra Reid

Did You Know. . .?

UNF mathematics associate professor Dr. Faiz Al-Rubaee was named Florida's Professor of the Year by the national Council for Advancement and Support of Education (CASE).

UNF music professor Bunky Green received five stars from *Down Beat* magazine for his album "Healing the Pain."

Special education student Vicki Chappell was elected president of the UNF chapter of the Council for Exceptional Children.

Former student J.B. Scott was named leader of the famed Dukes of Dixieland Jazz Band in New Orleans, La.

Visual arts student Christopher Walsh was selected as a Rising Senior in a statewide program honoring outstanding student visual artists.

Seven African-American graduate students received from $2,500 to $5,000 each for the Delores A. Auzenne Fellowship for Graduate Study for the 1990-91 academic year.

61 percent of UNF's 17,000 alumni reside in Florida.

UNF's faculty members now number 283, 85 percent of whom hold terminal degrees in the disciplines in which they teach.

56 UNF students were named to *Who's Who Among Students in American Universities and Colleges*. They will join an elite group of students from more than 1,400 national institutions of higher learning. *Who's Who* nominations are based on academic achievement, community service, leadership potential and extracurricular activities.

Library Director Andrew Farkas co-authored and published the book *Enrico Caruso: My Father and My Family*.

Jacksonville, Florida's City of Tomorrow

The Jacksonville story began with the earliest settlers in the Jacksonville area, the Timiqua Indians. The first European settlers, the French Huguenots, arrived in North America on the banks of the St. Johns River in 1564. It was here they established a colony known as Fort Caroline. It still exists today as a national park.

The colony was destroyed in 1565 when Spanish forces, led by Pedro Menendez de Aviles, captured and destroyed the colonists. Following that first massacre, many Europeans and North Americans clashed for control of the land.

On June 15, 1822, the town of Jacksonville was established when the residents of what was then known as Cowford petitioned Secretary of State John Quincy Adams to make Jacksonville a port of entry. Jacksonville was named in honor of Major General Jackson. Duval County was created the same year and was named after Florida's first governor, William P. Duval.

Today, Jacksonville has a population of more than 686,340, a median age of 31 and its growth projections show it as Florida's City of Tomorrow. Its strong business base, increasing importance as a corporate center, vibrant transportation industries, growing military community and widening recognition as a sports and leisure capital have combined to create the critical mass for growth.

Source: Jacksonville Chamber of Commerce

A seascape is printed in dark blue ink. The sky fades off skillfully into the text area. Visually, this is altogether a well-conceived, single-page feature.

Two columns of miscellany, heavy on graphics, light on copy, is an eye-catching feature. Illustrations are a mixture of clip art and the designer's collection of old engravings.

143

**International Business
Machines Corporation**

HIGH-ENERGY GRAPHICS

Designer
Beth Singer
Design Communication Inc.
Washington, DC
Assistant Designer
Joanne Zamore
Publisher
IBM Federal Systems Division
Bethesda, MD
Text Type
ITC Garamond
Display Type
Differs with each feature
Page Size
$8\frac{1}{2} \times 11$
Printing
Three Color

Outstanding corporate newsletters come and go. Their days are sometimes numbered not because of their quality but because corporate policies and objectives change over a period of time. IBM publications have long been noted for their superior design and editorial standards. Beginning decades ago with the famous in-house magazine *Think,* the company has brought out a succession of fine publications.

In the 1950s the company appointed a brilliant New Canaan architect, Eliot Noyes, to assume design leadership. He attracted people like Paul Rand who helped achieve new heights of design excellence.

The *FSD Manager,* an award-winning newsletter/magazine, was aimed at company managers at various levels who were specifically involved in systems for the U.S. defense efforts.

Prominent Washington designer Beth Singer was called in to design and style the lively editorial content of this sophisticated publication. She developed pages with elegant typography and memorable illustrations. "The budget was modest, so we found ways to stretch dollars and still design 'FSD Manager' to rank among the best at IBM," said Ms. Singer.

Displayed on these pages are a few examples of the graphic content that define and should help inspire high standards. The cover illustration (opposite) by James Yang has the dash and vitality of a genuine pen-and-ink rendering. It is witty and at the same time powerfully suggests the sober theme of security. The logotype, based on Caslon, has dignity and strength.

International Business Machines Corporation

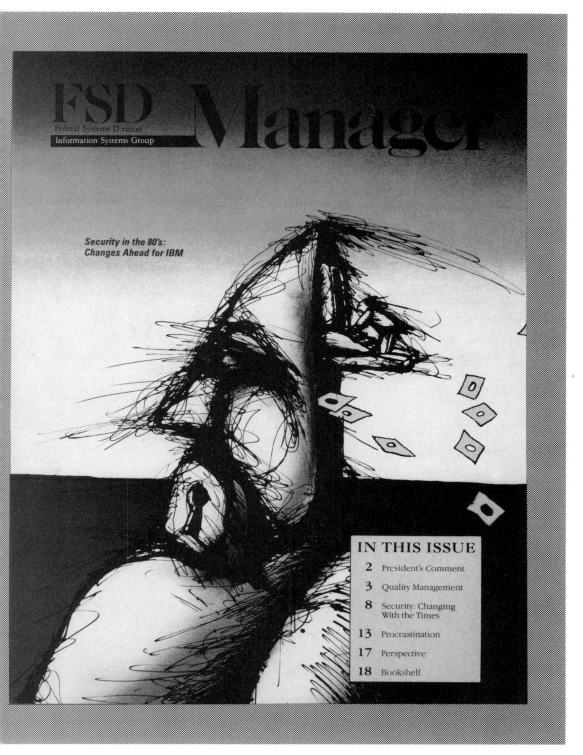

FSD
Federal Systems Division
Information Systems Group

Manager

Security in the 80's:
Changes Ahead for IBM

IN THIS ISSUE

Designs for Study

A conventional three-column page is made distinctive by illustrations that are creative in concept and execution. This pen-and-ink freehand rendering with gray washes projects strongly in a target position on the page. Title type, set in italics, is restrained but, surrounded by white space, conveys a sense of urgency.

An article begins with the three corporate initials set in Caslon to match the logotype. This occupies the position of a typical three-line initial and helps move the reader into the text.

The clean simplicity of this page is typical of the tasteful, understated layouts that follow. This newsletter won several awards within IBM and was featured in both the New York and Washington Art Directors shows.

Your Part in the Employee Appeal Process
Some Key Points to Keep in Mind

by Norman L. Koestline

IBM expects a great deal from its management team. We've never been ashamed to admit that our managers must demonstrate technical expertise, a commitment to quality, the ability to balance workload and adherence to schedules. And, they must always have a sensitivity to human resources and a steadfast dedication to respect the dignity and the rights of each person in the organization. "A nice balance between Peter Drucker and Albert Schweitzer, with just a touch of Thomas Edison's creative genius," an observer once remarked.

While we don't always achieve perfection in this pursuit, we do remarkably well. We strive to select management candidates who have the greatest potential for success, and we invest heavily in providing them the best training. And, we tell our employees to let us know when something isn't right.

The IBM employees' right of appeal—through the Open Door/appeal process—is critical to the continued success of IBM. Despite the fact that we approach the management job with an intent to succeed, things can go wrong. We need to know about employee problems, admit any mistakes and fix them quickly. This will insure our employees know that's how we

want to run the business.

FSD middle managers are receiving briefings to assist them in maintaining or improving the perceptions employees have about the Open Door/appeal process. In turn, they are being asked to coach their subordinate managers toward this end.

The emphasis is on the appeal process; how it can work better, and what can cause it to fail. Most important, we want to improve employee perceptions about the process through positive management actions. The following summarizes some of the key points that apply to all levels of management.

First, we challenge managers to assume the role of employee advo-

cate in the appeal process. Stated most simply, employees have the right to assume that if they appeal to management, the manager or investigator will represent their viewpoint objectively as they investigate the facts. Nothing else in the appeal process is more important, and nothing else is more difficult. This is particularly true if the manager to whom the appeal is being made is a second or third line manager in the same organization as the employee.

Think for a moment about the temptation to argue with the issue(s), with the employee, to become defensive, to disbelieve what he or she is telling you, to doubt the employee's motives, or to short circuit the investigative process because you "assume" certain "facts." Or, you may want to defend the management team, to look good to your management, to avoid impacting a business objective, and so on. Being an employee advocate isn't easy! But the simple fact remains that advocacy is critical to our role in handling appeals. If we fail to maintain that posture, employees will perceive that management is defending management and the process is a sham. Your ultimate decision should be a balanced one, based on the facts—but advocacy must be your starting point.

Illustrations by Marsha Leukerman

146

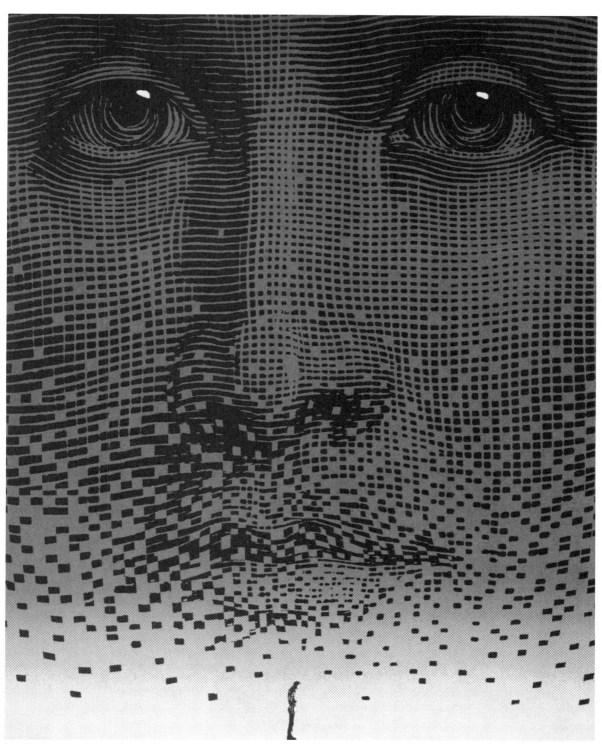

Look closely and you will see a tiny, cowering figure contrasted before the giant image. This dynamic page is the central visual element in an article on stress. The powerful symbolism of the page results from the extreme enlargement of a fine, traditional steel engraving similar to the portraits on U.S. currency. The simple technique of blowing up a minutely detailed image many times larger creates an illustration with a totally new look.

Lotus Development Corporation

SUBTLE TYPOGRAPHY HANDLED SKILLFULLY

Design Director
Ronn Campisi
Designer
Kimberly Wedlake
Publisher
Lotus Development Corp.
Cambridge, MA
Text Type
Caslon
Display Type
Differs with each feature
Page Size
$4\frac{1}{4} \times 10\frac{1}{2}$
Printing
Two Color

Not quite pocket-size—but almost—this is a breezy, youthful employee newsletter for a youthful company. Circulated from the home base in Cambridge, MA, it not only reaches staff members as far away as 10,520 miles in Melbourne, Australia, it also pulls in the news from Lotus locations throughout the world. It's one among a very few newsletters that has an international correspondent on its masthead.

The single text column starts out unabashedly on the front cover where it grabs your attention with 20-point type that subtly slides down to 16, then 14, then 11, and finally 10 point before it continues overleaf onto page 2. From that point, the text moves ahead breathlessly page by page with diverting sketches in the wide outer margins and some active black-and-white photographs. Even the portraits look unposed and alive.

The typography is strong and distinctive. Secondary heads set in a script, Typo Upright, add a welcome touch of ornamentation. The size of type throughout is never large but it is handled so skillfully that it keeps you moving with it. The designer was furnished text copy on disks preceding design. Copy fitting was fairly simple because the layout plan is uncomplicated and practical.

At first glance, this publication may not look exceptional. But look closely. Its unique design and detailing make it one of a kind and it is well worth close study.

Editorial and writing was handled by the publications office at Lotus and each issue was designed and produced out of house by Ronn Campisi Design.

Lotus
Notice

· ·

1991

Riding the Ups and Downs

· · · · · · · · · · · ·

1991 was a year full of ups and downs. Expectations were high for new products, company acquisitions and for a general uplifting of Lotus's stature in the marketplace. Sales rose to record highs worldwide and programs such as diversity shone as examples of Lotus's commitment to employees. 1-2-3 for Windows, greeted by mixed reviews, entered the market as the company began to face tough economic realities. As pressure on Lotus's bottom line increased, the com-

· · · · · · · · · · · · ·
DECEMBER 1991-JANUARY 1992

A handy size and shape, easy to read "on the run," the format is a unique departure from traditional newsletters.

Photos occupy one-column positions or smaller insets on the outer edges of pages. Flush-left captions, set in condensed sans-serif type, are leaded to the maximum for easy readability. Captions are printed in dark red.

At least one picture for each news item is the editorial/design style. Expressive photos result from explicit instructions to offices far afield to submit candid and casual photos of people in their work environments.

Bold-faced folio, publication name, and date are centered for a subtle typographic detail. A simple system of hairline rules run vertical at the side margins.

Robert Weston (Sales/New Orleans) with receptionist and juggler Kathleen O'Donnell. His customers trust him from Day One.

has always asked us to really know the products and use them in our daily lives before Cambridge said it was necessary. I use them all."

Rudolf says Weston knows his customers equally well. "They trust him from Day One. When he gets up in front of 300 people, it's real. He's sort of the Gary Cooper of sales. When he complained that the demos from Cambridge felt artificial, I said, 'Just show them how you use the products in your daily life.' Now, when he demos Agenda, he picks out a name from the audience that's already in his program. Even the resellers trust him, and they don't usually trust people on this side of the desk."

International

La Voix Chantante

. . . .

MARIE-JOSE BIDAUT, RECEPTIONIST, France, is gifted with what the French call

Marie-Jose Bidaut (Lotus France). Knowing how to calm les clients mécontents.

"la voix chantante" (English translation: a singing voice) and she knows how to use it to calm unhappy customers. Says Bidaut: "Customers call the office when they are unable to get through to the [customer support] hotline, and they may not be very happy with Lotus. I'm the first person that they reach. I just try to stay calm. I think they can sense that I'm a laughing, smiling person and most of the time they calm down. Sometimes, the problem is something they can fix by looking at their manuals. Most of the time it's something simple."

When she's not on the Lotus switchboard, Bidaut is busy registering incoming invoices, checks and orders, greeting visitors, arranging meetings and dispatching copies of documentation to customers.

Bidaut says July was the toughest part of the year for her. She was manning the front desk during her usual morning stint, and filling in for the afternoon receptionist, who was on holiday. "Much of the hotline staff was also on holiday," she recalls. "But the customers were apparently not on holiday."

Fortunately for Bidaut and for Lotus customers in France, dramatic increases in call volume to the hotline have highlighted the need to add customer support staff. Lotus France recently hired five new specialists for the hotline and the ever-sunny Bidaut is beaming.

Flat Chat in Australia

. . . .

FOR LOTUS'S CUSTOMER SERVICE team in Australia, the year has been "flat chat," says Jim Quilty, supervisor. "Now that we are a buy-sell subsidiary, allowing us to sell new releases and upgrades directly, we are very, very busy on the phones," he explains.

Jim Quilty (Lotus Australia). Customer Service sells directly to customers now.

This year, Lotus Australia's four customer service reps handled an average of 1,100 inbound calls per week and sold more than 2,000 upgrades and cross-grades in October alone. All this despite the troubled Australian economy, now in a deep recession. "Right now we're getting a lot of praise for the work we've been doing," Quilty says. "When you consider that Microsoft's sales force outnumbers ours four-to-one, that means Customer Service plays a bigger role."

Quilty attributes a lot of the customer interest to two recent promotions, Double Up and the Great Lotus Offer, as well as the Art of Business show that brought the "full suite" to Sydney, Melbourne, Canberra, Brisbane and New Zealand.

"There's a huge interest in 1-2-3 for Windows and the Double Up is excellent for seeding Ami Pro," says Quilty, adding that he believes Ami Pro will rival WordPerfect and Microsoft Word over the next 16 to 18 months.

Placement of pictorial matter prevents long text columns from appearing formidable on pages that are a tall $4\frac{1}{4} \times 10\frac{1}{2}$.

So while Primero may not have all the functionality that Lotus's corporate spreadsheet users demand, it does have the features that home users are seeking. Tim Daly, product planning manager, Paris, and a development team in Dublin headed by Alan Barrett, helped see to that. Says Barrett, "What makes Primero especially easy to use is the WYSI-WYG environment. The graphical interface has users up and running straight away."

Tim Daly (Product Planning/Paris). The templates are the essence of Primero.

And what makes Primero truly unique is the set of templates included in the package, says Daly. "The templates are really the essence of the product. We took them to the ex-president of the Spanish Small Business Association, and with his help we came up with a product specially designed for the market," he says.

BIG BLUE BUNDLING DEAL NEEDED A NUDGE

Apparently Lotus is not the only one who thinks Primero hits its mark. Big Blue does too. IBM has agreed to bundle Primero with their hardware offering for the domestic market in Spain, the PS/1, making an initial order of 6,000 units, to be followed quickly by 5,000 more. And IBM made that decision despite the fact that they already bundle Microsoft Works, which comes complete with its own spreadsheet, with the PS/1.

But according to Fieger, the deal with IBM was not always a given. Early on in the negotiations, the deal nearly fell through precisely because of IBM's prior agreement with Microsoft. "Although they liked and wanted Primero from the start, IBM stalled on the deal, citing 'internal practices' that prohibited them from putting a second spreadsheet on the PS/1." he says.

Thanks to a nudge from Jim Manzi, IBM headquarters finally gave its okay and the bundling deal was signed. "It was fantastic to see how we elevated the issue up through Lotus and we were able to revive what we thought was dead," Fieger says. "I think Primero is a great example of working together to meet our objectives."

As Lotus's first truly European product — built from the ground up for Spain — Primero has a bright future. "We can deliver Primero in many different flavors, simply by changing the templates to serve a specific market niche," says Daly.

Inset photos are never allowed to interfere with the easy, readable flow of words. This avoids erratic word or letterspacing.

All photo illustrations are outlined with rules so that even those with pale backgrounds hold their rectangular shape.

DATELINES

MOSCOW — "Orders continued to come in from all cities — except for Moscow and Leningrad. It was pretty much business as usual," reports Jane Kitson, business development manager, USSR, referring to the aftermath of the failed Soviet Coup. "In fact, in August we took in more orders than in any other month thus far."

The Soviet Union still "hasn't finished falling apart," and the state-run software distributor is being "tossed back and forth between the union and federal levels," Kitson says. Yet Lotus continues to build a solid retail infrastructure, she points out. With more than 120 retailers, the distributor (VNIPI), and two sub-distributors, "there is no corner of the Soviet Union that doesn't now have a dealer. We've also recently signed on two new training centers in Kiev and Omsk, bringing the total number of training centers to six."

Kitson's own views on Soviet people in the post-coup environment: "I've never known them to be jubilant. But after the coup, they seemed genuinely glad to be alive and motivated to change, knowing they have a future. It's clear, though, that the situation is going to get a lot worse before it gets better."

KISTA — Meanwhile, across the Baltic Sea, Lotus marketers in Sweden have cooked up a little coup of their own. As the headquarters for Lotus Nordic, the Kista office is charged with developing and orchestrating marketing plans for Sweden, Norway, Denmark, Iceland and Finland. The team has created a contest to promote sales of the "Windows Suite" by retailers. According to Anders Broms and Per Lindholm of Nordic, they've lured more than 1,200 dealers into participating in the contest so far, with portable CD player giveaways and promises to send the top 100 salespeople to the 1992 Summer Olympics in Barcelona. The marketers have also created a "Windows Bag" for retailers, containing the full suite of Lotus products for Windows and marketing communications materials to help them sell the products. The bags are sold to retailers at a very tempting price, says Broms.

Anders Broms (Lotus Nordic)

Per Lindholm (Lotus Nordic)

Capped by a distinctively curved title, a special feature of overseas stories is accented top and bottom by double rules. Text type in sans serif emphasizes idea of news bulletins.

**Association Typographique
Internationale (ATypI)**

A DESIGN TO ATTRACT TYPE LOVERS

It's an awesome task to create a typographic newsletter that will please an audience of typophiles. Association Typographique Internationale, a prestigious organization of typographic professionals, holds periodic meetings in various countries. The newsletter "Type 90 Report" was the principle promotional item for a conference at Oxford, England. It was designed by conference Chairman Roger Black, a prominent U.S. designer. Interestingly, this was an example of a designer doing the writing and editing as well as the design.

The typographic style is classic Caslon—except for the huge "90" on the cover and some subheads in a sans-serif Grotesque. The pages are eye-catching and elegant. A smashing logo contrasts massive red numerals against delicate Caslon type elements. Also notable on the cover is the center column. Typematter is welded together with a handsome photo for a powerful vertical pattern.

The designer chose pale buff-colored, uncoated paper stock for easy readability of black text type. Halftones were printed strong and clear on a calendered surface. Rich red typographic accents were used throughout the pages as well as decorative rules and slender dash leaders (dotted lines). Typography is designed with sensitivity to subtle gradations of type sizes, leading, and letterspacing.

There is no question that this quality presentation was important in attracting a large attendance to this major conference at Oxford.

Designer/Editor
Roger Black
Publisher
Association Typographique Internationale
Switzerland
Text Type
Caslon Old Face
Display Type
Caslon Old Face
Grotesque
Page Size
$8\frac{1}{4} \times 11\frac{1}{2}$
Printing
Two Color

Type 90

REPORT

Nº 1 : APRIL 1990

An occasional review of events leading up to the international conference on type and design in Oxford, England, from August 31 to September 4. Sponsored by Association Typographique Internationale (ATypI).

Type90 is a world-class meeting of designers and graphic artists concerned with the future of type. During four days at the end of the summer in one of the most beautiful university towns in the world there will be:

500 Conferees
20 Speakers
50 Workshop
   Leaders
2 Typographic
   Playrooms
12 Type
   Design
   Exhibits
20 Exhibits of
   New Type
   Technology
And a Blizzard
   of Parties

O*xford, England, is a delightful site for a design conference. Type90 conferees can lodge at the historic college, Christ Church, a short walk to most events. Nearby is the Bodleian library and a wealth of bookstores and other attractions of a college town. To the west are the Cotswold hills. Oxford is less than an hour from London's Heathrow airport, and easily reached by train from Paddington station. [More on travel, accommodation– page 6]*

Late this summer Oxford will attract the world's leaders in typographic design

Traditionally the domain of publishers, type is rapidly becoming a tool used by everyone. We are at an important juncture. Type is leaping the old boundaries of the printing world and is coming into everyday life. A world conference, Type90 has been called this summer in Oxford to look at the issues from every possible angle–aesthetic to technical, legal to lighthearted.

[Continued next page]

All editorial pages are on a four-column grid. Flush-left setting is used throughout and results in uniform word spacing in the restricted character count caused by the narrow columns.

By the year 2000 everyone

Some of the Type90 Participants

John Aston
Colin Banks
Fernand Baudin
Ed Benguiat
John Benson
Harold A. Berliner
David Berlow
Roger Black
Ronn Campisi
Edward Booth Clibborn
Neville Brody
Matthew Carter
Nicole Croix
Ari Davidow
John Downer
Paul Hayden Duensing
John Dreyfus
Veronika Elsner
Louise Fili
Adrian Frutiger
Allan Haley
Steven Heller
Jonathan Hoefler
Cynthia Hollandsworth
Cleo Huggins
Peter Karow
David Kindersley,
Renee Le Winter
Jeff Level
Walter Jungkind
Masahiko Kozuka
Günter Gerhard Lange:
Zuzana Licko
Frans Lases
Jerry Lee
Lida Lopes Cardozo
Bruno Maag
John Miles
James Mosley
Stan Nelson
Robert Norton
Matthias Noordžij
Mike Parker
Jim Parkinson
Aurobind Patel
Fiona Ross
Robert Slimbach
Poul Søgren
Jack Stauffacher
Paula Scher
Erik Spiekermann
Sumner Stone
Tari Tamamoto
Ittai Tamari
Wesley Tanner
Kirti Trivedi
Carol Twombly
Petr van Blokland
Gerard Unger
Jim von Ehr
Susan Winman
Günter Zorn

Oxford is for Type Lovers

For four days starting August 31, 1990 an international panel of experts on type, design with type, and marketing type will assemble in Oxford—Type90.

The greatest type designers

Including Ed Benguiat, Matthew Carter, Adrian Frutiger, Günter Gerhard Lange, Sumner Stone, and Gerard Unger.

Leading graphic designers

Neville Brody, Zuzana Licko, Paula Scher, Franz Lasès, John Miles, Erik Spiekermann, Petr van Blokland and more.

Lida Lopes Cardozo

Typographic experts

To name a few: John Dreyfus, Peter Karow, Rene Kerfante, Mashiko Kozuka, James Mosley, and Michael Twyman.

In all, almost one hundred top typographers and designers have been invited to present their work, steer discussions, and demonstrate new and ancient techniques. Five hundred participants will have the opportunity to join these experts for four days of lectures, seminars, informal discussions and hands-on experience.

Type90 promises to be an unforgettable event, held at the crucial juncture in the history of type, design, and printing.

Here are the details:

Adrian Frutiger

The Program: Breadth and Depth

We have carefully designed a program that should respond to the needs

Town Hall, a picturesque Victorian in Oxford is the venue for registration and lectures.

2

PHOTOGRAPHS COURTESY PARTICIPANTS, YVONNE SCHWEMER-SCHEDDIN, AND BEATRIX HOFFMANN

TYPE90 REPORT NO. 1

A column of names is distinctively set in caps and small caps, sensitively set off by a delicate vertical dash rule. Bold-faced subheads contrast effectively against gray typematter.

Photos of conference speakers and a building facade combine to give the reader a glimpse of personalities and the conference environment, all in the sweep of an eye.

The editorial tone is breezy and conversational. The layout is an example of short bites of information that can be read and assimilated with ease.

Association Typographique Internationale

will have a favorite typeface

of anyone deeply involved in type design and publishing, but Type90 is not a series of dry lectures and quiet sherry receptions. There will be academics —and radicals. There *will* be designers working on the cutting edge of style—and classicists who challenge the assumption that the mainstream of Western printing design should be discarded.

Type90 is fast-paced, more complete than the landmark Type1987 conference TDC. At the core is a

GERARD UNGER

single-track program of presentations. But some speakers will make presentations no longer than five minutes. Over the three full days of lectures, the format will vary and the proceedings will be filled with lively give-and-take.

Some of the highlights include:

JOHN BENSON

The subtext of the conference is that type has leapt the bounds of the printed page.

JAMES MOSLEY

History and Post-History

The post-postmodernists Neville Brody and Zuzana Licko will show their forward-looking work, and John Dreyfus will examine the legacy of Charles Peignot (the greatest champion of typography in France this century who, with Dreyfus, founded ATypI).

Breaking the Rules

James Mosley will chronicle the colorful British display types of the nineteenth century—Ian

FRANS LASES

Mortimer's collection will be exhibited. The brilliant, young Dutch typographers, who are rallying under the slogan "Ban the Bezier" and creating "Times New Random." will be introduced by Petr van Bloklund (winner of ATypI's Peignot Prize).

Technology, Power, and Aesthetics

On the technical front, Type90 sponsors will demonstrate cutting-edge machinery and techniques—a private show not open to the public. BBC's Alan Jeeps and John Aston and Dutch television's Frans Lasès will demonstrate their innovative video work. (Lasès calls his lecture "The Good Morning Type Show.")

LIZ DALTON

It's a Small Type World

With the advent of new technology, non-Roman letterforms are easier to generate and manipulate. The potential impact on aesthet-

GÜNTER GERHARD LANGE

ten most distinguished British designers who use type and demonstrating why London has supplanted New York as the commercial typographic trendsetter.

Of Lettering Duels and Novelty Faces

Ed Benguiat has challenged a computer-based designer to a lettering duel, which we'll cover on video. Steven Heller of *The New York Times* will be leading an

ics and culture in general is staggering. Edward Booth-Clibborn is organizing a fast-paced, portfolio-based presentation highlighting the

ED BENGUIAT

informal encounter group on "Truly Disgusting Novelty Faces and How to Use Them."

Bruno Maag and Liz Dalton will present a multimedia installation of changing images and visual reflexes examining typographical readability.

The complete program is shown on the next pages.

3

Hairlines surround each photo and give a crisply uniform structure to the spread. Note the subtle letterspacing in the type at the foot of the page.

155

Nurses Service Organization

DESIGNED WITH FLAIR, EDITED WITH STYLE

Read by a nationwide audience of professional nurses, "NSO Risk Advisor" is an award-winning newsletter. Its pages are handsome and appropriately conservative since it has serious objectives: It provides 625,000 readers with information about personal liability risks in the field of nursing.

Every inch is designed and edited with style. The designer uses Quark XPress on a Mac with fine-tuned skills. These pages demonstrate the degree of quality possible when computer-aided design is in capable hands. The type content is composed with the reader in mind. Text, in three- and four-column grids, is inviting and readable, set in 10/12 Minion, an Adobe face with classical origins. Illustrations take their places with natural ease. For the most part they're decorative—a few are informational—and you can easily recognize their "custom designed" quality. Printing is on recycled offset stock.

The designer has used a clever production technique. The white paper is tinted overall with a 10% screen of PMS 128 to give it a pale ivory look. Using this printed tint, the designer can create white spaces by simply knocking out areas of the 10% screen to let the paper show through. This is used to highlight short items, charts, and surveys.

Designer Robert Perry has a background in magazine design. He describes the collaboration with the editor that makes this newsletter succeed visually: "Sometimes she will rewrite copy right on the Quark to make it fit—or, sometimes I modify the layout." This cooperative spirit has made these smartly-styled pages possible.

"NSO Risk Advisor" won a gold medal for design in the 1993 Newsletter Clearhouse competition, as well as a number of other national awards.

Designer
Robert J. Perry III
Publisher
Nurses Service Organization
Trevose, PA
Producer
Springhouse Corporation
Springhouse, PA
Text Type
Minion
Display Type
Poster Bodoni
Page Size
$8\frac{1}{4} \times 10\frac{1}{2}$
Printing
Three Color

NSO Risk Advisor, March 1993, ©1993 Aon Direct Group, Inc., Trevose, PA, and Springhouse Corporation, Springhouse, PA. Reprinted with permission of the publishers.

MARCH 1993

NSO RISK ADVISOR

A new educational benefit from Nurses Service Organization, providers of insurance to over 1 million nurses since 1976

HOW PROFESSIONAL LIABILITY INSURANCE PROTECTS YOU

"Like so many other nurses I know, I thought that lawsuits only happened to other people. But when a uniformed deputy rang my doorbell and handed over a 25-paragraph complaint against me, I was devastated. The first thing that caught my eye was a notice that I had the right to designate $4,000 worth of assets that could be taken to satisfy a settlement. The person suing me could take my car, jewelry, savings, and even a percentage of my future wages if he won this lawsuit...."
— Excerpt from a customer letter (J.G., Tennessee)

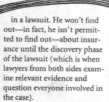

From time to time, we receive letters from policyholders who want to know whether they really need their professional liability insurance. Colleagues, nurse-managers, even hospital risk managers have told them that a separate policy is unnecessary because they're covered by their employer's policy.

Have you been hearing the same thing? Maybe you've even been thinking it yourself. Before deciding that you don't need your coverage, consider these facts:

• *Your employer's policy will cover you, but only to a point.* That policy is designed to fit the institution's needs and protect its interests, which won't always be the same as yours. In other words, the insurance carrier may well defend the institution more vigorously than it would defend you.

Also, your employer's policy covers your actions only when you're at work. So if you give advice to a neighbor after hours or volunteer to work at a community event, you'd be on your own—and that means you'd be solely responsible if you committed a negligent act and someone was harmed.

• *Contrary to what you've been told, having your own insurance doesn't make you a more likely target for a lawsuit.* But if you're sued for malpractice, it'll protect you financially by paying for your defense and any settlement or judgment against you (up to the limits of your policy). Your risk manager, though, may tell you that you're taking a bigger risk if you have insurance. But the patient's lawyer doesn't know whether or not you have your own professional liability insurance when he names you

in a lawsuit. He won't find out—in fact, he isn't permitted to find out—about insurance until the discovery phase of the lawsuit (which is when lawyers from both sides examine relevant evidence and question everyone involved in the case).

Another thing to consider: Access to the courts is one of our basic rights, so anyone can sue anyone else for any reason. Even if you've done nothing wrong, you still have to mount a defense against a malpractice lawsuit. That alone could cost thousands of dollars—but it won't cost you anything if you're covered by CNA's professional liability

insurance policy.

• *If your institution has to make a payment because of your negligent action, it could turn around and sue you.* This rarely happens—institutions can't afford to alienate nurses—but it *is* possible. If your institution sues you for malpractice, its policy certainly won't cover you. But CNA's policy would.

What happened to the customer who wrote to us? She called and talked with one of our claims representatives. Here's more of her letter:

"The claims representative told me to send the document to her by express mail; she would take care of the rest.

Within a week, someone from the Nashville office called and told me that a lawyer had been hired to represent me. My lawyer kept me informed of the progress of the lawsuit from discovery through settlement—a process of 11 months."

 Printed on recycled paper

Functionally elegant typography with headlines set in Poster Bodoni is the appropriate style and mood for the subject. Subheads on reverse panels strongly underscore the headlines and repeat the front cover style.

LEGAL TIPS & TIDBITS

Stay up-to-date and informed on safe practices, legal trends, and more.

BEWARE OF PATIENTS LOOKING FOR LITIGATION

Although not all unhappy patients sue their nurses, most who do give fair warning by:
• questioning everything
• complaining habitually
• overreacting to any perceived slight or negative comment, real or imagined
• openly expressing hostility to their nurses and other health care providers
• asking for the names of their nurses
• taking notes of discussions with doctors and nurses
• continually behaving in an uncooperative, combative, or noncompliant manner
• requesting their charts just before being discharged.

When you're assigned to a patient like this, you may be tempted to run the other way. But don't. Instead, be especially polite and professional when you care for him. Going the extra mile now could head off a lawsuit down the road.

If a patient or a family member just can't be satisfied, ask the hospital's risk manager to intervene. Patients are less likely to sue when their fears and complaints are acknowledged and dealt with promptly.

HOW TO BE A GOOD SAMARITAN WITHOUT RISKING A LAWSUIT

You aren't obligated to stop and assist at the scene of an accident or similar emergency (unless you live in Minnesota or Vermont, which have a duty-to-rescue law). But if you do stop, remember that you've established a nurse/patient relationship, so you must observe the nursing standard of care.

To reduce your malpractice risk, follow these guidelines:
• Care for the accident victim in the vehicle; move him only if he's in danger.
  • Keep his airway open.
  • Stop his bleeding.
  • Make sure he's warm.
  • Determine his level of consciousness.
  • Ask him where he's feeling pain.
  • Assess the possibility of fractures.
• Don't try to straighten the victim's arms or legs. And don't carry him unnecessarily or force him to walk.
• Don't speculate about who or what caused the accident.
• Stay with the victim at the accident scene until emergency medical technicians arrive to assume his care.
• Guard the victim's personal property. Release it only to the police or members of his family.

COUNTERSIGNING: WHAT DOES IT MEAN?

If you're an RN, you may sometimes have to countersign notes made by an LPN, LVN, or nursing assistant even if you haven't supervised those actions.

To protect yourself legally, find out what your hospital's policy manual says. Does the hospital interpret countersigning to mean that the LPN, LVN, or nursing assistant performed those nursing actions in your presence? If so, don't countersign unless you were there.

If your hospital acknowledges that you don't always have time to witness your coworkers' actions, then your countersignature implies that:
• the notes describe care that you know the LPN, LVN, or nursing assistant had the authority and competence to perform
• you've verified that all required patient-care procedures were actually carried out.

What if another nurse asks you to document her care or sign her notes for her? In a word, don't. Unless your hospital policy authorizes or requires you to witness someone else's notes, your signature will make you responsible for anything put in the notes above it. So you could be liable for an error in another nurse's care.

NSO RISK ADVISOR is intended to inform Nurses Service Organization customers of potential liability in their nursing practice. It reflects general principles only and shouldn't be regarded as legal advice. Readers should consult with a lawyer if they have specific concerns. Neither NSO nor NSO Risk Advisor assumes any liability for how this information is applied in practice or for the accuracy of this information.

NSO RISK ADVISOR is published three times a year by Aon Direct Group, Inc., formerly part of Rollins Burdick Hunter of Illinois, Inc. Headquarters are located at 4850 Street Rd., Trevose, PA 19049. Phone: (215) 953-4600. ©1992 by Aon Direct Group, Inc. All world rights reserved. Nurses Service Organization is a registered trade name of Aon Direct Group, Inc.

EDITORIAL INFORMATION: Send comments and questions c/o NSO Risk Advisor at 4850 Street Rd., Trevose, PA 19049. Due to space limitations, all editorial sources and references may not be listed, but they're available on request.

REPRINT INFORMATION: Quotes of up to 300 words are permitted with credit to NSO Risk Advisor, except for articles bearing the copyright of others. Photocopying of articles (up to 100 copies) is permitted only for educational use by hospitals, schools, and charities; proper credit to NSO Risk Advisor must appear on the first page. Other reproduction without written permission of the publisher is prohibited. For further information, contact: NSO Risk Advisor, 4850 Street Rd., Trevose, PA 19049.

ADVISORY BOARD
Mary M. Baker, RNC, MSS, FNP
President and CEO of a home nursing service and nursing practice, Sacramento, Calif.

Diana Brocheugelige, RN, MSN
Renal Clinical Specialist and Nursing Instructor, Abington, Pa.

Gail DeMarco, RN, MSN
Associate Director, Nursing Practice and Services Program, New York State Nurses Association, Guilderland, N.Y.

Terry Douglas, RN, ARNP, MN, EdD
Pediatric Nurse Practitioner (private practice) and Health Services Administrator, Washington State DSHS, Spokane, Wash.

Anne Helm, RN, MS, JD
Associate Professor, Health Law, Portland, Ore.

Esther Sangster, RN, MSN, ARNP
Director of Education, Tampa, Fla.

MEET NSO REPRESENTATIVES

You can meet some of the faces behind the Nurses Service Organization (NSO)—and receive a free gift—at the following conventions:
• November 1 to 3, 1992, AJN Conference on Medical-Surgical and Geriatric Nursing, Philadelphia
• April 11 to 18, 1993, National Student Nurses' Association Convention, Kansas City, Mo.
• May 12 to 15, 1993, Oncology Nursing Society Convention, Orlando, Fla.

Editor: Susan Doan-Johnson
Designer: Robert I. Perry III
Copy Editors: Karen Brodbak Barlow, Lori Cramer

LESSONS FROM COURT

Avoid charges of negligence by reviewing these nurses' errors.

MISSING SPONGE
Can a doctor rely on the nurses' sponge count?

Two nurses who were assisting a surgeon told him that the sponge count was correct. So he sutured the surgical wound and sent the patient to the postanesthesia care unit.

Later, he couldn't recall whether he'd removed one of the sponges. He questioned the nurses, who told him they'd counted the sponge while it was in the patient's body. And it was still there, an X-ray revealed. The patient

sued the surgeon and hospital. The court held the surgeon liable. (The hospital had admitted its nurses' negligence and settled out of court.) The surgeon appealed.

The appeals court reversed the lower court's decision for two reasons:
• The nurses were responsible for counting the sponges. The surgeon had relied on their assertion that the count was correct.
• The surgeon didn't control the nurses' actions because they worked for the hospital and followed its written procedure for counting sponges.

RESTRAINT ISSUE
Did this patient wiggle out of a vest restraint...or did the nurse apply it incorrectly?

A nurse discovered her elderly, senile, postoperative patient trying to get out of bed. The patient was in a vest restraint. She settled the patient in bed, checked the restraint, then went on a break. Before leaving, she asked another nurse to look in on the patient.

The second nurse heard a call for help from the patient's room. She found the patient on the floor. With the help of two other nurses, she returned the patient to bed and reapplied the vest restraint.

The patient, who sustained a fractured left hip, sued the hospital for negligence. However, at the trial she didn't remember the fall. So she couldn't explain what had happened.

The location of the vest restraint then became the issue. The second nurse said it was still properly tied to the bed when she discovered the patient. (That fact wasn't in her notes though.) If so, the patient had somehow slipped out of it.

But the doctor's note said that the patient was wearing the restraint when she was found. In that case, the restraint would have been improperly applied.

The jury returned a verdict in favor of the hospital. The patient appealed.

Citation: Van Iheek v. Anderson, 824 P. 2d 509 (Washington, 1992).

So he wasn't liable for their error.

Citation: Kime v. Tallahassee Memorial Regional Medical Center, 579 So. 2d 701 (Florida, 1991).

MONITORING PROBLEM
Did these nurses give less than the standard of care?

A nurse was having trouble activating a child's apnea monitor. Although the child was breathing, the monitor's alarm would sound each time the nurse attached the electrodes to his chest. Finally, she used larger electrodes and the monitor began to work properly.

The child's mother was staying at the hospital with him. At about 4:20

a.m., she discovered that he'd stopped breathing and was cyanotic. The lead wires to the alarm, she said, were still attached. The mother contended that the alarms never sounded because the nurse who'd checked the child at 4 a.m. had forgotten to turn them back on. The nurse said she'd turned them off when she responded to the mother's call for help.

Nurses on the unit had difficulty resuscitating the child because the code cart was improperly equipped (for example, it contained adult laryngoscope blades and defibrillation pads). Eventually, the nurses obtained most of what they needed and improvised the rest.

Although the child was intubated and his heart began beating again, he died 4 days later. His parents sued the hospital.

The admitting doctor stated in an affidavit that nothing the staff did or didn't do caused the patient's death. But the plaintiffs' expert witness disagreed. Specifically, he claimed that
• the child's nurse took too long to connect the monitor, indicating that she wasn't properly prepared to use it.
• the monitor didn't sound when the child experienced an apneic event, indicating that the staff operated it negligently.
  • the code cart was inadequately and improperly equipped, delaying resuscitation and causing the severe and permanent damage that led to the child's death.

The trial judge granted the hospital's motion for summary judgment, meaning that he felt there wasn't enough evidence to try the case. The appeals court, however, has reversed this decision. The trial hasn't taken place yet.

Citation: Estate of et al. v. Memorial Hospital of Adel, Inc., 408 S.E. 2d 473 (Georgia, 1991).

Two companion pages with brief text items have parallel layouts. The masthead and tabular matter occupy a full column with subdued simplicity.

A page of court cases avoids a look of blandness with two small but graphically strong illustrations. White space on these informational pages is confined to the top area.

A bold six-line drop initial commands attention and invites the reader into this feature story. Without this device, this heavy text area would lack articulation.

The designer conceived this layout design as a spread in typical magazine fashion. The center position in an eight-page publication, type and illustration are not affected by the gutter area.

THE LEGAL BURDEN OF QUESTIONABLE DRUG ORDERS

Feeling the heavy responsibility of unclear drug orders? Here's some advice to help you decide when to call the doctor for clarification.

You've heard or participated in countless discussions about illegible or confusing drug orders. They've probably gone something like this:

"I can never read Dr. Jessup's orders," one nurse complains to you. "Look at this. Does he mean *4 mg/day* of Stelazine P.O. or *40 mg/day?* He must mean 4 mg."

You look at the order. "I don't know. You'd better ask," you say. "Forty milligrams does sound like too much."

"I know," your colleague says. "But I hate to call him. He's always so irritable."

Obviously, an irritable doctor isn't reason enough to take a chance with an illegible or confusing drug order. Common sense tells you to question orders you don't understand—no matter what reaction you expect from the doctor. The courts have confirmed this point in several rulings.

Still, acting on common sense may be easier said than done. So here's some advice for dealing with questionable orders from doctors—and with difficult doctors.

"It's not a mistake."

Suppose you're the nurse who's faced with the unclear Stelazine (trifluoperazine HCl) order. You look up the drug in your unit's drug reference book and discover that the usual dose for a nonpsychotic patient who's anxious (which is the case with your patient) is 4 mg/day. Now what?

The doctor could have meant to order 40 mg/day, even though that seems excessive for this patient. But *assuming* either dose is the correct one invites liability if the patient is injured. Remember, the law protects you only when you follow orders that a reasonably prudent nurse would follow.

So you have to call the doctor, no matter how unpleasant he may be. You've got the facts in hand—that's one point in your favor. Another is common courtesy. Be professional and call at a reasonable time (if waiting won't harm your patient).

BY CAROLYN L.G. LANGDON, BSN, JD
Des Moines, Iowa

4 NSO RISK ADVISOR

When you call the prescribing doctor, ask him if he meant 40 or 4 mg, and tell him what the recommended dosage is for a nonpsychotic, anxious patient. He may tell you that he meant 40 mg after all—and why.

But if his explanation isn't convincing, consider how important your difference of opinion is. If the variation were small and wouldn't harm the patient, pursuing the matter probably wouldn't be in anyone's best interest. But a dose that's 10 times higher than *usual is* worth pursuing.

What if you don't call the doctor and decide to give a smaller dose—in the range mentioned in your drug reference book? That's the path to legal liability and chaos. Legally, you can't decide to give less than the doctor ordered—that would amount to prescribing. Also, patient care would be inconsistent from one shift to the next, and doctors would be unable to assume that their orders were being followed.

The best alternative is to tell the prescribing doctor that you can't give the medication and why. (Don't just ignore the order—that's legally risky too.) If you think the order is too dangerous for anyone to follow, consult with the pharmacist and your nurse-manager. They'll probably work through channels to clarify the order.

Above all, don't follow an order if you're convinced it's inappropriate. *You're* responsible for your actions, not the prescribing doctor.

What if the doctor isn't available?

What do you do at night or on weekends when the doctor's office is closed and he isn't taking calls? The courts require you to contact the doctor responsible for the order you're questioning. But if another doctor is taking calls for him, the on-call doctor has assumed responsibility for the patient and you can ask him.

This isn't quite as safe as consulting the doctor who wrote the order. That means you'll have to be especially careful and follow these steps:

• Read the order to the on-call doctor. If the prescribing doctor's handwriting is unclear, make sure the on-call doctor knows why you're having problems understanding the order.

• Tell him who wrote the order and when and why he wrote it.

• Tell him your question and what prompted it. Make sure he understands your interpretation.

• In the nurses' notes, document your conversation.

• On the order sheet, note the new order from the on-call doctor and add his name. Ask him to cosign the order when he next comes to the unit. As a courtesy, tell the prescribing doctor about your question and the result when you see him.

Deciding when to ask

I've discussed a couple of specific problems you may face with drug orders, but how about the big picture? What does the law say about following doctors' orders? Put simply, it requires you to follow all proper orders and to question orders you know—or should know—could harm the patient.

To decide whether a drug might harm a patient, you must know:

• the usual doses, administration routes, desired effects, contraindications, and adverse effects of the ordered drug

• whether the patient has a documented allergy to the drug

• whether the patient is taking any other drugs that might interact with this drug

• whether the patient's condition has changed significantly since the doctor wrote the order.

Don't try to save time by going to the nearest doctor and asking "Is this order okay?" (except in an emergency). You need to investigate the drug yourself, consulting reference books on your unit and talking with the pharmacist. For two reasons, this is time well spent. First, you'll learn facts about the drug that will help you in the future. Second, you'll avoid the potentially embarrassing situation of asking questions based on incomplete or incorrect information.

Your investigation will give you sound reasons for asking the prescribing doctor about the order. If you say, "I have a question about this order for 10% dextrose in water because we usually use isotonic fluids for diabetic patients," the doctor is obviously more likely to listen to you than if you say, "This order doesn't seem right."

Timing your questions

The time your questions take may be less important than when you ask them. Delaying an order while you find out whether it's safe or appropriate can create two problems: an unmedicated patient and an angry doctor. To at least avoid the former, ask your questions *before* you're supposed to administer the drug.

Sometimes, though, you can't do this. Let's say that you're assigned to a new patient. An emergency keeps you busy all morning. You're about to give the 10 a.m. medications when you realize that the ordered dose of your new patient's antihypertensive medication seems unusually high. When you read the package insert, you discover that it is considerably higher than the recommended dose.

The patient is only moderately hypertensive, so you decide to hold the medication until the doctor makes rounds in a half-hour. Is this a good decision or not?

If the doctor can't be reached by phone, holding the medication is a wise decision: The dose is considerably higher than normal, the patient isn't in imminent danger of a cerebrovascular accident, and you expect the doctor to arrive on the unit soon.

Make sure you document any decision to give or hold a medication. Include any attempts to reach the doctor and the information you considered in making your decision. This documentation may not save you from the doctor's anger, but it will protect you legally.

Documenting your decision

Even a professional explanation may make the prescribing doctor angry. He may complain to your nurse-manager about your "insubordination." You can protect yourself and your job with careful documentation.

• *In the nurses' notes,* describe in detail the order as written, your questions and what prompted them, the doctor's answers to your questions, and your response to him.

If the doctor ends up giving the medication himself, he should chart the dose, route, and time. You should document your assessment of the patient's condition before and after the medication was given. Don't add any criticisms: Stick to the facts. The patient's chart is no place to accuse the doctor of incompetence or negligence or to attempt to exonerate yourself from any liability.

• *In a memo to your nurse-manager,* include all the information you wrote in the nurses' notes and add an explanation of your efforts to solve the problem before you refused to give the medication. Keep a copy of this memo for yourself, but don't put it in the chart. This memo is *not* an incident report—it's a record of your side of the story.

• *When an incident report is appropriate,* simply record the facts. Filling out an incident report may be a good idea if the doctor frequently strays from recommended dosage ranges.

If you're reprimanded for the incident, insist that your explanation of the events be included in your personnel record. And if your employment contract allows you a hearing for reprimands, you may want to take advantage of this right to clear your record.

NSO RISK ADVISOR 5

The story title and a theme illustration that was specially assigned go together with visual harmony, resulting in a distinctive book jacket affect.

Jake's Attic (TV Program)

SCIENCE NEWSLETTER FOR KIDS

Jake is popular among kids in the Midwest. His TV program, "Jake's Attic," brings science in palatable form to a youthful audience through regional TV channels.

Like the TV show, "Jake's Notes" is designed to please bright kids and stir up an interest in science. Appropriately, it features science facts and concepts in enticingly colorful graphics symbolic of the subject matter. Some of the spot illustrations are "found" material but most are created by the designers. The design work is performed on a Mac. However, the designers say they "like to draw on paper, then streamline their graphics on the computer."

Cover and inside pages go all out for graphic display. The tall, bold sans-serif logotype dominates the cover and has the smashing affect of a colorful poster. All four pages are a panoply of richly muted colors. The text type was chosen for quick, painless reading. Set in ITC Century Book Condensed, lines are leaded more than average, suitable for young readers.

This is a first issue. The editorial content and copy is produced by Steve Jacobs, who is the star of the program. Graphic design is prepared freelance by the Wichita design group, Gardner & Greteman. Circulation is handled by individual TV stations who purchase copies, which they then mail to readers.

Designers
Sonya Greteman, Karen Hogan
**Creative Design
and Art Direction**
Gardner & Greteman
Wichita, KS
Publisher
Jake's Attic
Wichita, KS
Text Type
ITC Century Book Condensed
Display Type
Differs with each feature
Page Size
$8\frac{1}{2} \times 11$
Printing
Four Color

The theme of the spread is strung across the top in bold sans-serif type. Note the successful use of wide letterspacing. A black panel bleeding off the top with type reversed in color effectively caps the spread.

Three step-by-step experiments open with decorative numerical graphics followed by single-line titles in capitals set in refined condensed type. Other short features intersperse with decorative display titles and graphics. Text type is flush left, ragged right for a relaxed, casual look.

S P A R K   Y O U

E X P E R I M E N T

DISPOSABLE DIAPER

DESCRIPTION: Some brands of disposable diapers contain a specially designed polymer molecule. You will separate crystals of the polymer from the lining of the diaper and see why they are often called "super absorbers!"

YOU WILL NEED: One or two disposable diapers, an empty paper grocery bag, a mixing bowl and spoon.

HERE'S HOW:

1. Tear open one of the diapers and remove the fiber filling.
2. Hold the filling over an open paper bag and shred the filling into very small pieces.
3. Close the top of the paper bag and shake the bag for ten to fifteen minutes.
4. Open the bag, and remove the filling. A small amount of white powder or crystals will be on the bottom of the bag.
5. Place the white powder in the mixing bowl. Add a cup or two of water. Observe what happens.
6. The water will be drawn into the absorbing powder, forming a very thick paste. What's Happening: Chemists are able to design molecules which can do many different things. The special polymer molecule used in most disposable diapers is called sodium polyacrylate, or S.P.A. Diaper manufacturers put crystals of S.P.A. on the fibers which make up the filling of the diapers. One molecule of S.P.A. can absorb and hold over 1,000 water molecules.

THE CHALLENGE:

1. You can reverse the absorbing process! Try this: after you have used the S.P.A. to absorb water, sprinkle some common table salt on the paste, stir, and watch what happens.
2. Can you think of other uses for the super absorbing molecule? Write a list in your journal.

E X P E R I M E N T

DANCING PENNY

DESCRIPTION: You can make a coin mysteriously "dance" on the top of an empty soft drink bottle

YOU WILL NEED: Several pennies, nickels, and dimes, pop bottle, water, and your hands.

HERE'S HOW:

1. Chill your bottle for 5 min. in the fridge.

2. Select a coin that will fit in the opening of the bottle, without falling into the bottle.
3. Place a few drops of water at the edge of the coin, where it contacts the lip of the bottle.
4. Carefully wrap your hands around the bottle and watch the coin. In a few seconds it should start tapping!

WHAT'S HAPPENING: The empty soft drink bottle contains air. When you wrap your hands around the bottle, the heat from your hands warms the bottle and the air inside. When the air is heated, it expands. The expanding air pushes up on the coin, causing the coin to "tap." The few drops of water act as a sealing liquid, to prevent the expanding air from leaking out between the bottle lip and edge of the coin.

THE CHALLENGE: Jake challenges you to design the best coin tapping system possible, using materials found in the kitchen. Try using different size bottles and temperatures; bottles that have been cooled in the refrigerator or warmed by the sun. Try different liquids for the sealing fluid; soapy water, cooking oil, etc. Remember to make observations and keep record of them in your science journal.

FACTOIDS

How **BIG** is an **ATOM**? The piece of paper this newsletter is printed on is approximately one million atoms thick!

The **BUTTER** that is squirted on your popcorn at the movie theater isn't really butter at all! It is flavored soy bean oil, with a little coloring added to give it that **GOLDEN BUTTER LOOK!**

Did you know that lightning strikes the earth approximately **1,000** times every second?

A minor feature with brief science facts becomes a focal point that gets attention. The bold sans-serif head, running vertical, neatly aligns at top and bottom and results in a unique, visual typographic feature.

A strong headline has been designed effectively within an extremely narrow (10-pica) column. The combination of thick and thin type and bold sans serif makes the title eye-catching.

Jake's Attic

IMAGINATION

Back yard ZOO

GARTER SNAKES: Have you ever found a garter snake in your backyard? They are not poisonous, but be careful, they can bite. A typical garter snake is dark green or reddish-brown in color, with three lighter colored stripes running the length of its back and sides. Garter snakes can grow to be 15" to 25" long.

HOUSING YOUR SNAKE: You can design your own snake cage, but it should have good ventilation, smooth walls, a secure lid, and ample room for the snake.

DIET: Garter snakes eat earthworms, small amphibians, and small fish. Handle the snake as little as possible. It is stressful for the snake to be handled.

The snake should be returned to its environment after 3 or 4 weeks of captivity and observation. The snake should be released between early spring and autumn. They need time to find a safe winter hibernation site.

Element
OF THE MONTH

TUNGSTEN A hard, brittle, metals. Its melting point is higher than that of any known metal; 3370°C. That's why it is used to make the filaments in your light bulbs.

The **W** symbol comes from its original name Wolframium, which means "Heavy Stone".

EXPERIMENT 3

HOMEMADE PUTTY

DESCRIPTION: Using everyday materials, you will make a plastic polymer similar to the plastic putty sold in toy stores.

YOU WILL NEED: White glue, powdered hand soap containing borax, and water.

HERE'S HOW:

1. Sprinkle a very small amount of the powdered soap onto the palm of your hand.

2. Add a few drops of water and stir with a finger to make a very thin paste.

3. Squirt some of the white glue onto the paste and mix with your finger.

4. The glue/soap/water mixture will form a rubbery plastic putty!

WHAT'S HAPPENING: Chemists often connect atoms into long chain molecules called polymers. Most plastics are polymers. The sodium borate which is in the hand soap causes the glue to form a polymer.

THE CHALLENGE: Jake did not give you the exact amount of the three ingredients to use. Try a series of experiments to see if you can determine a good formula for the homemade putty. For each experiment, change the amount of one of the ingredients. Record the amount of each ingredient and the results of the experiment in your journal.

Casey Bones SAYS

POLYMER:

POLY = Many

MER = Particles or Atoms

A very long molecule, made of a chain of atoms or smaller molecules.

New York City Transit Authority

WORDS AND PICTURES DRAMATIZE BIG-CITY TRANSIT

Designer, Art Director
Melissa Feldman
Manager, Photography
Philip Bartley, Jr.
Publisher
New York City Transit Authority
New York, NY
Text Type
Times Roman
Helvetica Heavy
Franklin Gothic
Display Type
Franklin Gothic
Page Size
$5\frac{1}{2} \times 11$
(12 pages, accordion folded)
Printing
Two Color

Late on a night in August, five cars of a New York City subway train were derailed at Union Square. There was twisted steel, smoke, and loss of life.

It was a rare happening—but it's the stuff that makes dramatic photo-journalism in the pages of "At Your Service." The readers of this unusual newsletter are the 50,000 people who manage, service, and run New York's buses and subways.

The publication uses words and pictures to document forcefully the complex world of big-city transit. This is a no-nonsense newsletter with credibility—appreciated and read by the field's vast workforce.

"At Your Service" is produced internally by a creative staff that includes an art director. Significantly, the masthead also lists a Manager of Photography, which indicates a commitment to the value of vivid, compelling black-and-white photographs.

Its pages are accordion-folded, six panels, 5 1/2 × 11 on white paper stock, 33 inches wide. A president's letter on the inside cover is set in well-leaded Franklin Gothic. This is followed by a five-page editorial feature that has three-column grids set 10/12 Times Roman. Callouts, initials, and bold leads are set in Franklin Gothic. This publication is designed to be simple, easy-to-read typography. One of the pages on the reverse side is a mailing panel.

Average reading time is about 20 minutes. This short-term communication from management encourages a sense of belonging, which is an important objective of "At Your Service."

Designs for Study

The title panel for a feature story is a full-bleed page. Title, photo, and text form a strong unit. Note that reverse text type is bold and has ample leading for readability.

The complete newsletter consists of 12 pages folded into $5\frac{1}{2} \times 11$ panels, printed both sides. The layout style is totally functional with no distracting decorative content.

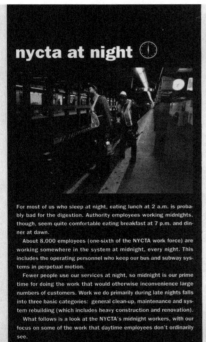

nycta at night

For most of us who sleep at night, eating lunch at 2 a.m. is probably bad for the digestion. Authority employees working midnights, though, seem quite comfortable eating breakfast at 7 p.m. and dinner at dawn.

About 8,000 employees (one-sixth of the NYCTA work force) are working somewhere in the system at midnight, every night. This includes the operating personnel who keep our bus and subway systems in perpetual motion.

Fewer people use our services at night, so midnight is our prime time for doing the work that would otherwise inconvenience large numbers of customers. Work we do primarily during late nights falls into three basic categories: general clean-up, maintenance and system rebuilding (which includes heavy construction and renovation).

What follows is a look at the NYCTA's midnight workers, with our focus on some of the work that daytime employees don't ordinarily see.

8:17 p.m. Grand Central Station, mezzanine at Lexington Avenue. A team of Revenue's collection agents are ready to descend to the southbound platform and board a revenue train.

Collection crews make their way through the system every night to collect bags of money and tokens and deliver them to the Jay Street money room. Each crew has a schedule of stations to visit, known only to them and the RTO train operator running the revenue train. Each night before 4 a.m. about a dozen of these work crews manage to make pick ups at all 468 active stations.

If you don't catch them at the beginning of their journey—before they start collecting revenue—you'll never catch them. They won't answer any questions about their schedule that night and they won't allow photographs taken of the train.

Two-year Collecting Agent Steven Fair says that working with the same people every night on a dangerous job builds close relationships. "We've got a lot of comradery. Working together like this, we're a close-knit group."

9:20 p.m. Transit Police Homeless Outreach headquarters on Manhattan's

Vestry Street. Outreach officers are boarding a Surface bus that they will use to transport homeless people to shelters.

The staff of eight outreach officers work two separate operations every night in Manhattan and the Bronx. Since last year, Surface has provided the Transit Police with dedicated buses for Homeless Outreach during cold-weather months. In addition to these buses, every night the City's Human Resources Administration supplies a school bus that one of the Outreach officers drives.

The HRA bus goes to terminal stations, where social workers and police officers offer food and shelter to people. The Surface bus sweeps the system and usually goes to at least a dozen locations every night. Officers also respond to calls from their fellow officers or other NYCTA employees who report seeing homeless people needing transportation to shelters. (The phone number for reporting is 718-330-3881.)

Homeless people committing rules violations are ejected but are offered transportation to a shelter. People not violating rules are still offered transportation to a shelter, but they don't need to accept.

Though only about 10 percent of the homeless people the officers approach accept outreach services, the job has its rewards. "Even if it's just one in a hundred that accepts [transportation to a shelter]," says Police Officer William

Amendolare, "you're doing something. It gets cold in the tunnels at night and it's dangerous. You get that person to get on the bus, you're saving that person's life."

10:10 p.m. On the local tracks north of the IRT's Chambers St. station, RTO construction flagger Henri Bonner is setting a train-tripping device next to a red lantern. If an approaching train fails to stop when the train operator sees the red lantern, the trip will cause the train to brake automatically.

The flagger's job is to protect construction workers.

About 60 yards away from Bonner, on the middle track (where power is off), contractors are doing rail-welding work. They have some of their equipment on the local track, where power is still on. Before a train can crawl past the workers, Bonner removes the trip and other flaggers blow their whistles to get the crew to clear the track.

When the work is done outside on elevated tracks (only during the day), flaggers signal trains with flags. Where it's dark, in tunnels, they wave yellow and red lanterns—yellow for trains to proceed with caution and red for stopping.

Looking up at a passing train from the roadbed can be

pretty frightening. "If you've never stood next to a train before, you're in for a surprise. They're a lot bigger than you think," says Bonner.

Most flaggers are conductors by title who prefer dark tunnels to train cabs. According to 20-year flagger Rodester Timmons, many conductors pick flagging jobs because they like being a solo act. "You pick a flagging job knowing you're working midnights and that you'll be left alone."

11:18 p.m. Queens Village Bus depot. Bus Operator Mable Teague is using the "Keene" machine to suck tokens and coins out of a bus fare box. The money is carried through a hose into a vault.

Queens Village has 200 buses, and each day about

180 operate in passenger service. The midnight tour is a time for fueling, cleaning and making minor repairs (such as fixing side-view mirrors) on all the buses. Each bus gets scrubbed and a run through the bus wash. About 40 buses a night need repairs.

The midnight tour is also the time when the depot's yard dispatcher makes a "schematic": a map to show where each bus is located among 24 tracks. The schematic shows which bus will run on which routes the next day and which buses need more extensive repairs at a base shop.

Artie Biazzo is a 21-year "shifter"; his job is moving buses to different parts of the depot. He says, "I like nights. I like being free to do my job in peace."

12:32 a.m. Queens' Court Square station. Infrastructure plumbers are installing new pipes for an employee lavatory.

Infrastructure maintainers are rehabilating the station complex that includes 23rd St-Ely Ave. While the plumbers are working down on the tracks, up on the platform masons are laying and grouting cinder blocks to build a new wall.

We get one of the plumbers, Structures Maintainer Martin Ryan, to look up from his work to tell us what he likes best about working midnights. "You see how quiet it is?" he says, even though other workers are continuing to bang and clang, hack at concrete, cut, drill and weld. "With less passengers in the station, we can get more work done in less time."

1:50 a.m. Manhattan's 23rd Street/Seventh Avenue station. Station Cleaner Daniel McKenley is blasting away grime with the mobile-wash gun.

During late nights, Stations closes down fare control areas and platforms scheduled for mobile washing. Mobile-wash units park on the street and shoot 200-degree water through a hose at 3,000 pounds per square inch. Says Cleaner Daryl

Text narrative documents the story of nighttime transit workers in fast-paced type columns, much like newspaper copy. Small photos achieve dynamic contrast surrounding the larger blowup. Hours of the night are marked by bold lead-ins of Franklin Gothic.

Like a film title, the headline, in a commanding position, parallels a strong pattern of photos and effectively takes the place of picture captions.

Three photos, perfectly aligned side by side, form a discursive visual narrative. This demonstrates the power of sequential images in still photography.

getting back on track

COMMAND: Are you an 1133 Woodlawn?
CONDUCTOR: Yes, 1133 Woodlawn.
COMMAND: And you're just north of 14th Street on two track?
CONDUCTOR: Yes.
COMMAND: All right. Do you have a problem, sir?
CONDUCTOR: [inaudible]
COMMAND: Say it slowly. Do you have a problem?
CONDUCTOR: The first five cars are derailed.

We'll always remember what happened at Union Square just after midnight on Aug. 28: the twisted steel of a derailed No. 4 train, the smoke, the rubble, the loss of life.

A month, a year, 20 years from now, let's also make a point of remembering the events following the crash:

the rescue, the clean up and the rebuilding, and how we as an organization rallied together to get one of our busiest subway lines safely back in service—faster than anybody thought possible.

The Rescue. About 40 Transit Police officers at Union Square's District 4 office heard the crash and ran to assist passengers at the smoke-filled scene. Along with the city's EMS and the NYPD's Emergency Service Unit and the Fire Department, workers from the Transit Police's Emergency Medical Rescue Unit helped get people out of the train and then provided medical assistance.

The police and other rescue units led people on the last six cars through the tunnel to the 23rd Street station. Those on the first four cars were evacuated at 14th

Street. Surface dispatched buses to transport people to outer-borough hospitals, as did the Red Cross, which also provided sandwiches and juice for people at Union Square.

Transit Police Lieutenant Robert Wheeler says, "Transit Police and people from city agencies were working hand-in-hand, risking their lives to save people." For example: Transit Police Officers Emanoel Bowser and Dennis Micozzi were riding the train when it crashed. Despite their injuries, they assisted in the evacuation until about 5 a.m.

Cleaning Up and Rebuilding. "Nobody had ever seen a derailment as bad as this, so nobody really knew how long it would take to repair such an extensive amount of damage," says Rapid Transit's Senior Vice

President Tom Prendergast.

The train had ripped out 22 steel-girder support columns, used to hold up the tunnel ceiling as well as the street above the subway. Five subway cars were off the track, with two cars mangled beyond recognition. Two tracks and a third rail had been ripped out, and two sets of signals, two switches and the air compressor room destroyed. The street above had sunk a half inch; there was no electricity.

According to System Safety's Neil Yongue, the key to organizing the clean up was getting people from different groups to work together. "Right from the outset, we coordinated our efforts to get people from all different departments to attain a common goal. The attitude wasn't, 'You can't do this.' It was, 'What can

we do to get it done.'"

Line-equipment electricians supplied electrical power for lights, fans and machinery from emergency AC panel boxes and by running cables from the third rail at 19th Street down to the accident site.

But workers had to wait more than 24 hours before they could begin the clean up. Representatives from the National Transportation Safety Board and other safety agencies needed to investigate the crash scene with the damage left intact.

Infrastructure workers set up a command center for the operations at the abandoned 18th Street station. To open the station from street level, they busted through the sidewalk with jackhammers.

The Materiel Division got workers the supplies they'd need, including steel beams,

15 timbers for support columns, two pieces of rail, 20 fans, water coolers, bunker lights, portable toilets and an electrical generator. They issued emergency purchase orders for most of the supplies. But Materiel's Pat D'Ambrosio was particularly impressed by the civic spirit exhibited at an A&P near 18th Street. "The manager told us our workers could go in and get whatever food they wanted. We'd just have to keep the receipts and figure out the charges later, after the work was finished."

The bulk of the clean up and rebuilding began at around noon on Thursday August 29, under the watchful eyes of System Safety workers, who monitored the air to make sure workers weren't being exposed to toxic fumes or doing any-

thing that would result in injury. Says Yongue, "When you consider the number of people out there and the fact that they were being exposed to glass and sheet metal, the fact that there were no injuries is a tribute to their abilities as workers."

Car Equipment's Joe Hofmann adds, "It's all about teamwork, working together and looking out for one another. That's the key to the job, and the reason you didn't see any injuries."

We had more than 200 workers at a time on the job, 24 hours-a-day. A hundred yards of tunnel full of people—dark, close, dusty and hot. Working 12- to 16-hour shifts all through the weekend, right through their RDOs and the Labor Day Holiday. Says Structures Maintainer Tony James, "If you think about the heat, it'll

> "The attitude wasn't, 'You can't do this.' It was, 'What can we do to get it done.'"
> –System Safety's Neil Yongue

get to you. You just gotta forget about it and just think about the job—trying to get it done, no matter how tired you are."

The pictures show some of the work that went on down there.

RTO crews manned six work trains—crane cars and flatbeds— to help move out the cars and debris. "I personally saw us fill up eight flatbed cars," says Track's Benjamin Everson.

Diesel trains pulled out the five cars that didn't derail. But getting out the first five cars, which weren't

on the track, was trickier.

Working alongside more than a dozen Authority Track workers were workers from Metro-North. Metro-North supplied a new hydraulic jacking system which could lift a 44-ton car, slide it sideways and set it back down on the rail.

Larry Gamache, whose job was to oversee the work by all the different departments, says, "Before the accident, Metro-North had been letting us test out their Hornsh hydraulic jacks, and [Track Division's Chief Engineer] Fred Smith was interested in purchasing one for the Authority. Based on the performance we got out of them, we found out they can really do the job."

The fourth and fifth cars were jacked, rerailed and pulled off to the Bronx's Concourse Yard. Car

2   3   4

The text for a dramatic story of a subway derailment begins typographically like a play with tense, emphatic dialogue and a degree of understatement. The body of the story opens with a three-line capital initial in Franklin Gothic.

Text columns set in 10/12 Times Roman are interrupted by bold leads printed in a second color and a quotation lifted from the body of the story. Two more pages, not illustrated, continue the layout motif with two more identically sized photos.

Boston Center for Adult Education

DESIGN STYLE SUPPORTS EDITORIAL AND VICE VERSA

As you might expect, Boston, the center of education and scholarship, has an outstanding newsletter dealing with education— "The Center Point." This superb publication reads well, looks lively, and is a model of fine typography. Designer Ronn Campisi styled this first issue on the Mac. Successive issues brought out by the editors have followed his prototype. Campisi says, "The format is flexible enough so that it's easy for them to follow style."

He designed the newsletter with sensitive typographic detailing: classic Roman text type, italic bylines, and sans-serif picture captions that capture your attention. The smooth integration of three- and four-column text blocks is an example of the range of choice built into the design.

The editorial content is rendered to effectively complement the design. Text is written to fit the layout. The length and content of the stories are well-planned for adequate coverage. Photos from existing files are chosen to enhance as well as inform. Headlines not only have journalistic flair but they're well-shaped as typographic units. The name of the publication is worth noting. It is appropriate as well as a clever play on words. Set in Galliard, the text type style, the designer crafted a low-slung letter "o" for a logo that's subtle and distinctive. This newsletter represents a balanced approach to design and editorial planning.

Designer
Ronn Campisi
Editor
Wendy Seller
Publisher
Boston Center for
Adult Education
Boston, MA
Text Type
Galliard
Display Type
Galliard
Futura Light
Futura Bold
Page Size
$8\frac{1}{2} \times 11$
Printing
Two Color

The Center POINT

NEWS FROM THE BOSTON CENTER FOR ADULT EDUCATION

Message from the executive director

by Paul Fishman

REMEMBER the fable of the blind man and the elephant? Each man tried to describe the animal from his limited knowledge of a leg or ear or trunk? There never was any agreement about the whole beast. Well, the Boston Center for Adult Education is a kind of elephant and this newsletter is our way of piecing together the various components of the Center's identity.

To those who teach here, the Center is represented by a historic Back Bay mansion with awkwardly sized classrooms that may once have served as a dressing room or servant's quarters. To those who conduct courses at our recently acquired facility on Arlington Street, the Center may reflect the more modern look of the 80's, including well-equipped studio and dance space.

For the student, the whole Boston Center experience might be summed up in one three-hour Main Course lecture in which classes meet in participants' homes and are accompanied by dinner or dessert. For the fortunate, the BCAE experience is a series of
Continued on page 6

BECAUSE ADULTS SHOULD KNOW BETTER

The beginning of adult education in Boston

by Wendy Seller

In 1933, the new concept of an adult education center in Boston was so well received that 350 people enrolled for the first term, far exceeding what the Center had expected, and nearly 700 people had to be turned away. The idea was initiated by Dorothy Hewitt, originally President of the Adult Educational Department of the Boston Y.W.C.A., and Kirtley Mather, a geology professor at Harvard University. Both felt that Boston needed an informal educational program for both adult men and women, regardless of their economic means. The Center was established to enable small groups of people from various sectors of life to gather with a dynamic instructor, in a comfortable environment, and exchange ideas on a topic of current interest. The program would emphasize the importance of each person to develop individually under circumstances that would recognize his or her uniqueness.

Without any mailing list or financial backing, the Boston Center was launched through a city-wide distribution of catalogues, and endorsement from many leaders of major business, social and political organizations throughout greater Boston. In addition, the Center's ideas were presented in a series of broadcasts by Dr. Mather over Boston's four major radio stations.

The program, first named the "Twentieth Century Adult Education Centre," met at the Twentieth Century Club at 3 Joy Street. Classrooms consisted of a dozen or so rooms in the five-story brick building. Instructors usually sat at a large center table in the room, surrounded—at the table and in easy chairs—by their adult students.

The Center's first term offered a
Continued on page 7

With six terms a year, BCAE students are able to experiment and test their talents.

BCAE TODAY

Fifty-five and still growing strong!

by Jamie Jaffe

The current Boston Center catalogue contains five hundred exciting course selections that include financial management, career exploration, art, dance, languages, cooking, travel and more. The subject areas and formats in which courses are offered are more varied now than when the Center's first catalogue was published in 1933, but the essence of its mission shines through—to provide quality, informal educational opportunities for adults.

Classes at the Center are offered six
Continued on page 7

VOLUME 1 NUMBER 1 SPRING 1988

Headline type throughout is Galliard upper and lower case. The head at right has an introductory top line set in caps. Capital letters also lead into the opening text paragraph. A horizontal hairline separates the story areas.

A subhead dominates the spacious margin and cuts into the text for an imaginary "panel" affect. The tall initial is a useful device to get attention. The photo is a bridge between this story and the elevator story at the right.

THE CENTER POINT

THE NEW BCAE ELEVATOR

What you don't see is what you pay for

by Paul Fishman, Executive Director

THE BCAE'S ORIGINAL elevator—surely a marvel in its time—was well past its prime when we decided to replace it (or her... see "Arabella, the elevator," this issue). The machinery was cranky, hard to use by generations brought up with automatic elevators, and expensive to maintain.

Installing the new elevator first required the drilling of a 54 foot hole in the ground for a hydraulic piston. The procedure involved the temporary use of a huge drilling rig that was placed in and around the shaft. The machinery was the same sort used to drill for oil. Happily neither petroleum products nor anything else unexpected was found in the deep fill under the building.

Assembling the elevator cab and equipment took two months of precision work inside the cramped space of the original elevator shaft. Elevator mechanic Bob Wesson of the Upright Elevator Company patiently explained his work to interested staff as he cut, bolted, wired, fitted, measured, and plumbed the new machine into life.

Five months and $140,000 later the new elevator - not yet named - awaits all. Be our guest and take it/her for a lift.

A TIME TO CELEBRATE!

Champagne and free rides mark completion of project

BCAE HELD A SPECIAL thank you party on Sunday afternoon, February 21st, for donors who contributed to the new elevator at 5 Commonwealth Avenue. Stepping into the mansion on this cold, winter afternoon, one felt as though they had walked into another era. Champagne was being served in the main lobby. Tea, in the mansion's finest silver, accompanied appetizers in the Edwardian Loomis Room. A large chandelier of German glass hung overhead; a blazing fire illuminated the room with a warm light. With classical music playing softly in the background, Bob Galvin, President of the Board, thanked the elevator contractors and donors for their important contribution to the Center and invited all guests to take a ride in the new elevator. The elevator marks the completion of the building renovation made possible by the 21st Century Drive and will provide wheelchair accessibility to all floors in the building.

Stepping into the mansion one felt as though they had walked into another era

You no longer need to take the staircase to the top— with BCAE's new elevator.

Arabella, the elevator

by Linda Goldstein

AT LAST, the BCAE must bid farewell to "Arabella," the original elevator installed at 5 Commonwealth Avenue more than 80 years ago. Arabella received her name from John "Pappy" McLean, the Gamble Building's superintendent who retired in 1986. While she was aesthetically pleasing, Arabella was quite undependable and difficult to run. The new elevator, completed in February, is not only easy to operate, but fully accessible to those in wheelchairs. Funding for the elevator came from the 21st Century Drive, a three year endeavor raising $315,000 to upgrade the facilities at the Center. Contributions were received from corporations, foundations and individuals. BCAE christened the new elevator with a champagne reception for major donors held (appropriately) on February 21st.

Linda Goldstein is the Publicist at the BCAE.

Folios are small, bold, well-positioned, and easy to find. They align neatly with the vertical hairline. Name and date add a subtle, horizontal touch of interest to the folio area.

A story about a new elevator symbolically occupies a tall column with numbers that cleverly represent floor levels from basement to top.

THE CENTER POINT

THANK YOU TO DONORS!

THE STAFF, leaders, and Board of Directors of The Boston Center for Adult Education wish to thank the donors of the 21st Century Fund for their generous contributions which have enabled the Center to renovate its facilities and install a new elevator. Donors contributing $100 or more are listed below:

Benefactors
Sandra Bakalar
Richard B. Gamble
Family of Sarah Gamble
Estate of Betty B. McAndrew
Anne C. Rubenstein
Katherine B. Winter

Ida S. Barter Trust, Bank of Boston, Trustee
Boston Edison Company
The Boston Globe Foundation
Gibbett Hill Foundation
The Gillette Company
John Hancock Mutual Life Insurance Company
Agnes M. Lindsay Trust
The New England Amelia Peabody Charitable Fund
Raytheon Company
William E. & Bertha E. Schrafft Charitable Trust
Stop & Shop Foundation

Patrons
S. Alan Becker
Sidney B. Smith
C. Vincent Vappi
Abigail W. Washburn*

Eastern Gas & Fuel Associates
Liberty Mutual Insurance Group
The Harold Whitworth Pierce Charitable Trust
A. C. Ratshesky Foundation
State Street Bank & Trust Company

Sponsors
Leo L. Beranek
Estate of Frederick W. Clapp
Elinor L. Coggin
M. L. Coolidge
James G. Gallaher
Robert J. Galvin
Joan and Saul Goldweitz
Carol A. Rennie

Angela F. Winthrop

The Paul & Edith Babson Foundation
Bank of Boston Charitable Foundation
Cahners Publishing Company
The Cricket Foundation
Ellen A. Gilman Trust
Walter R. & Helen P. Hennessey Charitable Foundation
Honeywell Bull
IBM
Mitchell B. Kaufman Charitable Foundation
Polaroid Foundation
Saunders Hotels
Shawmut Bank. N.A.

Donors
Mr. and Mrs. Oliver F. Ames
James L. Bildner
Richard P. Breed, III
Victor Brogna
Nancy L. Cahners

Daniel J. Coolidge
David Friend
Milton L. Grahm
Richard I. Kaner
Janet and Walter Koltun
Therese A. Maloney
Anne McCormick
John L. McCrea
Ann Dins Nemrow
Peter Nessen
Anthony and Geraldine Pangaro
Harriet F. Parker
Herbert J. Richman
Deborah A. Robbins
Abram Segel
Donald and Willona Sinclair
Paul R. Snider
Mr. and Mrs. Stephen A. Swets
Mrs. Albert H. Wechsler
Mr. and Mrs. Thomas Whitney

Creative Gourmet
Filene's
Prudential Insurance Company

Contributors
Mrs. David Ames
Sheelagh Anzoni
Joanne and Richard Arnaud
Lenore and Norman Asher
Judith and Joseph Auerbach

Frederick D. Ballou
Michael Barza and Judith Robinson
Edward A. Berman
Lawrence M. Bernstein
Joseph J. Bloomberg
Herbert Bremner
Elizabeth C. Case
Hugh M. Chapin
Mrs. Clarence A. Dauber
S. Sydney De Young
Paul L. Fishman
Emily P. Flint
Paul Garrity
Mr. and Mrs. Richard Glovsky
Mr. and Mrs. William Glovsky
Maynard Goldman
Mark and Jill Goldweitz
Priscilla L. Grindell
Groman Family Foundation
Carolyn J. Harrigan
Dr. and Mrs. Bradford Holt
Emily C. Hood
Andrew A. Hunter
Christopher P. Kauders
Barbara and Louis Kane
Sandra G. Krakoff
Helen Ladd
Hamilton DeF. Lockwood
Lorraine Lyman
June McCourt
Laurence T. Perera
Holly Parker Safford
Carol Shea
Richard S. Shuman
Irwin H. Silver
Elsa G. Sonnabend
Faye G. Stone (Mrs. David G.)
Family of Leah Carver Toabe
Libby and Herbert Tobin
Marian Ullman
Susan J. Velleman
Charlotte G. Ventola

Bar Services, Inc.
Different Tastes, Inc.
New England Telephone
Nordberg's Caterers

Deceased

PHOTOGRAPH BY MARC B. MALIN

BCAE Executive Director Paul Fishman tests out the new elevator when racing to a Board meeting.

A widely letter-spaced running title at the head of each page is set in Futura Light. Black panels with theme titles in reverse type emphatically cap each page and provide a unifying pattern throughout.

A four-column page, appropriate for a listing of names, relates well to the identical column width on the opposite page. This spread illustrates how to successfully combine differing column widths to accommodate editorial needs.

A casual, seemingly unposed photo represents, all in one shot, the facility and an active view of an executive. Note the elevator numbers in the upper-right corner.

LaGuardia Community College

IMAGES OF A BIG-CITY COLLEGE

Across the river from Manhattan, this two-year community college includes two specialized high schools on its campus. Altogether these facilities provide education and enrichment for hundreds of inner-city and new immigrant students. There is abundant subject matter on this busy campus for "LaGuardia Report."

For the staff of the school, this newsletter provides vital information about their institution. "LaGuardia Report" is also a P.R. medium for a large external audience of opinion makers such as the press, political office holders, and community leaders. It is a worthwhile investment in image and goodwill.

Graphics are plentiful and the editorial content is varied. Its large, 10 1/4 × 16 pages are produced desktop on a Mac by Editor/Designer Bill Freeland, who is also the school's director of communications. The lengthy text columns could be formidable but they are paragraphed often and interspersed with decorative spots, clever illustrations, and photos. The editors believe in paying for the talents of outstanding graphic artists. A recent cover was designed by the nationally known artist/designer, Seymour Chwast, who has contributed a number of illustrations over the years.

Mr. Freeland says, "The pages of 'Laguardia Report' are for the bigger, more significant stories on specific themes. We run all the routine stuff in a separate, more modest, in-house newsletter."

During its 20 years, the college has developed a highly visible publishing program including posters and many print items. "LaGuardia Report" is clearly a centerpiece of the program.

Designer/Editor
Bill Freeland
Publisher
LaGuardia Community College
Office of Communications
Long Island City, NY
Text Type
Bodoni Book
Display Type
Bodoni Condensed
Page Size
10¼ × 16
Printing
Four Color

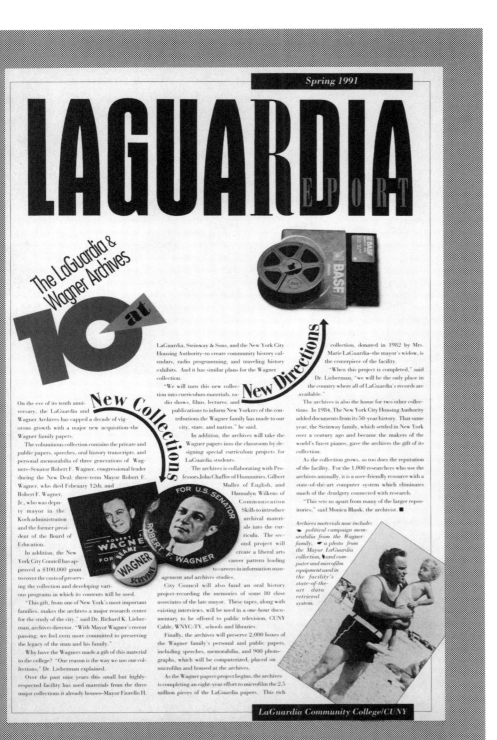

Spring 1991

LAGUARDIA REPORT

The LaGuardia & Wagner Archives at 10

New Collections

On the eve of its tenth anniversary, the LaGuardia and Wagner Archives has capped a decade of vigorous growth with a major new acquisition–the Wagner family papers.

The voluminous collection contains the private and public papers, speeches, oral history transcripts, and personal memorabilia of three generations of Wagners–Senator Robert F. Wagner, congressional leader during the New Deal; three-term Mayor Robert F. Wagner, who died February 12th; and Robert F. Wagner, Jr., who was deputy mayor in the Koch administration and the former president of the Board of Education.

In addition, the New York City Council has approved a $100,000 grant to cover the costs of preserving the collection and developing various programs in which its contents will be used.

"This gift, from one of New York's most important families, makes the archives a major research center for the study of the city," said Dr. Richard K. Lieberman, archives director. "With Mayor Wagner's recent passing, we feel even more committed to preserving the legacy of the man and his family."

Why have the Wagners made a gift of this material to the college? "One reason is the way we use our collections," Dr. Lieberman explained.

Over the past nine years this small but highly-respected facility has used materials from the three major collections it already houses–Mayor Fiorello H.

LaGuardia, Steinway & Sons, and the New York City Housing Authority–to create community history calendars, radio programming, and traveling history exhibits. And it has similar plans for the Wagner collection.

"We will turn this new collection into curriculum materials, radio shows, films, lectures, and publications to inform New Yorkers of the contributions the Wagner family has made to our city, state, and nation," he said.

In addition, the archives will take the Wagner papers into the classroom by designing special curriculum projects for LaGuardia students.

The archives is collaborating with Professors John Chaffee of Humanities, Gilbert Muller of English, and Hannalyn Wilkens of Communication Skills to introduce archival materials into the curricula. The second project will create a liberal arts career pattern leading to careers in information management and archives studies.

City Council will also fund an oral history project–recording the memories of some 80 close associates of the late mayor. These tapes, along with existing interviews, will be used in a one-hour documentary to be offered to public television, CUNY Cable, WNYC-TV, schools and libraries.

Finally, the archives will preserve 2,000 boxes of the Wagner family's personal and public papers, including speeches, memorabilia, and 900 photographs, which will be computerized, placed on microfilm and housed at the archives.

As the Wagner papers project begins, the archives is completing an eight-year effort to microfilm the 2.5 million pieces of the LaGuardia papers. This rich

New Directions

collection, donated in 1982 by Mrs. Marie LaGuardia–the mayor's widow, is the centerpiece of the facility.

"When this project is completed," said Dr. Lieberman, "we will be the only place in the country where all of LaGuardia's records are available."

The archives is also the home for two other collections. In 1984, The New York City Housing Authority added documents from its 50-year history. That same year, the Steinway family, which settled in New York over a century ago and became the makers of the world's finest pianos, gave the archives the gift of its collection.

As the collection grows, so too does the reputation of the facility. For the 1,000 researchers who use the archives annually, it is a user-friendly resource with a state-of-the-art computer system which eliminates much of the drudgery connected with research.

"This sets us apart from many of the larger repositories," said Monica Blank, the archivist. ■

Archives materials now include:
➤ political campaign memorabilia from the Wagner family; ➤ a photo from the Mayor LaGuardia collection, ➤ and computer and microfilm equipment used in the facility's state-of-the-art data retrieval system.

ROBERT WAGNER FOR SAME · **WAGNER** · **FOR U.S. SENATOR ROBERT F. WAGNER** · **WAGNER SCREVANE**

LaGuardia Community College/CUNY

Headlines set in Bodoni Condensed have a sober quality that is a foil for lively and varied visual shapes. Decorative illustrations were commissioned to clearly symbolize editorial themes.

A system of hairlines surrounds and separates the editorial features. Horizontal black bands strongly accent the head and foot of pages.

A free-form illustration spanning four columns is the focal point of the spread. The designer used the Mac to smoothly fashion the text to follow the contour.

Seizing A Special Mandate:
Cultural Pluralism and Economic Development

Math Team Triumphs

In a feat which seemed unattainable only one year ago, the college's student Math Team captured first place in this year's CUNY Math League Contest for two-year colleges.

The five-member team toppled defending champion Queensborough Community College and four other opponents in a two-part competition which tests students' ability to solve pre-calculus problems within a designated time.

Along with an over-all high team score, all five LaGuardia team members individually scored near the top.

"We are very excited because it's the first time our team ever won any kind of competition," said Professor Andrew Berry, the team's faculty advisor.

His strategy was to simply teach students how to methodically solve a problem within a strict time limit and to "bombard" them with questions from old competitions, as well as original problems similar to those encountered during contests.

The math team has also fared well in other competitions. Last winter the team came in third in the New York State Mathematical Association for Two-Year College Team Competition, and in the spring competition, the team landed in second place.

Professor Berry says his plan for next year is to "keep entering the team in more and more tournaments." ■

Professor Andrew Berry

When Dr. Raymond C. Bowen assumed the presidency of the college last year, he came with two visions:

"I see the special mandate for community colleges to break down barriers based on race, cultural background, age, sexual preference, or other artificial differences," he announced at his first official meeting with faculty and staff.

At the same gathering he praised the college's tradition of both preparing its students for the workplace and reaching out to the business community. Saluting these efforts, he announced that the natural next step would be to more clearly define the college's role in the economic development of the city.

Just one year later, as he is inaugurated as the college's second president, Dr. Bowen has already seen these themes transformed into full-fledged initiatives. This has been accomplished by two presidential committees which have been given the task of defining the college's new direction.

The Task Force on Pluralism has developed a plan to confront racism and promote pluralism within the college, while the Committee on Economic Development is establishing a far-reaching policy which will affect the college's students as well as the city's business community.

For the current academic year, according to Pluralism Task Force Chairperson Eleanor Q. Tignor, the committee has identified major goals related to cultural awareness, curriculum review, students' perceptions of pluralism, gay and lesbian concerns, and multicultural involvement in the community.

Last year one major focus was a series of cultural awareness sessions attended by the Task Force on Pluralism, the Personnel & Budget Committee, the Curriculum Committee and department and divisional representatives responsible for curriculum-related policy. This year the goal is to expand the program to other members of the college community.

The process began during Opening Sessions.

The Committee on Economic Development is working on a two-pronged program affecting both students and the business community.

For students, the committee is examining how programs which have successfully prepared students for the workplace can more effectively link them to the city's

Professor Tignor and Dean McGaughey

economic mainstream.

"Statistics show that it is our students—minorities, women, and immigrants—are the workers of today and tomorrow," said Dean Judith McGaughey, committee chairperson. "This makes efforts to effectively educate them increasingly important."

In examining ways to better equip credit and non-credit students for careers, Dean McGaughey indicated the committee will focus on three areas: cooperative education; career-related academic programs; and programs in the Division of Adult and Continuing Education directly related to training and entrepreneurship.

For example, one question under discussion is how to integrate into the curriculum the skills a student needs to become an entrepreneur.

To help business deal with our rapidly changing economy, the committee has proposed the creation of an on-campus unit—The LaGuardia Urban Center for Economic Development (LUCED)—to enable the college to link employers [...] to a host of [...] services such as [...] nical assistance, entrepreneurial training, as well as government contracting, cross-cultural business practices and a wide variety of referral services.

"With establishment of LUCED, the college is positioned to be the leading economic development provider in this community," said Julian Absid, economic development specialist. ■

6

Partners In The Prisons:
Giving Detainees A First–A Second Chance

T he college has received a $150,000 grant from the New York City Department of Corrections to launch a first-ever educational and vocational training program for prison inmates with substance abuse problems.

The program, developed by the college's Correctional Education Program, working with the Correctional Department's Substance Abuse Intervention Division to provide a full range of academic and vocational classes, as well as career and educational counseling, to over 700 detainees who have been placed in city detention facilities while awaiting sentencing. Classes began in September at three centers on Rikers Island, one on Wards Island, and one at the Forbell Street facility in the East New York section of Brooklyn.

"This is a very innovative program," said Shirley Miller, acting director of Community Service Programs here

has never before been an academic component within the Correctional Department's Substance Abuse Unit."

This special division was established a year ago to serve inmates who have been identified as having drug or alcohol problems.

"The college will be part of the whole therapeutic approach to helping inmates," said Philippe Magloire, the program's coordinator.

Because most of these inmates will eventually transfer to another facility, the program serves primarily as an educational stepping stone. Inmates choose from among adult basic education, high school equivalency preparation, and college preparation classes. Then once sentenced to a state facility, they can continue their studies there.

"Students are unable to complete an entire academic program due to the shortness of their stay," said Ms. Miller, "but the instruction may indicate to them that they have a capacity for learning and thus encourage them to continue in a

Top Honors For Robin Kearse

A LaGuardia student was among ten collegians from two-year institutions across the country to be awarded one of the most prestigious honors bestowed upon a community college student—the National Distinguished Students Scholarship.

Robin Kearse, a 21-year-old single mother who manages a full-time college schedule, a part-time job, and her two-year-old daughter, received a $1,000 IBM Corporation-Academic Information Systems gift that will be doubled when she goes on to a four-year college next spring. Ms. Kearse plans to enter Brooklyn College and major in television production.

The competition, sponsored by Phi Theta Kappa, the national honors society for community college students, considered over 300 of the country's brightest two-year college students.

In describing her achievements, Ms. Kearse revealed a story of individual determination to overcome formidable obstacles to attain her goal.

The first obstacle came in 1986 when,

shortly before graduating high school, she contracted an illness which prevented her from accepting a scholarship to Florida A&M University. When she recovered, it was too late to enroll. Instead she secured a data entry clerk position at World-vision Enterprises, a TV production company. Within six months she was named a manager, but soon thereafter left for maternity leave.

She decided to attend LaGuardia in 1988 because she believed a two-year college would provide an easier transition than a senior institution.

After achieving a perfect 4.0 index as a liberal arts major, her successful transition seemed assured.

In a question posed in the written portion of the scholarship application, Ms. Kearse wrote that her challenges "lay not only in maintaining acceptable grades but rather a positive attitude, so others would look to me as a role model."

"I have a driving force that won't let me stop," she said. ∎

classes on such topics as resume writing and interviewing techniques.

"When someone is attempting to turn their life around," said Ms. Miller, "clearly new goals are needed. That process can be facilitated by this counseling sequence."

This program with the Substance Abuse Intervention Division is the latest addition to the college's expanding correctional education program. The college first responded to the needs of inmates in 1975 when it created a small program in the nearby Queensborough Correctional facility. In those 15 years LaGuardia has developed programs on Rikers and Wards Islands, and at the Forbell Street facility which together serve over 5,000 inmates annually.

As the program has expanded, so have the offerings.

The first classes covered purely academic material, with inmates choosing among GED, college prep, or adult basic education courses. Then in 1988, when the Corrections Department decided to include vocational training in the program, it selected LaGuardia to provide the bulk of the instruction.

In addition to serving detainees, the program also works with inmates who are soon to be released. With the support of the federal Vocational Education Act, the program has established a center where such inmates from Queensborough and Lincoln Correctional Centers can take advantage of career exploration workshops, career-skills training, and referral services which lead into credit and non-credit continuing education programs.

"Through its various programs, LaGuardia offers inmates a second chance to change their lives through education," Mr. Magloire said. ∎

similar program at an upstate facility."

In the vocational training component, Mr. Magloire said, the college has developed three courses—pesticide control, keyboarding skills, and baking—which a student may complete in a relatively short time. For example, the pesticide control course which prepares students to take

the exam for New York State certification can be completed in just 30 hours.

Complementing the instruction is a counseling component which provides academic and vocational guidance and life-skills

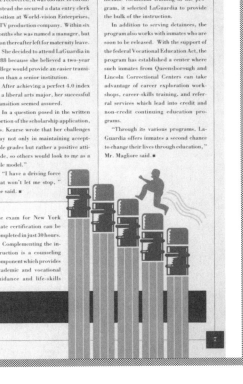

A personality story, boxed within hairlines, dominates the center of the page, surrounded by another major text feature. Initial letters are consistently positioned as reverse type on black squares.

Ascending a pencil staircase, an animated figure cleverly represents the opportunities and challenges of a special training program. This design is an effective example of computer-generated art.

Step-By-Step Publishing

AN ULTIMATE TEACHING MEDIUM ON PAPER

Art Director/Designer
Michael Ulrich
Director of Art & Production
Mike Hammer
Publisher
Step-By-Step Publishing Division of
Dynamic Graphics, Inc.
Peoria, IL
Text Type
ITC Century Light
Helvetica Condensed
Display Type
ITC Century Light Condensed
Helvetica Bold Condensed
Page Size
$8\frac{1}{4} \times 10\frac{1}{2}$
Printing
Four Color

"Step-By-Step Electronic Design" is the ultimate in instructional page layout. Not one square inch of its 8 1/4 × 10 1/2 pages is wasted. This is a subscription newsletter aimed at the reader/user who is totally committed to a sequential learning experience. Its jam-packed content, sometimes set in small type, is perfectly organized.

The editors describe its visual and verbal data as "surpassing the information found in specialized program manuals." A talented staff, which divides its time between this and other projects, often develops new techniques through ongoing experimentation. The publisher is Dynamic Graphics, Inc., who bring out the much-admired *Step-by-Step Graphics* magazine.

This is a handsomely printed four-color newsletter whose pages have a two- and sometimes three-column grid that bears close study for its sequential presentation of material. Its two-track information plan works like this: (1) A wide outer margin displays numbered captions set in 8/8.5 Helvetica Condensed, which correspond with numbered illustrations. (2) The remaining two or three columns contain narrative copy, numbered in sequence, set in 9/11 ITC Century Light. Altogether, this is fine typographic detailing and clear, concise writing. Reading the copy and scanning the graphics is in some respects equal to a classroom experience.

Obviously, the electronic techniques taught on its pages are demonstrated by the design execution of the newsletter itself. It is produced with Quark XPress 3.1 on a Mac IIci. Text is imported from Word and graphics (in EPS format) from the programs covered in each issue, primarily Illustrator, Freehand, Photoshop, PageMaker, and Quark XPress.

PHOTOSHOP

Seamless Photography

■ *by Janet Ashford*

STEP·BY·STEP *Electronic Design*

THE HOW-TO NEWSLETTER FOR DESKTOP DESIGNERS ■ JULY 1992 VOLUME 4, NUMBER 7

NEW YORK-BASED PHOTOGRAPHER Greg Heisler likes to create portraits that contain metaphors. With traditional photography this means setting up the photo shoot with the metaphors already in mind, and often enlisting the help of the subject. But with digital imaging, many photographs can be combined in one image, allowing more flexibility. So when Heisler accepted an assignment from *Time* magazine to do the 1991 Man of the Year cover, he decided to use Photoshop to create the composite of more than 40 photo images.

FROM TRADITIONAL TO DIGITAL PHOTOGRAPHY

Heisler, who had often worked with Kodak on promotions and as a lecturer, was among photographers, illustrators and art directors invited to participate in "open house" workshops on Macintosh-based photo editing when Kodak opened its Center for Creative Imaging (CCI) in Camden, Maine in May 1991. He had never used a computer before, didn't like the high-tech look of the computer images he'd seen, and was very skeptical about becoming involved. But after four "very frustrating" days producing a self-portrait with Photoshop, he came away convinced that the new medium had potential. "The piece I made looked different from any of my other work," says Heisler. "It looked like photography-based illustration, a completely new thing." Now, if only he had the equipment and "a spare lifetime" to learn the software!

Between May and November, when *Time* offered him the Man of the Year assignment, Heisler visited the Center twice more—once to design a black-and-white poster for a *pro bono* assignment and again to develop a series of black-and-white portraits of creative business leaders for *Viewpoint* magazine. For

Photographer Greg Heisler used Photoshop to combine a conventional portrait of Ted Turner with edited screen grabs of CNN's live news coverage for *Time* magazine's 1991 Man of the Year award. A computer novice, Heisler used the facilities and technical support of Kodak's Center for Creative Imaging in Camden, Maine.

Wide side margins are the consistent location for numbered, descriptive captions that run close by and have direct reference to the illustrations and information graphics.

The two-column grid provides a framework for easy-to-read text columns and functional illustrations. Small subheads set in Helvetica Bold Condensed punctuate the subject matter.

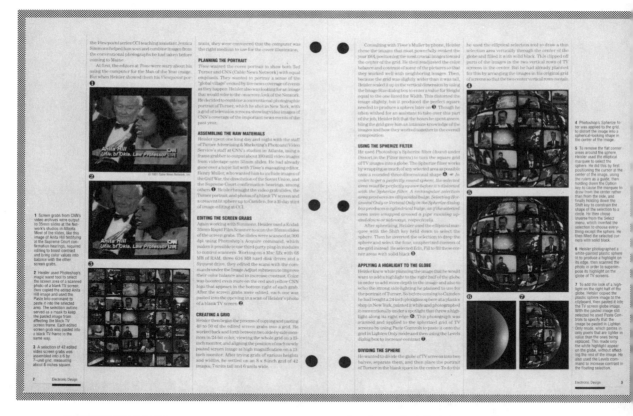

Helvetica Condensed, a somewhat formal typeface, is set in a narrow, very readable column width with flush-left lines. Note that hyphenation is kept to a minimum.

A running narrative in the text blocks functions as the voice of an instructor. The number system in these pages assures that readers will never lose their way. Columns are neatly divided by vertical hairline rules.

Pages are printed with high-resolution EPS at 2540 dpi and 150 lpi on 80# Sequoia Matte Text paper stock. Three holes are punched so that issues can be compiled in a loose-leaf notebook.

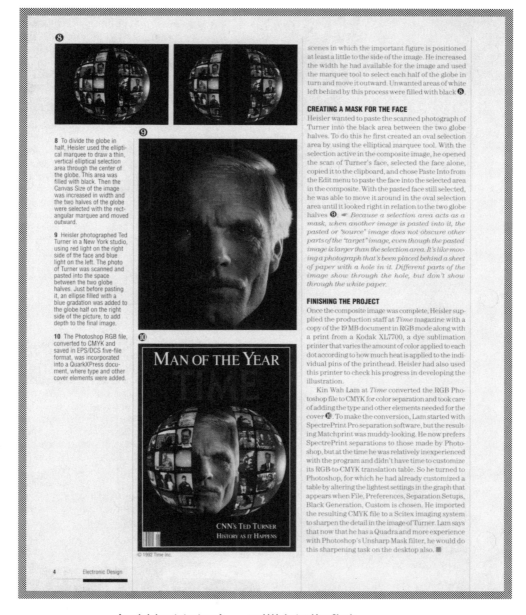

8 To divide the globe in half, Heisler used the elliptical marquee to draw a thin, vertical elliptical selection area through the center of the globe. This area was filled with black. Then the Canvas Size of the image was increased in width and the two halves of the globe were selected with the rectangular marquee and moved outward.

9 Heisler photographed Ted Turner in a New York studio, using red light on the right side of the face and blue light on the left. The photo of Turner was scanned and pasted into the space between the two globe halves. Just before pasting it, an ellipse filled with a blue gradation was added to the globe half on the right side of the picture, to add depth to the final image.

10 The Photoshop RGB file, converted to CMYK and saved in EPS/DCS five-file format, was incorporated into a QuarkXPress document, where type and other cover elements were added.

4   Electronic Design

scenes in which the important figure is positioned at least a little to the side of the image. He increased the width he had available for the image and used the marquee tool to select each half of the globe in turn and move it outward. Unwanted areas of white left behind by this process were filled with black **8**.

CREATING A MASK FOR THE FACE

Heisler wanted to paste the scanned photograph of Turner into the black area between the two globe halves. To do this he first created an oval selection area by using the elliptical marquee tool. With the selection active in the composite image, he opened the scan of Turner's face, selected the face alone, copied it to the clipboard, and chose Paste Into from the Edit menu to paste the face into the selected area in the composite. With the pasted face still selected, he was able to move it around in the oval selection area until it looked right in relation to the two globe halves **9**. ☞ *Because a selection area acts as a mask, when another image is pasted into it, the pasted or "source" image does not obscure other parts of the "target" image, even though the pasted image is larger than the selection area. It's like moving a photograph that's been placed behind a sheet of paper with a hole in it. Different parts of the image show through the hole, but don't show through the white paper.*

FINISHING THE PROJECT

Once the composite image was complete, Heisler supplied the production staff at *Time* magazine with a copy of the 19 MB document in RGB mode along with a print from a Kodak XL7700, a dye sublimation printer that varies the amount of color applied to each dot according to how much heat is applied to the individual pins of the printhead. Heisler had also used this printer to check his progress in developing the illustration.

Kin Wah Lam at *Time* converted the RGB Photoshop file to CMYK for color separation and took care of adding the type and other elements needed for the cover **10**. To make the conversion, Lam started with SpectrePrint Pro separation software, but the resulting Matchprint was muddy-looking. He now prefers SpectrePrint separations to those made by Photoshop, but at the time he was relatively inexperienced with the program and didn't have time to customize its RGB-to-CMYK translation table. So he turned to Photoshop, for which he had already customized a table by altering the lightest settings in the graph that appears when File, Preferences, Separation Setups, Black Generation, Custom is chosen. He imported the resulting CMYK file to a Scitex imaging system to sharpen the detail in the image of Turner. Lam says that now that he has a Quadra and more experience with Photoshop's Unsharp Mask filter, he would do this sharpening task on the desktop also. ∎

An orderly layout structure of illustrations is characteristic of these pages. This is all-out functional design. Content is primary. There are no extraneous design elements that would hinder teaching. Clearly, this is a staff production with a meeting of minds between the verbal and visual players that makes the pages work so well.

The Art Institutes International

ALL-OUT PICTORIAL PAGES

It is axiomatic that graduates of professional schools often become employers of each year's new crop of graduates. A highly successful group of art institutes* published "The Design Schools Alumni Newsletter" to acquaint working alumni with the achievements of students and recent grads.

The approach: all-out pictorial. The strategy: Show education in action, students at work, being honored, and anything else that represents employable skills. Photos and graphics vividly reflect the schools' positive image and encouraged alumni professionals to remember their alma mater when hiring.

The text is brief: Sometimes only a picture caption tells the story. While photographs and art carry the major information load, content planning has different priorities. The editor and designer spread out a three-month's collection of pictorial subject matter and make choices on the basis of eye appeal as well as information content. This approach to visual criteria is similar in many ways to the techniques of photojournalism traditionally practiced at *Life* magazine.

The Photography Department at the schools is a never-ending source of photos that provide this newsletter with a vital sense of things happening. Its page layouts display a simple selection of typefaces combined with black-and-white photos—once again proving the power of strong B&W.

Headline type is Kabel Black, a style that's popular in advertising. Its individual characters have a posterlike effect that is in harmony with the journalistic photos.

---

*Art Institute of Atlanta, Art Institute of Dallas, Art Institute of Fort Lauderdale, Art Institute of Houston, Art Institute of Philadelphia, Art Institute of Pittsburgh, Art Institute of Seattle, Colorado Institute of Art.

Designer
Leslie Oscher
Publisher
Education Management Corp.
Pittsburgh, PA
Text Type
ITC Bookman Light
Display Type
Kabel Black (Stempel)
Page Size
$11\frac{1}{2} \times 15$
Printing
Two Color

Art Institute of Atlanta
Art Institute of Dallas
Art Institute of Fort Lauderdale
Art Institute of Houston
Art Institute of Philadelphia
Art Institute of Pittsburgh
Art Institute of Seattle
Colorado Institute of Art

The Design Schools Alumni Newsletter

Spring 1985

Dear Alumnus:

Do a friend a favor . . .

The Art Institutes are always looking for gifted new students. If you know of a friend or family member who is contemplating a career in design, photography or fashion, get in touch with us. The Institutes can't promise lectures by Bob Peak

Illustrator Bob Peak stresses a point during the recent Art Institute workshop he conducted.

(pictured above) every week. But the caliber of the instructors and the quality of the programs continue to be among the best offered in the country. Send in the coupon on page 4, and we'll guarantee a quick response. Who knows? You may be helping a deserving young designer on the way to success!

Art Institute of Fort Lauderdale graduate Victoria Horner in her office at *Beauty Fashion.*

Onward and Upward

Opportunity Knocks in New York City

NEW YORK–"I've always known that New York was where I wanted to be," says Art Institute of Fort Lauderdale graduate Victoria Horner, "so I'm really glad I was able to relocate here." Victoria does illustration, layout and mechanicals for *Beauty Fashion* magazine, a trade publication for the beauty and cosmetic industry, pub-

lished in New York City. She first learned of the job opening through the Institute's Employment Assistance Department, came to New York for an interview and was hired then and there. "I just love it here," Victoria says. "I'm learning something new every day–and I've learned so much about meeting publication deadlines!"

Designs for Study

In mosaiclike patterns, stories occupy discreet rectangular spaces with no overlap or intrusion of any part. This orderly arrangement of stories is designed to assure quick, easy readability.

Headlines are restricted to two sizes—one for single-column and a larger point size for multiple-column stories. With one exception, picture captions are single lines.

Judges: *Life* magazine's Bob Ciano, center, flanked by Will Hopkins, right, and Ed Hamilton.

$100,000 in Scholarships Awarded

NEW YORK—A panel of prominent judges recently selected 10 winners from among the 400-plus entries received by The Design Schools offices for the annual Art Institutes Scholarship Competition. The 10 winners, high school seniors from 10 different states, were awarded two-year, full-tuition scholarships worth a total of $100,000. Judges included *Life* magazine's Art Director Bob Ciano, former Art Director of *American Photographer* Will Hopkins, Young & Rubicam's Klaus Schmidt, record album designer Paula Scher and The Design Schools Ed Hamilton.

Atlanta Students 'Disney' With Excitement in Florida

ORLANDO, Fla.—Last year, a group of students from the Art Institute of Atlanta spent two days at Disney World participating in a workshop with the art and design staff there. It was such a hit that Disney's staff invited Atlanta students back this year—for five days!

During that time, students worked directly with Disney artists, toured the entire complex, and learned about the history and philosophy behind the famous Disney cartoon characters. Disney's staff even critiqued an assignment the students did: designing a promotional piece for the new Moroccan Pavilion at Epcot.

Student tries her hand at that famous mouse.

Graduate Makes Medium Serve Corporate Message

CHICAGO—When Commercial Art student James Cavaliere graduated from the Art Institute of Philadelphia last March, he'd already been chosen by Du Pont's Printing Systems Division to illustrate the company's theme at "Print '85," the largest print exhibition in the western hemisphere. Du Pont had one of the major displays in the show, with James's art appearing throughout.

One particular full-color piece was enlarged into a mural and placed at the entrance of the exhibition hall. The piece also appeared on the covers of two publications: one, a special supplement to *American Printer* magazine, and the other, Du Pont's "Print '85" brochure. And, as if all this weren't enough, James and his art will soon be featured in an article in *The Register*, a Du Pont publication.

Du Pont's choice: student James Cavaliere.

Prize winner Dennis Ryan poses in the sold-out stadium during a break in the tennis action.

Seattle Student Nets Lipton Logo Prize

DELRAY BEACH, Fla.—Dennis Ryan of the Art Institute of Seattle captured the $1,000 first prize in the 1985 Lipton International Players Championships logo design competition. The Visual Communications major was flown to Delray Beach for the tournament finals, where he accepted his award in front of thousands of cheering tennis fans.

Open exclusively to students of The Design Schools, the Lipton competition drew more than 1,000 entries. Of the 70 students who were among the finalists, 18 shared the $2,500 in prizes.

Ryan's design will be the official '86 logo.

facts

Little Known Facts About The Design Schools

During the last nine months (July 1984 to April 1985):
- Over 1,900 new graduates entered the work world.
- The Employment Assistance Offices received 3,750 job listings.
- More than 1,200 employers attended Portfolio Reviews.
- 90 percent of graduates available for employment accepted positions in their fields within 6 to 9 months after graduation.
- The Employment Assistance Offices helped 4,122 students find part-time employment.

By fall, a total of 158 Apple computers will be available for Computer Graphics classes at the Institutes.

Graduates and faculty from the Art Institute of Fort Lauderdale won 44 Addy awards in the Fort Lauderdale Advertising Federation competition.

Artist Jim McMullan's illustration on the cover of the Art Institute of Pittsburgh catalogue won a gold medal from the Society of Illustrators in New York.

A key principle in the planning of the spread is the juxtaposition of large photos against smaller ones and the relative elevations, one up and the other down.

The Kabel Black display type, running vertically and blown up, creates an effective graphic feature for a column of editorial miscellany.

A broad illustration "jumps the gutter" to form a strong horizontal pattern. The free-form figures provide welcome contrast among the rectangles.

Chris Boucher models sweatshirt design.

Presidential Shirt: No Sweat

VIRGINIA BEACH, Va.–Art Institute of Pittsburgh graduate Chris Boucher would give you the shirt off his back. That's because it bears his design for the sweatshirt featured in the official Inauguration Day souvenirs catalogue. Chris's employer, T-Body Inc., specializes in such shirts, two of which were sent to President and Mrs. Ronald Reagan. "We got a nice thank-you from both," says Chris.

How vedy, vedy British is this unique illustration by Art Institute of Seattle graduate Kurt Hollomon. "That's because I did it while on vacation in Britain," says Kurt, who's been freelancing in the Seattle area for over a year now and doing very well.

Hairlines subtly emphasize the structure of story areas. The technique, borrowed from newspapers, is widely used in publications.

'Animated' Graduates Set Up Their Own Studio

PITTSBURGH–Do you miss old-fashioned, quality animation–the kind that's hardly ever seen anymore? Well, so did Art Institute of Pittsburgh graduates Jim Allan and Phil Wilson. So much so that the talented twosome decided to form their own animation studio, Allan & Wilson Studio Inc. At the studio, they create TV commercials and specials, such as the recent "Allison and the Magic Bubble" and "A Star for Jeremy," a Christmas charmer.

"A Star for Jeremy" was shown on cable TV.

Jim Allan, left, and Phil Wilson in their studio.

Rod Swanstrom reviews his portfolio with CBS Creative Director and VP Louis Dorfsman during an inspiring weeklong visit to New York City.

Young Illustrator From the West Spurred by His Visit East

NEW YORK–"You've got to be versatile to be a freelance illustrator in Colorado," says Art Institute graduate Rod Swanstrom. "You have to work in a lot of different styles because employers expect you to do just about everything." Rod should know! He's kept busy these days illustrating for Den-

ver magazine, *Ski* magazine and the *Rocky Mountain News.*

Recently, Rod traveled to Manhattan to go on several interviews arranged by The Design Schools. Included were meetings with CBS Vice President Louis Dorfsman, noted illustrator Braldt Bralds and several

artists' representatives. "Everyone was so encouraging about my work that the trip was really inspiring," Rod says. "You know, I invested everything I had to attend the Institute, but it was worth it. What an education! It was fantastic, and I wouldn't have changed a minute of it!"

3

Large, tabloid-size pages make blowups possible and open up a great variety of layout possibilities.

The text type, ITC Bookman Light, has a strong presence that brings to mind newspaper columns. Recently redesigned for photo and digital setting, this traditional type style is smooth and even in appearance and easy on the eyes.

Grene Cornea (Eye Surgery Clinic)

MEDICAL AND DESIGN EXCELLENCE GO TOGETHER

Physicians have long been on the receiving end of "ethical promotion" literature, a soft-sell approach to advertising medicine and medical supplies. This material is often designed by top-talent graphic designers.

Here's a reverse situation—a doctor who is promoting his own services and staff through a well-designed newsletter, "New Vision." As designer Sonya Greteman says, "This doctor is on the cutting edge. He's not only a highly successful eye surgeon but he has a keen appreciation for typography and graphic design." In fact, the doctor selected Berkeley, the typeface used in his newsletter. And that isn't all. As in any successful service organization, there is a marketing director who is responsible for editorial content and copy writing.

"New Vision" (a first-rate name) is dispensed 10,000 strong to optometrists, as well as to current and previous patients in the Midwest area. Despite the fact that it deals with the sober problems of eyesight, this newsletter looks and reads lively. The design was executed on a Mac using the PageMaker and Freehand programs. Printing is in four color with graphic features designed in shades of rich, muted colors. Well-chosen photos are printed in black and white.

Designers
Sonya Greteman, Karen Hogan
Creative Design and Art Direction
Gardner & Greteman
Wichita, KS
Publisher
Grene Cornea Clinic
Wichita, KS
Text Type
Berkeley
Display Type
Differs with each feature
Page Size
8½ × 11
Printing
Four Color

VISION

WINTER 1992

PATIENTS

CHANGING LIVES

When Dennis Thrower had his eyes checked in November, 1991, his natural vision was 20/15, without glasses or contact lenses. Great vision? Yes, but it wasn't always that way. Eight years ago, at age 26, Thrower was 20/80 in one eye, and worse than 20/200 in the other eye. As a firefighter, he knew his need to wear glasses could have a negative affect on his career. Most fire departments have very strict vision requirements. So Thrower decided to learn more about radial keratotomy (RK) surgery.

"I had read several articles in my trade magazines about the surgery. After looking around the country, I found out Dr. Grene was doing the procedure. I may have been the first RK in Kansas, but I know I wasn't Dr. Grene's

first case. I was impressed with his credentials. He had a lot of background and experience with RK, so I felt very comfortable with that. I knew I wasn't anyone's guinea pig."

Dr. Grene first learned of RK during his

8 YEARS

Fellowship at Harvard, when a professor encouraged him to find out more about the procedure. After training with colleagues in Chicago and Oklahoma City, Dr. Grene returned to Harvard, where he and his professor performed the first RK for the Harvard staff. Their first patient is still doing very well.

At the time of Thrower's surgery, there were few statistics for long-term RK results. "I had a lot of questions about the long term effects of the surgery. Dr. Grene was very honest about it, and told me there were

R. BRUCE GRENE

no guarantees. But he also made me feel very comfortable that my results would be good."

"He was right. I haven't had any side effects. Although, sometimes if I get real tired, I notice my left eye becomes blurry. If I'm up 24 hours working on a fire, I may start to notice it."

"I had been wearing glasses for twenty years, since I was six, so it was really strange not to have to wear them any more. It's made a tremendous difference. My good vision really helps in my work, especially when dealing with hazardous materials. It's been eight years now, and I'm really happy with my RK results."

GRENE
CORNEA
CORNEA & REFRACTIVE
EYE SURGERY

Graphics were sketched on paper, then streamlined by computer. Display type is used effectively as a graphic feature, equally decorative and informational.

A two-page spread is framed with bands of rich, muted color that bleeds off on all four sides. Pictorial inserts project into text areas smoothly and do not obstruct readability.

What's a better way to introduce the clinic's good-looking staff than a picture stretching from left to right, a full spread wide? The designers skillfully posed the group and sensitively silhouetted the wide-angle shot for a result that has an upbeat, appealing, human quality.

EDUCATION

CORNEAL MAPPING

New and innovative eye testing equipment appears almost monthly. These instruments are designed to give doctors more effective tools to diagnose and treat eye disease. As a corneal and refractive surgeon, Dr. Grene recognized the EyeSys™ computerized corneal mapping system as an exciting new tool. The first of it's kind in Kansas, the EyeSys™ produces maps of the corneal surface. By providing a clear map of the cornea, corneal diseases can be diagnosed and followed with greater accuracy. Dr. Grene is working with EyeSys™ to evaluate different uses of the computer maps. The computer maps are being used to study the corneal surface of patients with dry eye syndrome, astigmatism and corneal transplants.

Authentic pasta was only a secondary consideration when Dr. Grene visited Milan, Italy this fall. Dr. Grene and Dr. Lee Nordan of San Diego were invited to Milan to teach current cataract and astigmatism surgical procedures. Although Dr.'s Grene and Nordan specialize in corneal and refractive surgery, their extensive cataract surgical experience resulted in this invitation. "It's an honor to be able to teach others about my love – eye surgery. It's also a real thrill to be able to travel abroad. I grew up in western Kansas and didn't fly until I was 19. I will admit, though, I also hoped to pick up a few hints in Italy to improve one of my favorite hobbies, making my own pasta."

TOMORROW'S TREATMENTS

research

"COOL" LASER

Over the past ten years, extensive research has been underway in the use of excimer ultraviolet lasers in eye surgery. The excimer laser, for use in correcting nearsightedness, is awaiting approval from the U.S. Food and Drug Administration (FDA).

Dr. Grene has closely followed the development of the laser. He has visited laser sites in Germany, Italy, Canada and throughout the United States. Close to home, Dr. Grene has worked with Dr. Dan Durrie in Kansas City. As one of 20 FDA study sites, Dr. Durrie's study results will be compiled for the FDA. Several of Dr. Grene's patients have been enrolled at the Kansas City site to undergo the experimental laser procedure. Enrollment in the laser study will be completed this year and those patients will be monitored for the next two years.

Lasers currently used in eye surgery destroy the tissue with heat. Excimer laser is different. A computer signals the excimer laser to emit short, high energy pulses of "cool" ultraviolet radiation. The excimer vaporizes microscopic sections of corneal tissue by breaking down the chemical bonds between molecules, and minimal harm is done to adjacent tissue.

At present, disadvantages of the excimer laser compared to RK surgery include: 1) more pain following surgery, 2) slower recovery of vision and, 3) an increased risk of corneal scarring.

Grene Cornea will continue to monitor the excimer laser studies. Dr. Grene is cautiously optimistic about the excimer laser's eventual FDA approval. The thumbs-up signal from the FDA for this experimental surgery could come as early as 1994.

SANDY MARILYN HEATHER SONIA MARC ANN PAT

A horizontal band of gold hue displays the names of staff members set in two centered lines to occupy suitably vertical spaces. Note the subtle, distinctive use of caps and small caps.

The three-column grid pattern is effectively broken, below, by a vertical line of giant type, a logo, and a human eye, all assembled into a very readable column.

REFRACTIVE SURGERY

NEW VISION

By now, you've probably heard about radial keratotomy, an eye surgery to improve visual function in those who are nearsighted (myopic). It is estimated that 50 million people in the United States who suffer from myopia could be eligible for the surgery. If you're nearsighted, you may be one of them. Here's a quick and simple way to find out: Call Grene Cornea and ask about our RK seminars. Seminars are usually scheduled each Monday evening for one hour. You'll learn about the history and current success of surgery for nearsightedness and astigmatism.

Following the seminar, your next step is to make an appointment for a consultation with Dr. Grene. The consultation fee is waived if you've attended an RK seminar. During the consultation, Dr. Grene will evaluate your vision, measure your cornea and discuss the possible risks and complications of eye surgery. He'll also consider your life style, work and hobbies, and determine if you are a good candidate for surgery.

The Grene Cornea staff will schedule your surgery for a Friday afternoon. The actual surgery takes from five to ten minutes, and you'll spend less than two hours at the Cataract Surgery Center. An anesthetic eye drop is given to numb the eye, and patients receive a mild sedative to help them relax. After the surgery, you'll receive eye drops, but no eye patching is generally required. You'll be ready to leave within the hour, but plan to have a friend or family member drive you home.

Over the weekend, stick to your normal routine, but don't swim or participate in high contact or racquet sports. Shortly after the surgery, you may experience scratchy eyes, light sensitivity and glare. You may also notice that your vision varies from morning to evening. These conditions generally disappear in a month or two.

On the Monday morning after surgery, Dr. Grene will check your eyes, and adjust your medications if necessary. After this follow-up visit, you can return to work. Many RK patients

RK INFORMATION

EDUCATION

ATTEND A SEMINAR

CONSULTATION

MEET WITH DR. GRENE

SURGERY

FIVE TO TEN MINUTES ON FRIDAY AFTERNOON

POST-OP CARE

NO PATCH, HOME FOR A NAP BACK TO WORK MONDAY

experience improved vision within a few hours of the surgery. However, remember that your cornea continues to change in the weeks following surgery, so it may take several weeks for your vision to completely stabilize.

RK surgery can reduce, and frequently, eliminate the need for corrective lenses. More than a decade of clinical experience has shown that, under the care of an experienced RK surgeon, RK is a safe, successful, and permanent means to reduce nearsightedness. Dr. Grene has performed more than 2,000 RK surgeries. One hundred percent of Dr. Grene's RK patients have experienced a dramatic improvement in their natural vision, and 96% are seeing 20/40 or better. Call to reserve a seat at our next RK seminar, and bring your glasses.

A listing of information, modestly promotional, is organized in an easy-to-follow series of slim, reverse type panels.

ROSS   HUBERTINA   SUSAN   JUDITH   PENNY   WENDY   DENISE

CREDITS

2—International Business Machines Corp.
13—Wentworth Publishing Co., Time Inc., University of North Florida, *Nutrition Action Health Letter*
14—Art Center College of Design, A&E Network
15—John Abrams
16—San Francisco Museum of Modern Art
21—Museum of Contemporary Art, San Diego
22—Lotus Development Corp., Com/Electric, Historic Hudson Valley, Rochester Institute of Technology, School of Printing Management and Sciences
23—The AIGA Washington Chapter
24—WGBH Educational Foundation, The Hudson River Museum
26—Art Directors Club of New York
27—Metro North Commuter Railroad
28—The Council of Economic Priorities

29—International Business Machines Corp., Inter-American Development Bank
30—Crocker Nurseries, The Art Institutes International
31—Warner Communications, Inc.
35—Morningstar, Inc.
36—A. Sue Weisler
38—Wide World
42—*Lear's Connection, Twin Cities Reader*
43—Herman Miller, Inc.
45—Dover Publications, Inc.
46,47—John Abrams
50—New York Public Library Print Collection
57,64—John Abrams
70,71—Parsons, Brinkerhoff, Quade & Douglas
72—Edward A. Hamilton
73—Zoological Society of Houston
74—Inter-American Development Bank, The Art Institutes International
75—Council of Fashion Designers of America

76—Hots for You
80—LOOK Magazine Collection courtesy of the Library of Congress
81,82,83—Inter-American Development Bank, Edward A. Hamilton
84—Edward A. Hamilton
85,86—LOOK Magazine Collection courtesy of the Library of Congress
86,87—John Abrams
88—Argosy Book Store Print Files
91—Dover Publications, Inc.
92—*United Nations World*
93—International Business Machines Corp., USDA/DHHS, *The Whole Idea*, National Cancer Institute
94—City of Denver, John Hancock Mutual Funds, National Cancer Institute, *The Whole Idea*.
95—*Step-By-Step Electronic Design, Nutrition Action Health Letter, The Whole Idea*, Hots for You
98,99—Courtesy of Nigel Holmes
101—John Abrams
103—Edward A. Hamilton

BIBLIOGRAPHY

Arnheim, Rudolph. *Visual Thinking*. Berkeley: University of California Press, 1972.

Bewick, Thomas. *1800 Woodcuts By Thomas Bewick and His School*. New York: Dover, 1962.

Binns, Betty. *Designing With Two Color*. New York: Watson-Guptill Publications, 1991.

Bruner, Jerome S. *On Knowing: Essays for the Left Hand*. Cambridge: Harvard University Press, 1963.

Craig, James. *Designing With Type*. New York: Watson Guptill Publications, 1980.

Eisenstaedt, Alfred. *Witness to Our Time*. New York: The Viking Press, 1966.

Halsman, Philippe. *The Jump Book*. New York: Simon and Schuster, 1959.

Hamilton, Edward A. *Graphic Design for the Computer Age*. New York: Van Nostrand Reinhold, 1970.

Hicks, Wilson. *Words and Pictures*. New York: Harper, 1952.

Holmes, Nigel. *Designers Guide to Charts and Diagrams*. New York: Watson-Guptill Publications, 1984.

Holmes, Nigel. *Designers Pictorial Maps*. New York: Watson-Guptill Publications, 1984.

Holmes, Nigel. *Designers Pictorial Symbols*. New York: Watson-Guptill Publications, 1984.

Hurlburt, Allen. *Publication Design*. New York: Van Nostrand Reinhold, 1971.

International Paper Corporation. *Pocket Pal*. New York: International Paper Corporation, 1974.

Kerlow, Isaac Victor and Rosebush, Judson. *Computer Graphics for Designers and Artists*. New York: Van Nostrand Reinhold, 1986.

McLuhan, Marshall. *Understanding Media*. New York: McGraw-Hill, 1964.

Miller, Thomas H. and Brummitt, Wayne. *This Is Photography*. New York: Garden City Publishing Company, 1945.

Rand, Paul. *A Designer's Art*. New Haven: Yale University Press, 1985.

Sontag, Susan. *On Photography*. New York: Farrar, Straus and Giroux, 1977.

Strunk, William, Jr. and White, E.B. *The Elements of Style*. New York: Macmillan, 1959.

Zachrisson, Bror. *Legibility of Printed Text*. Stockholm: Almqvist & Wiksell, 1965.

Zinsser, William. *On Writing Well*. New York: Harper Perennial, 1990.

Newsletter Studies, Chapter 10

A photo release is necessary for legal purposes and should be signed by all photo subjects at the time of shooting. This includes models and even your best friend. The only exceptions are people in groups in public places and individuals who are well-known public personalities.

NAME OF YOUR PUBLICATION OR COMPANY

Consent for Publication of Photograph

Location _____ Date _____

For valuable consideration, I hereby give my consent to _____ (and to anyone else whom it may authorize) to photograph me and to publish, at any time in the future, photographs of me, with or without my name, for any editorial, promotion, trade or other purpose whatever, except for testimonial and endorsement of product advertising.

SIGNATURE OF SUBJECT OF PHOTOGRAPH _____

ADDRESS _____ TELEPHONE NO. _____

WITNESSED BY (PHOTOGRAPHER OR EDITOR) _____

SIGNATURE OF OTHER WITNESS (IF ANY) _____

ADDRESS _____

INDEX